THE OJAI VALLEY

An Illustrated History

by

PATRICIA L. FRY

COMPLETELY REVISED

MATILIJA PRESS
PMB 123
323 E. Matilija St., Ste. 110
Ojai, California 93023

THE OJAI VALLEY
An Illustrated History

Publisher's Cataloguing-in-Publication
(Provided by Quality Books, Inc.)

     Fry, Patricia L., 1940-
        The Ojai Valley : an illustrated history / by
        Patricia L. Fry.-- 2nd ed.
          p. cm.
        Includes bibliographical references and index.
        ISBN: 0-9612642-4-1

        1. Ojai Valley (Calif.)--History. 2. Ojai
     (Calif.)--History. 3. Ojai Valley (Calif.)--
     Description and travel. 4. Ojai (Calif.)--
     Description and travel. I. Title.

     F868.V5F78 1999   979.4'92
                    QBI99-1109

Cover photo by Phil Harvey
The Mystique of Ojai
805-646-8679

Cover design by Mary-Anne Reed
Amazing Graphics
805-646-7656

Book design by Linda McGinnis
530-623-2613

Dedicated to

Ojai pioneers

and their descendants.

Table of Contents

Photo Index

About the author...

It was twenty years ago when I launched the research that resulted in the first edition of this book. Little did I know that *The Ojai Valley: An Illustrated History* would become the first and sometimes the last word in many inquiries to the personnel at local libraries, the Ojai Valley Museum, the Chamber of Commerce office and City Hall. This book has helped countless local school children complete their history projects. It has provided a guide for visitors and, in some cases, an enticement for them to stay. It's been a popular gift for newcomers and those who are leaving the valley, a welcome addition to many private history collections and a delight to those whose roots are deeply imbedded in the Ojai Valley.

Practically every week, someone tells me how much they appreciate having this book for reference purposes or how much they enjoy just reading it.

As my supply of copies dwindled, I had to decide whether to reprint the book or to let it die. Knowing what this book has meant to the community these past sixteen years and realizing that it could be enjoyed by many generations to come, I had to find a way to reprint it. But it wasn't a simple process.

The first edition was handwritten and then typed on a manual typewriter. It was then edited and typed and edited and typed over and over again in preparation for the printer.

Most of the pictures were second generation photos. I took pictures of the old photographs to eliminate the risk of losing any of them in transit to a photo lab. I spent hours on the back steps of the museum when it was in the old fire station on South Montgomery Street, for example, snapping pictures of the museum's original photographs.

For this edition, we used computer technology all the way, including in the handling of the photographs. The photographs are as sharp as they can be. Hopefully, readers will find fewer typographical errors, as well.

That's about the book, now about me: I'm a fifth generation Ojai resident and my grandchildren are seventh generation. My great great grandfather, Dexter Munger came to the valley with his two sons in 1876. Great, great grandfather and grandmother, Thomas Jefferson and Laura Robison came here in 1886 and another set of great grandparents, Hiram and Allie Belle Watkins, settled in Oak View in the early 1900s.

Since I wrote the first edition of *The Ojai Valley*, I've continued my writing career. I've published an additional 5 books, including two more local histories: *Nordhoff Cemetery* and *A Thread to Hold: The Story of Ojai Valley School.*

As with the first edition of *The Ojai Valley: An Illustrated History*, I've derived a great deal of pleasure from preparing this book for you and I hope that reading it gives you equal pleasure.

Preface

Ojai might not be, had the numerous self-proclaimed publicists who were first intrigued by the valley cast aside their pens. Had someone collected this material over the decades, it would fill several volumes. The words, however, were not amassed. They dotted distant hometown newspapers, appeared in national magazines, filled descriptive advertising pamphlets and dominated personal letters. The intentions of the authors were to lure Eastern friends, family and strangers to this valley. While most early writers concentrated on the charm and beauty of Ojai, however, scant few thought to preserve its historical aspects.

The local newspaper is by far the best record of day-to-day life in any community. All back issues of *The Ojai*, our early weekly publication, are preserved in the Ojai Library. Although nearly everyone wonders about some historical aspect of his town, few people would read through a hundred years of old newspapers just to satisfy a curiosity. They hope that someone else will go the trouble.

Elizabeth Chase was the first to consolidate the history of Ojai Valley. Her 1933 research resulted in a thesis for her master's degree and she donated copies to the local library and museum.

In 1946, Walter Bristol wrote *The Story of Ojai Valley* using the personal knowledge acquired during his thirty-seven year residency. In his introduction, he states that there is nothing particularly exiting about the history of Ojai. His book dealt primarily with the personalities of early settlers and influential people, many of whom he knew personally. Mr. Bristol also used some previously researched material: Chase's manuscript, Zaidee Soule's card index of important events and the Ojai Valley Woman's Club scrapbook. Bristol's 35,000 word book contained the first collection of historical facts about Ojai ever offered to the public.

In 1959, Arthur Erwin Woolman wrote *The Ojai Valley, Gateway to Health and Happiness*. Like Bristol's publication, Woolman's 20,000-word well illustrated book brought readers up to date.

The next history was written in 1971 by Fred Volz and Polly Bee. Their informative *Golden Book* celebrated the fiftieth anniversary of Ojai. All of these publications are out of print.

Within the pages of this book, the history lives once again. *The Ojai Valley: An Illustrated History* represents six years of diligent research and an additional fifteen years of random history collecting. I've read all of those old newspapers several times now. I've interviewed numbers of old timers, pioneer descendants and history buffs. I've questioned hundreds of so-called facts, seeking to verify or disprove each of them. I've countered popular beliefs when they were positively refuted.

The history can be elusive, especially when relying on memory. And the more time that passes, the less reliable the memory. As an illustration, local historian, David Mason, who was instrumental in having the pergola rebuilt in 1999, says that as the pergola took shape across the street from his arcade florist shop, citizens frequently stopped in to voice their opinions. Many of them told Mason that the dimensions on the new pergola were off.

"It was smaller," one person would say. "It was longer," said another. "It was farther west than you've built it," offered another. The truth is that the pergola was built using the original architect, Richard Requa's blueprints and when workers began preparing for the new structure, they discovered the foundation for the old fountain and found that they were only a scant half-inch off in their calculations.

As present day architect David Bury and his craftsmen have endeavored to give you an exact replica of the beloved pergola, I have made every effort toward harmony in truth as I present this revised history of the Ojai Valley to you with pride and with love.

Acknowledgments

With great pleasure I publicly thank those who offered the benefit of their knowledge and memories so that this important project could become a reality. Following, I've listed the names of individuals who contributed in some way to either the first or the second edition or both. We are fortunate to have gleaned what information and anecdotes we have from these folks, for over thirty of them are now deceased.

Name	Connection
Richard Adams	Robison, McGlinchey, Jordan familes
Betsy Armstrong	Brandt family
Howard Bald	Bald and Clark families
Leah Edde Beard	arcade history
Elmer Beckett	history buff
Sarah Beeby	Ojai Band
The Beese family	Meiners ranch house
Eunice Berry	long-time resident
Ron Biggers	Biggers family
Betty L. Middleton Britton	historical author
Mel and Bim Burckes	Oak Glen Cottages
Alice Caldwell	protégé of the Libbeys
Juanita Callender	Tico, Carnes, Camarillo families
Elizabeth Clark	Clark family
Tom and June Conrad	Clark family
Pat Clark Doerner	Clark family
Miriam Dumer	Watkins family
Elmer Friend	Friend and Beers families
Sidney Gally	Gally family
Bert Gates	Ojai agriculture
Max and Lillian Green	long-time residents
Pete Hall	long-time resident
Roy Hall	long-time resident
Eula Hammons	Ojai Valley Woman's Club
Winifred Hirsch	Voice of the Valley
Alan Hooker	Ranch House Restaurant
David Hopkins	Boy Scouts
Ruth Houk	Houk and Jones families
Richard Hoye	historical researcher
Mary Lapham Hunt	Biblical Gardens
Lillian Jackson	long-time resident
Marguerite Jenks	Garland family
Harriet Kennedy	Leslie family
J. Kilbourne	Kilbourne family
Gussie Linebarger	Lundine family

Name	Connection
David Mason	local historian
Ann McGarrity	long-time resident
Ginger Morgan	Berry and Blumberg families
Claude and Kathleen Munger	Munger and Robison families
Dalton and Emy Lou Munger	Munger, Robison, Watkins families
Leon and Vivian Munger	Munger and Robison families
Mel and Robert Mushaney	long-time residents
David F. Myrick	history buff
Vivian Noren	Smith and Wolfe families
Wilma and Robert Perry	long-time residents
Les Peirano	long-time resident
Philip Pierpont	Pierpont family
Alan Rains	Rains Department Store
Lynn Rains	Rains Department Store
Margaret Reimer	Clark and Hunt families
Cindy Reynolds	City Clerk
Helen Baker Reynolds	Baker family
Marion Ring	Fraser family
Dortha Clark Roberts	Clark family
Walter Robie	Presbyterian Church
Monica Ros	Monica Ros School
Carl Rynerson	Rynerson family
Joe Sarzotti	Sarzotti family
Richard Senate	history buff and author
Nancy and Jack Selby	long-time residents
Julie Tumamait-Stenslie	Tumamait family
Clarence Sterling	historical author
Marsha K. Strong	Montgomery, Robinson families
Anson and Peggy Thacher	Thacher family
Elizabeth Thacher	Thacher family
John and Verna Thompson	Thompson, Clark, Bullard families
Katherine Van Dellen	long-time resident
Arthur Waite	Waite and Gibson families
Craig Walker	pergola history
Connie Wash	Gorham family
Margaret Walter	Bennett family
Percy and Effie Watkins	Watkins family
Nadine Webb	Henderson family
Mary Frances and Jack Weedon	long-time residents
Ann Yant	Linnel family

I would like to offer a special thanks to the following people:

Robert Browne, former curator for the Ojai Museum.
Sherry Smith, former Ojai Museum director.
Ellen Hall, Mary Kay Porter and Claudia Harris, current Ojai Museum staff.
Charles Johnson, librarian at the Ventura County Museum
Luke Hall, geologist.
June Laurie Behar, editorial assistant for the first edition.
Gary Schlichter, whose idea this book was in the first place.
Dennis Mullican, for his ongoing support, creative ideas and research assistance.

and the staffs of:

Ojai Library
Ojai Valley News
Ventura Branch Library
Thacher Library
Krotona Library
Title Insurance Company of Ventura
Santa Barbara Historical Museum Library
Santa Barbara Branch Library
Casitas Recreational Area
Casitas Municipal Water District
Toledo Museum of Art
Ventura County Recorders office
Santa Barbara County Records office
Olympics Committee

Credits appear under each photograph, with the following abbreviations used for major lenders:

Ventura County Historical Society	**VCHS**
Ojai Valley Museum	**OVM**

Statistics

Ventura is fourteen miles south of Ojai on Highway 33. Los Angeles is eighty miles from Ojai and can be reached either by driving south on Highway 101 from Ventura, or east from Ojai on Highway 150 to Highway 126 and then east to Interstate 5. Santa Barbara is thirty miles from Ojai when traveling west on Highway 150 and then north on Highway 101. Continuing north on Highway 101 brings one to San Francisco, which is 350 miles from Ojai.

The elevation of Ojai ranges from 700 feet (lower valley) to 1,500 feet (upper valley) above sea level. The valley is surrounded by coastal range mountains averaging 4,500 feet above sea level. Ojai Valley is ten miles long, three miles wide and encompasses ninety square miles. The average high temperature is 80.9 and the average low is 47.5 degrees Fahrenheit. Average rainfall is from fifteen to seventeen inches per year with eighty percent of the rain falling between November and March. Humidity runs between twenty and forty percent.

Chapter One
In the Beginning

Ojai wasn't always as we know it today. Many diverse cultures have come here over thousands of years and they molded areas and aspects of the valley to suit their individual needs. The change having the greatest effect on what we know as the Ojai Valley, however, occurred long before humans discovered and began using the land.

The Geology of the Valley

An investigation into the geology of the Ojai Valley is significant because it helps us to know more about the physical landscape that provides the backdrop for the human experience. To understand the forces that molded this land is to further appreciate Ojai.

The discernible geologic history of the valley dates back about sixty million years – sometime after the demise of the dinosaur. At that time, an ancient, unnamed ocean covered this area. The constantly changing shoreline was located in the general vicinity of Pine Mountain, fifteen miles north of modern Ojai. Some geologists believe that when the shoreline receded, our valley remained a great salt lake into which ancient rivers deposited layers of silt, sand and boulders. This debris eventually accumulated to a vertical depth of 47,000 feet in areas of maximum deposition, creating what is now our valley floor.

The episode that left the greatest mark on the structure of the valley occurred during the last one to two million years. This segment, in the gradual evolution of our terrain, included the emergence of the land from the water for the last time and the dramatic role of the San Andreas Fault.

The explosive forces of the Pacific Northwest volcanoes, as well as the slow bending of the earth's crust, helped create the West Coast of the United States as we know it today. These tumultuous events are directly related to the recently supported concept of plate tectonics (formerly known as continental drift).

According to this concept, the earth's crust is divided into six major plates and a dozen minor ones. Each mammoth plate moves against or slides past the other at a rate of from one to five inches per year, creating enormous friction and energy along plate boundaries. The San Andreas Fault system represents the plate boundary between the Pacific Plate, on which Coastal California is located, and the North American Plate, on which the rest of the United States is situated. The Pacific Plate is moving Southern California northward at a rate of about two inches per year – an action that experts say should place Los Angeles opposite San Francisco in about ten million years.

Ventura County lies in a geologic region referred to as the Transverse Range Province. Transverse means *lying across*. Mountains and valleys within this area have been deformed from the state's general north-south trend to an east-west configuration. Current geologic thought holds that this arrangement is due to movement along the 300 mile San Andreas Fault zone.

A compensation resulting from this phenomenon is one we all take for granted. Besides providing positive visual impact, the east-west positioning of our valley creates one of the most basic and pleasant of Ojai's charms – early morning and lingering evening sunshine.

The First Cultures

It's alleged that California was once part of Lemuria (also called Mu), the legendary continent that supposedly extended from our coastal ranges westward to Africa. As the story goes, when the bulk of the ancient land mass sunk beneath the Pacific Ocean, California, which is thought by some to have once been an island, and a few mountain tops remained above the water. We know some of those pinnacles as the islands of Polynesia and our own Channel Islands.

As a point of interest, early California natives called Santa Cruz Island *Limu*.

Milling Stone Horizon

Anthropologists originally named the Southern California aborigines *Ancient Ones*. These people were also known as *The First Culture People, Oak Grove Dwellers* and then *Oak Grove People. Milling Stone Horizon* is the current appellation.

Archaeological records place this culture here at about 5000 B.C. Some experts theorize that these people migrated in small bands from Asia over a land bridge that once spanned what is now the Bering Strait. However, new evidence places an even earlier culture here between 12,000 and 25,000 years ago and there's speculation that they arrived by boat. Prehistoric remains discovered on the Channel Islands, for example, date back to more than 10,000 years.

The Milling Stone Horizon populace is thought to have flourished from San Diego to San Luis Obispo. Archaeologists have discovered evidence of early villages throughout the Ojai Valley on the crests of high hills and far from current water supplies. Since they needed to be near water in order to survive, their choice of home sites indicates that our rivers flowed much higher and wider during that period. One expert speculates that the Ventura River was two miles wide at some points in ancient times. The people lived in semi-subterranean homes in areas shaded by oak groves. The abundance of manos and metates (grinding tools) in their sites, indicate that they harvested wild seed for subsistence.

Robert Browne, one of the founders of the Ojai Valley Museum and curator from 1967 until his death in 1993, discovered a Milling Stone Horizon site in his backyard in the 1970s. His home, which he and his wife bought only after detecting the site, was in the Skyline Tract on a bluff overlooking Highway 33 between Mira Monte and Oak View. He and a crew of archaeology buffs excavated over 4,000 artifacts from the site. The most valuable find was an effigy of a toad made of diorite (a type of granite native to the Lockwood Valley, which is about twenty-five miles due north of Ojai). Experts believe this to be one of the earliest works of art ever discovered in North America.

Within 4,000 years the Milling Stone Horizon completely vanished from this county and another culture took its place.

Hunting People

A band called *Hunting People* inhabited the valley between 1000 B.C. and the birth of Christ. Artifacts from the only known site in Ventura County, Soule Park in Ojai, indicate that these people were of sturdy build with massive features and large foreheads. The Hunters' villages were located in coastal valleys around small mounds and usually near swampland. Excavators found no evidence of any sort of housing at the Soule Park site, however. Their artifacts, which include large flint weapons, closely resemble those found in the Pinto Basin area, indicating that these people probably migrated from Mojave. Just as the previous culture vanished, the Hunting People suddenly and completely vacated the land.

The Chumash

The culture we know as *Chumash* had full possession of a large area of Southern California by 1000 A.D. For over 500 years these people lived in relative peace with few intruders to disrupt their society. They enjoyed intermittent visits from early voyagers during the Spanish Exploration Period.

In October of 1542, Juan Rodriguez Cabrillo anchored his ships, San Salvador and Victoria, off the coast of what is now Ventura. His chief pilot, Bartolome Ferrelo, was the first to write about the Coastal California natives. Ferrelo was particularly impressed by their command of the sea.

Sixty years later, Sebastian Vizcaino, under orders from King Philip III of Spain, sailed up from Acapulco to record some of the geographic details of the region. He named Santa Catalina and San Clemente Islands, San Diego, San Pedro and the Santa Barbara Channel. He also documented some of his thoughts and observations regarding the Chumash.

Gaspar de Portola noticed the natives on his way from San Diego to Monterey Bay. He and three of his sixty-four crew members, Lt. Pedro Fages, Miguel Constanso and Friar Juan Crespi, wrote valuable accounts of the Californians, their appearance and their activities. In his diary, Fages mentioned that he and his men camped at the Rincon (Spanish for "corner" or "nook") just north of modern-day Ventura, which they called *Asuncion*, near a village containing thirty-eight huts. The natives, he said, inundated them with great supplies of roasted fish. Fages and company named the village *La Carpintero* or "carpenter" because of the native boat builders there.

In 1775, Father Pedro Font, diarist for the Juan Bautista de Anza expedition, added his impressions of the people. Font's map referred to Ventura as *Asumpta*. This was de Anza's second overland trip during which he led families from Sinaloa, Mexico to settle in the new country. They brought the sheep and cattle that began the great herds of the Rancho days to follow.

Father Francisco Palou recorded what he saw here in 1778. Thirteen years later, naturalist Jose Longinos Martinez wrote about the Chumash in his journal. Archibald Menzies of the George Vancouver expedition wrote the first English account of the people.

Although important and valuable, the data collected by early explorers is not complete. There remain more impressions of the Chumash than information about them. Padres of the five missions established in Chumash territory had an excellent opportunity to learn about and preserve the native culture during the Mission Period, but they spent more energy trying to civilize and Christianize the natives than to understand them. Soon, the Chumash culture was a dimming memory.

Within the last ninety years, anthropologists, archaeologists, ethnologists and historians have begun to assemble the scattered pieces of the great Chumash puzzle. Although, some precious fragments may lie yet undiscovered, many of them are gone forever. In more recent years, Chumash descendants have begun to embrace their heritage by learning their ancestral customs and sharing them in hopes of preserving the memory of their culture.

Who Were the Chumash?

The Chumash inhabited the area from Malibu Canyon to Morro Bay and from Cuyama to the Channel Islands. Prior to the 1800s these people were called *Santa Barbara Indians*. Some early investigators referred to the natives as *Canalino* or "people of the channel." And before that? Since they had no written language and since none of the explorers ascertained their cultural appellation, we will never know.

John Wesley Powell who, along with Stephen Powers, compiled the first significant data available regarding the linguistics of the California natives, developed the term *Chumash*. Chumash refers primarily to a group of people sharing a dialect of language belonging to the Hokan linguistic family.

The Chumash had round heads, Australoid features and well-formed bodies. All early visitors remarked that the natives were friendly, gentle people. Most diarists wrote that they were happy, contented, slow to anger, rather childlike, peaceful, but ready to defend their families and hunting or collecting grounds. The men wore their long, black hair tied up with thongs, fastening daggers or awls of wood, bone or flint in it. Chumash men generally went naked, but occasionally wore waist-length capes of animal skin or feathers. Every man tied a net around his waist in which to carry small objects. They also used these nets to capture small game, fowl and fish. Unlike most United States natives, Chumash men grew beards which they plucked with clam shell tweezers.

OVM
Petra Pico, Chumash basket-maker. Late 1800s.

Early observers reported that the women were neat and graceful in appearance. They wore their hair in short bangs, trimming them by singeing single hairs with hot bark. A Chumash woman commonly attached two aprons of buckskin or grass to her waist. She weighted each blade of grass down with a pinch of asphaltum or small sea shells. Women wore animal fur capes for warmth and basketry caps for carrying heavy loads.

Both sexes pierced their ears and nasal septums and adorned themselves elaborately with jewelry. Men and women painted their bodies to distinguish themselves from those of other villages.

The Chumash Village

The Chumash people lived in villages consisting of several dome-shaped huts. They framed their homes with willow branches and thatched them with corrizo or surf grass, tule, alfalfa or fern, leaving a hole at the top for smoke to escape and for light to enter. Some huts reportedly measured fifty feet in diameter and housed up to five families. Whale ribs were sometimes used for doorway arches. Villagers slept on raised platforms, often arranged in tiers. They hung reed mats to separate sleeping areas for privacy and to provide warmth.

There were reportedly about 500 Chumash living in Ojai Valley in 1779 and there were four main villages: *Matilija*, which was located in what is now Meiners Oaks; *Awhai*, situated in the vicinity of Soule Park; *Sitopatopa*, in the east end and *Sisa*, in Sisar Canyon.

Each village had one or more chiefs. This was an inherited position which required the people's approval. It was a case of seniority by birth which made it possible for a woman to take leadership as well as a man.

Every village had a smooth, level gaming area surrounded by a low wall where the Chumash played the pole and hoop game. This game involved throwing a pole through a moving straw hoop. They also played their version of shinney (a hockey-type game). Gambling and guessing games were also enjoyed by natives. They held dances and various ceremonies in a separate ceremonial enclosure.

The *temescal* or "sweathouse" was somewhat like a modern sauna. Each village had one or more, depending on its population. Men used them daily for spiritual and physical reasons and prior to a hunt to remove their human scent.

Pedro Fages once observed a Chumash woman giving birth. He said that she made a small indentation in the earth and warmed it with fire. After laying a little grass within the hole, she rendered herself tranquil for the birthing. Once the child was born, she stroked him and flattened his nose by deforming the cartilage. Then she bathed herself in cold water.

The Chumash practiced interment. Villagers established a cemetery away from their main dwellings. Some explorers noted that surviving family members placed basketry items on the graves of deceased women and deer antlers on those of the men.

Hunting, Fishing and Gathering

While coastal Chumash depended heavily on the ocean's products for subsistence, inland villagers enjoyed seafood less often. Venison was the primary food for all Chumash. Deer not only provided meat but also sinew for bow strings and sewing and bones for tools and musical instruments. Inland Chumash relied on acorns as a dietary staple. They also made use of chia, soaproot, wild celery, wild cherries, wild strawberries, watercress, cattail seeds and flour, mushrooms, clover, cactus, laurel berries, madrona and manzanita berries, pine nuts, reptiles, amphibians and insects such as grasshoppers, yellow jacket larvae and caterpillar chrysalis.

Not only did they use the yucca plant as a source of food but they also employed it to manufacture cradles, baskets, sandals, clothing, nets, mats and rope. Archaeological records show evidence that the natives also consumed rabbit, gray squirrel, pocket gopher, wood rat, coyote, fox and domestic dog. Small birds and an occasional bear rounded out their diets.

Chumash men spent a lifetime sharpening their hunting skills. They perfected two basic techniques for hunting deer. Either they would outrun the animal or, wearing a deer head disguise to fool the deer, a hunter would sneak up until he was within bow shooting range.

Deer hunters used live oak, chamise and wild lilac to make their arrows and they fletched them with feathers from the red-tailed hawk, golden eagle and other large birds. They secured the stone projectile point with bits of asphaltum. Self-arrows, made from a single piece of sharpened wood, were reserved for smaller game.

When villagers desired a rabbit dinner, they organized a

community rabbit drive using flat, curved throwing sticks in the pursuit.

Chumash Craftsmanship and Artistry

The Spaniards were impressed by Chumash craftsmanship. The plank canoe, or *tomol*, in particular caught the attention of most voyagers. Special carpenters, possibly just in certain villages, made the extremely sea-worthy vessels by first splitting pine logs with whale bone wedges. They smoothed and shaped the wood planks using flint and shells. The workmen then burned small holes in the ends of each plank, sewed them together with milkweed cords and filled the joints with asphaltum and pine pitch. Some natives painted their boats and inlayed abalone shell eyes in the prow.

Fry photo
Replica of a Chumash tomol, on display at the Albinger Archaeological Museum in Ventura, CA.

The tomols measured from eight to thirty feet in length and carried from two to six people. Crews of every alien ship to enter local channels took note of the swiftness and skill with which the coastal natives navigated their crafts. The owners of such boats were conspicuous, as they wore ornamental capes over their shoulders and seemed to hold a place of esteem in the community.

The Chumash were the only tribal group in the United States to build plank boats. Since there seems to be no period of evolution for the tomols, historians speculate that other people taught the Chumash how to assemble these crafts. Recent evidence indicates that ancient Chinese entered our waters hundreds of years ago. Divers have found huge, donut-shaped, stone anchors typical of those once used by Orientals, off the California shore. Some continue to wonder, could the plank tomol be a rough replica of an early Chinese junk?

The Chumash found ways to utilize their environment in order to survive and knew to treat their surroundings with respect lest they succumb to it.

They used sea shells to eat with and also as tools, money and adornments. Sweat scrapers were usually made of deer or bear bones or swordfish bills. Although few sweat scrapers are located in digging sites, written history tells us that they were at one time plentiful. Aside from their primary function – scraping sweat from one's body – they were supposed to have doubled as weapons. A squabble between two men usually resulted in a duel. Each would slap at the other with his sweat stick until one of them drew blood. That ended the quarrel.

Gally family photo
Unidentified man with Chumash artifacts.

Chumash basketry is considered to be among the finest in America. They used baskets in many sizes and shapes – from huge storage baskets to tiny trinket baskets. They made basket trays for parching and winnowing (sifting) and baskets for food preparation. They had basket strainers, bait baskets and even basket bottles that were sealed with asphaltum to hold water. Chumash basket makers used both coiling and twining methods.

The Chumash people imported steatite, or soapstone, from Santa Catalina Island and, because of its high resistance to heat, made it into cooking vessels. Steatite was also used to make smoking pipes and arrow straighteners. Although the Chumash had no knowledge of pottery, the workmanship in their stone implements and vessels is considered by experts to be superb, as were the few wooden items they created, each from one piece of root. Because of the high quality shown in their everyday implements, it's logical to accept the conjecture that specialists in each village made most of them.

The Southern California natives were considered by some to have been outstanding artists. Yet, others find their cave paintings, or pictographs, crude and insignificant. The meanings behind the cave paintings have been a subject of contention ever since the white man discovered them. While some experts feel that they are highly stylized, symbolic drawings, others wonder if they're simply random doodlings. There's speculation that the paintings were done by young maidens while separated from the rest of the tribe for several weeks prior to marriage. Because the caverns are so isolated, it's thought that they may have been religious retreats where shamans received visions while under the inducement of the hallucinatory plant, datura.

Many elaborate pictographs are still hidden in caves and in the shelter of steep sandstone cliffs throughout the back country of established Chumash territory. Although most of the paintings are well concealed from view and are protected from the effects of the weather, the elements and time have done irreparable damage as, sadly enough, have vandals.

Music was an important part of the Chumash life. A drum, however, usually synonymous with native cultures, was not one of the Chumash instruments. The musicians plucked bows and shook rattles made from split wood, turtle shells, sea shells and bunches of deer hooves. They blew whistles made of deer tibia and played flutes made from dried bones.

Fry photo
Chumash pictograph.

The Language

Many of our county place names were handed down by the Chumash. *Ojai*, for instance, came from the name of the Chumash village, *Awhai* – pronounced aw-ha-ee. It has long been thought that Ojai means *nest* in the Chumash language and it seems logical when you consider that Ojai is ringed by mountain ranges. That sense of logic is why I and others, who have pondered and studied this question, think the white man dreamed it up.

Throughout the 1920s and 30s, there were many references stating that Ojai means nest. But, nowhere, during twenty years of research, did I find anything to substantiate this. Nor did I locate the origin of this belief. Careful research has convinced me and most other local historians that, contrary to popular belief, *Ojai* does not mean nest. It means *moon* and probably in the cyclical sense.

I used more than twenty books in researching the Chumash culture and not one of those authors wrote that Ojai means nest. *All* of those who included a study of the Chumash language in their books, wrote that Ojai means moon.

Around the turn of the century, researchers recorded the voice of Candalaria Valenzuela, a local Chumash woman. I listened to some of the tapes and heard her state that Awhai (Ojai) means moon. I even went so far as to find out how the local Chumash pronounced their word for nest.

Dr. Richard Applegate, after an incredible amount of research, listed many Chumash villages by their original names and translated them into English. There was a Chumash village on Matilija Creek called *Kaspat Kahwa* (or Kaxwa), which Applegate found to mean "nest of the heron," and another village in San Fernando Valley named *Kaspat Kaslo'w,* which meant "nest of the eagle." By analogy it becomes obvious that Kaspat and not Awhai means nest.

The fact that Ojai doesn't mean nest disappoints some locals. But it could be worse: one Chumash village was called "urine of the deer." Shisholop or Sisolop, the name of a village near Figueroa Street in Ventura, means "in the mud."

Santa Paula was once Mupu and the Wheelers Gorge area was called Sixulky or Seshulkuy, meaning "one is seated on it." The Chumash word, Sisa, or the Americanized version, Sisar, means "eyelash." Sekpe or Sespe means "kneecap." Sitopatopa or Topa Topa means "much cane." Cuyama or Cuyam means "rest" or "wait." Weneme or Hueneme means "sleeping place." Muwu or Mugu is "beach," and Katz or Castaic stands for "my eye." Matilija, once thought to mean "laughing waters," means "division." Other familiar words that we adopted from the Chumash are Saticoy, Anacapa, Piru, Cachuma, Malibu, Sisquoc and Simi.

Hundreds of people have found Indian relics in both the upper and lower valleys of Ojai over the years. Many backyards have one or more pieces of local Indian culture lying forgotten and ignored. When Dorothy and Wallace Burr first looked at the wilderness that would become the upper campus for Ojai Valley School, they saw hundreds of Indian artifacts just lying around the area. "What a wonderful display this will make for an onsite museum," thought Dorothy. By the time they'd completed the transaction on the property, however, the relics had vanished.

Still, people find Indian baubles and trinkets in the Meiners Oaks area when searching for such after a heavy rain. This author has possession of a sandstone bowl that Grandfather Claude Munger found on his La Luna Street property many years ago.

The major local Chumash sites have either been tapped by experts for the relics, paved over to protect the treasures for now or secured to preserve them in their natural state. To see native artifacts, visit the Ojai Valley Museum at 130 West Ojai Avenue.

The Mission Period

The Chumash shared their land willingly, even when the Franciscan intruders came to stay. Natives of Shisholop helped the padres build a large, brush ramada. And there, in 1782, the Spaniards established Mission San Buenaventura. Aided by the natives, Father Junipero Serra completed the ninth link in the great California mission chain in 1809 and dedicated it to Saint Bonaventure, the Seraphic Doctor.

VCHS
San Buenaventura Mission Settlement.

The purpose of the Mission Period settlers was to tame and civilize the natives and to make Christians of them – strengthening Spain's hold on California. When that was accomplished, the neophytes would be released from mission discipline and the land divided among them. The Spanish government expected this phase to span a mere decade.

It wasn't until 1822, however, that Californians swore allegiance to victorious Mexican revolutionists. Ten years later the Mexican government relieved the missionaries of all duties pertaining to anything other than spiritual matters and confiscated all California land. The government then proceeded to divide this land among men who had proven themselves of political value.

14

The Rancho Period

Fernando Tico held the highest civil position in the San Buenaventura Mission settlement. He cared for the stock and was in command of the whipping post, which was used to discipline unruly neophytes. Tico lived in the upper valley of Rancho Ojay (Spanish spelling) as early as 1831. He built a frame house among free roaming cattle, few and scattered Chumash and abundant wildlife. On April 6, 1837, Governor Juan B. Alvarado granted Tico the Rancho Ojay which encompassed 17,716.83 acres. Tico then built what was described as a "fine adobe house" in the lower valley in the vicinity of what is now Bryant Street.

VCHS
Fernando Tico.

Fernando Tico was proud of his accomplishments and loved being one of the elite California Rancho owners. But according to old stories passed down through history, his wife wasn't so happy here. Maria (Tico's second wife) missed her family in Santa Barbara and the social life she knew there. The Ojai Valley was desolate and she was lonely. When she found herself with child, she begged her husband to take her to Santa Barbara to be with her family and where there were doctors to take care of her.

Tico finally agreed and drove her to Santa Barbara where she stayed until the baby was born. Then she found new excuses to stay in the city. Her husband gave up and sold the Rancho to be with her.

While there, Tico ran a business and, with Pablo de la Guerra and Ramon Malo, he served on the first Santa Barbara County

Board of Supervisors. In 1851, Tico was considered to be a wealthy man, showing $12,655 on the tax rolls that year – twice as much as Juan Camarillo. Tico died in 1861 at the age of 63 and was the last adult to be buried in the mission cemetery in San Buenaventura.

Chrisogono Ayala, a Mexican soldier who helped the padres build the California missions, and his brother-in-law, Cosme Vanegas, officially accepted the Santa Ana grant of 21,522.04 acres on April 4, 1837. This ranch included the Ventura River Valley and sections of the Coyote and San Antonio Creeks in the Oak View area.

In 1841, Joaquina Alvarado petitioned for and was granted Canada Larga O Verde. As part of the possession ceremony, she, reportedly, walked over a section of the 6,659.04 acres throwing stones and pulling grass. She built an adobe house and lived there during the summer, spending her winters in Santa Barbara.

Governor Pio Pico granted Don Jose Arnaz, the administrator for the temporalities (mission natives), the right to purchase the ex-mission property of 48,822.91 acres in 1846. Arnaz, attempting the county's first land promotion, offered small parcels of his land free as an enticement to Easterners. His efforts were to no avail, however, and on November 10, 1852, Arnaz sold his entire grant to Manuel Antonio Rodriquez de Poli.

As promised, the government provided land for each native head of family. Being inexperienced in such ownership, the Chumash quickly traded away most of the small mission plots or lost them to swindlers.

By 1843, the short-lived Rancho Period had begun. The people who once made up the Chumash culture were free with nowhere to go. Disease, formerly unknown to the Chumash, and a change in diet had already weakened the race drastically. The demands and restrictions of the mission system had dampened their spirit. Within just fifty years, the Chumash were virtually non-definable as a culture, yet unprepared to assume a role in society.

They had become dependent on the missionaries for everything, including decision-making. They were accustomed to eating domestically raised meats and had forgotten how to hunt. It was impossible for them to return to the ways of their ancestors. Furthermore, the land was no longer theirs. Some Chumash accepted jobs on large ranchos.

As European Americans moved in, the natives were subjected to abuse. Plains travelers, having been confronted by hostile tribes, feared the Chumash and struck out at them. Some natives were killed and many died of syphilis. Those who were left, lost their self-respect and their frequent drunkenness became a social problem.

In 1855, the American government came forward with a solution. They purchased about 100 acres near the Santa Ynez Mission for the surviving Chumash and moved 109 people to the Santa de Cota Reservation.

California became a state in 1850 and the government began questioning the validity of Mexican land grants. Boundary descriptions were vague and their wording was difficult to understand. Squatters tried to claim the lands of others. Eventually, however, the United States courts deemed all grants final by a system of patent.

California was then divided into twenty-seven segments – Santa Barbara being the county seat for the Ojai Valley. And on January 6, 1873, the supervisors voted to form Ventura County. By then, thirty-seven years had passed since Fernando Tico received the Ojai land grant.

He held his land for sixteen years. On May 25, 1853, he sold the entire Rancho Ojai to politician Henry Storrow Carnes of Santa Barbara for the sum of $7,500. Carnes turned the land over to Juan Camarillo for $10,600 on June 24, 1856. Camarillo, a successful Santa Barbara merchant, had come to California from Mexico in 1834 with the padres. Later he purchased Rancho Calleguas, which is now known as Camarillo.

John Bartlett bought Rancho Ojai on September 8, 1864, for $17,754, and sold it four days later to John B. Church and John Wyeth, earning a profit of $246. During the next month, Church and Wyeth conveyed half of the property to Charles H. Russel and Henry Alexander, who soon bought Church and Wyeth out. This duo sold the entire property to John P. Green on behalf of Thomas A. Scott, whose express purpose in owning the land was for petroleum exploration.

Chapter Two
From the Ground Up

The Discovery of Oil in California

In 1855, while most residents gave little notice to the tar-like substance that oozed from the ground throughout areas of California, General Andreas Pico, Governor Pio Pico's brother, and their nephew, Romulo, dug for oil in the Newhall area and sold it in San Fernando as a healing substance and an illuminate. Six years later, a man named Gilbert built California's first oil refinery.

George Shoobridge Gilbert, a native of Kent, England, ran a whale oil business in Brooklyn. When he heard about the California Gold Rush, he sold his business and traveled to San Francisco, where he eventually established a sperm whale oil firm known as Phoenix Oil Works.

Once, while on his way to Los Angeles with a shipment, Gilbert stopped to investigate rumors of oil seepage in the mountains behind San Buenaventura. Some historians believe that it was the odor of the tar pits drifting out to sea that enticed him to anchor off our coast and explore the area. Pleased with what he found here, Gilbert leased the oil rights for Rancho Ojai from Juan Camarillo and built a refinery on land that was, in reality, just inside the eastern boundary of Rancho Santa Ana – at the confluence of San Antonio Creek and the Ventura River near the western slope of Sulphur Mountain.

Gilbert manufactured kerosene and lubricating oil. On May 2, 1861, just after he shipped a reported 12,000 gallons of illuminating oil to San Francisco, fire destroyed the refinery. Eager to resume operations, he rebuilt only to have his good name marred when one of his shipments to the East never arrived. Exhausted muleteers had evidently dumped the one hundred barrels in the Panama Jungle, where they were discovered years later.

When his refinery exploded a second time, Gilbert gave up the oil business, joined Walter Chaffee in operating the only store in San Buenaventura and built a house on Ventura Avenue for his large family.

Around that time, Yale professor Benjamin Silliman had earned national respect as a petroleum expert based on his analysis of the Titusville, Pennsylvania crude. In 1864, Silliman came ashore in San Buenaventura aboard a sailor's back and toured Rancho Ojai extensively by horseback in search of the rumored vast oil fields. He wrote and told his friend, Thomas A. Scott, about the twenty natural oil wells he found in the rugged, brush-covered region called Ojai. Estimating a million-dollar profit, he wrote, "Oil struggles to the surface at every available point and is running down the rivers."

Scott, acting Assistant Secretary of War under President Lincoln, was a living success story – a wildcatter who, with his partners, Andrew Carnegie and J.E. Thomas, had struck it rich in the Pennsylvania oil boom. Scott gambled on a repeat performance in the oil fields out West and formed a syndicate that purchased 277,000 acres of California land, including Rancho Ojai.

Scott's Eastern commitments made it impossible for him to handle this most recent enterprise personally, so he hired Thomas R. Bard to manage his California investment.

Bard, a former law student in the office of the Honorable George Chambers in Chambersburg, Pennsylvania, had left the law profession a few years earlier when he began experiencing poor health. The remedy in those days was an active lifestyle in the fresh air so Bard joined an engineering corps.

In 1861, when the Civil War broke out, 21-year-old Bard took a job as transportation agent for the Cumberland Valley Railroad. He was in charge of transporting troops and war materials to the Potomac and Shenandoah Valley. Bard's character and courage in this capacity so impressed Scott that he wanted him in his employ.

Bard's ship docked in San Buenaventura in 1865. He moved into the Swiss chalet that Scott's men had built for him near Sulphur Mountain, one-quarter mile from Jose Arnaz's adobe at what is now Rancho Arnaz.

Bard arrived just two years after the drought that killed hundreds of cattle and their carcasses were, reportedly, still strewn all over the county. It couldn't have been particularly pleasant under these circumstances, but Bard was not here on vacation. He had work to do – work he knew very little about.

One of the first things Mr. Bard learned was that the equipment he had ordered sent to the drilling site was inadequate in California. The steam drilling rig, for example, went through Pennsylvania soil easily, but would not penetrate this rocky ground. The oil men had to improvise.

OVM
Thomas R. Bard, 1859.

Despite setbacks, Bard completed the first well early in 1866. Number One, near his home, produced only sulphur water and gas. He put down the second well in the vicinity of what is now Camp Comfort, south of Ojai on Creek Road. That well also turned up dry. Bard's labor force at the two wells numbered thirty men plus a crew of wood choppers who earned $1.50 per cord providing fuel for the huge, black boiler.

Even with veteran oil man, J.A. Beardsley, working alongside Bard, things weren't going well. They punched down three more wells and still produced nothing. But the same story was being told all over the state.

By then, seventy oil companies were drilling in Southern California, but no one was getting rich. Bard had already spent $200,000 of his company's money. With nothing to show for it, he feared Scott would order him to quit. Number Six in Upper Ojai was his last hope. He moved into Tico's old frame house and turned all of his energy and attention to this well. He pushed his crew hard. Bard knew that Number Six would make or break them.

They were down 550 feet when, on May 29, 1867, Number

Six spewed forth. This well produced fifteen to twenty barrels of good grade oil per day – the best Western yield yet. But it was too little and too late. From Pennsylvania, Scott ordered all drilling halted. He felt that the pursuit was impractical and he reached this conclusion not only from his own failure.

Taylor and Welty, authors of *Black Bonanza,* state that the companies that were exploring California's oil potential during that period had collectively spent $1,000,000 to produce 5,000 barrels of oil worth $10,000. Eastern coal oil sold in San Francisco for 54 cents a gallon less than the cost of refining marketable kerosene from the California oil. Not only was it costly to drill here, but transporting the product over narrow cow paths by wagon was ridiculously time consuming, thus expensive. The once promising California oil future suddenly seemed doomed.

John Green arrived to oversee the disposal of Scott's property. But by 1869, he returned to Philadelphia leaving the entire burden to Bard, who managed Scott's affairs until his death in 1881. Then Bard became administrator to Scott's estate. He advertised the land, which included Simi, Las Posas, Calleguas, Colonia, El Rio de Santa Clara, Canada Larga, Ojai and part of San Francisco and San Buenaventura, in the *Ventura Signal* (the county's first newspaper). Bard promised perfect title to the properties for which he was asking $1 to $20 per acre.

Fifteen years after well Number Six erupted, there was another attempt locally to make it big in California oil. In 1882, Lyman Stewart, one of the first to take an interest in the Titusville oil, and his partner, Wallace L. Hardison, arrived in Santa Paula. They pooled all of their resources to gamble on there being oil. For seven years they drilled and searched and borrowed so they could drill some more. Things worsened, but the men persisted.

By then Thomas Bard was considered to be the richest man in the county. Stewart and Hardison approached him for a financial boost and Bard showed faith in their project.

On October 17, 1890, the trio formed the Union Oil Company of California with its headquarters in Santa Paula. Bard was the first president of the company, Stewart held the position of vice president, Hardison was treasurer and I.H. Warring was their secretary. John Irwin, Alexander Waldie, Dan McFarland, W.S. Chaffee and Casper Taylor served as directors.

There's a lot more to the Union Oil story and it is wonderfully told in the Santa Paula Union Oil Museum at 1001 East Main Street in Santa Paula.

There's a marker near Bard's well Number Six along Highway 150 between Ojai and Santa Paula crediting it as being the first well drilled for oil in California that yielded extended commercial production and the forerunner of California's oil bonanza.

Oil and land were not Thomas Bard's only interests. He was the first English-speaking supervisor of Santa Barbara County from 1868-72. He was instrumental in forming the new county of Ventura and his peers elected him to the state senate in 1900. It is said of Mr. Bard that he never sought office, but was sought out by it.

Bard laid out the town of Port Hueneme and built the wharf there in 1871. He helped organize the Bank of Ventura and served as its president for fifteen years. He also established the Hueneme Bank. Bard earned a reputation for never foreclosing on a mortgage. It is said that many farmers became successful because of Mr. Bard's generosity.

In his 1883 *History of Santa Barbara and Ventura Counties*, Jesse D. Mason described Bard as being, "clear-headed, firm-hearted, modest and courteous and not given to much speaking except when speech is of the essence of things."

Bard's brother, Cephas, was the first American physician in San Buenaventura and he built Ventura's Elizabeth Bard Memorial Hospital around the turn of the century in honor of their mother. The beautiful building still stands on the corner of Poli and Fir Streets but is no longer a medical facility.

Early Settlers

Visions of vast oil fields over this valley faded when Scott removed his petroleum people. Their wagon roads, however, led the way for the next distinct assemblage of folks in the valley – stout-hearted adventurers in search of a home. Ojai was not for the tenderfoot. Grizzly bears and mountain lions roamed the valley floor. Lack of water resulted in extensive flea infestation and dense oak forests made movement from one place to another difficult.

We know who came here to exploit the hidden wealth of the land. But who came to establish their homes? What sort of people chanced life in an unknown, untamed wilderness? Who were these people so willing to brave the elements and to stand up against the inevitable hardships that accompany settlement in virgin territory? Who were the pioneers facing untold privation to feather the way for us? The following pages provide a panoramic view of days past and animate those who lived them.

Dr. Isaac Chauncey and Olive Mann Isbell

Dr. and Mrs. Isaac C. Isbell occupied the abandoned Tico adobe sometime between 1864 and '66 according to Ed M. Sheridan, historian and early publisher of the *Ventura Signal*. Olive Mann was born one of fifteen children in Ashtabula County, Ohio in 1824. She came from the same stock as Horace Mann, the noted educator (1796-1859). At the age of 20, Olive married Isaac Isbell and they settled in Warren County, Illinois.

Dr. Isbell was born in 1815 in New York. He graduated from Western Reserve College in Hudson, Ohio and studied medicine in Cleveland. He was considered a roamer by nature and so it was that the Isbells left Illinois in 1846 expecting to join the Donner Party. They missed the ill-fated group, however, and fell in with other families at Mt. Pleasant, Iowa where they formed a wagon train heading westward.

John Fremont heard about the large caravan approaching Sutter's Fort and, representing the United States Army, he sent runners to enlist the men's help in a rumble with the Mexicans. As a safety measure, soldiers moved the refugees to the Santa Clara Mission. Dr. Isbell remained behind with them to administer necessary medical care.

The children had nothing to do and their boredom led to mischievousness. In order to occupy them, Mrs. Isbell volunteered to start a school. Her classroom was a fifteen-foot square stable from which they removed a few roof tiles to let light in. Her twenty pupils sat on boxes. Supplies consisted of what few books the children's parents had carried across the plains. And Olive wrote letters on her hand to teach the students the alphabet.

In April, five families, including the Isbells, moved to Monterey where Isaac reportedly built the first hotel. Mrs. Isbell hadn't been in town for thirty minutes when the United States consul, Thomas Larkin, approached her and requested that she teach their school. This time she held classes in a space above the jail. Because of the sloping roof, larger pupils sat at the ends and in the middle of the room while the smaller children sat along the sides. Olive had fifty-six pupils and enough books to accommodate only half of them.

In 1849, California created a school system. The first public school opened April 8, 1850, in San Francisco. Even though her career spanned a mere matter of months, Olive Mann Isbell will always be known as the first American teacher in California.

Later, the Isbells settled on a large ranch eight miles from Stockton and forty-five miles from Sutter's Fort. They provided food for the miners who passed by their place. Meals were $1, butter $2, eggs were $3 a dozen and they sold raisins pound for pound for gold. Some say that the Isbells made a fortune trading with Indians and miners. They often held gold in safekeeping for the miners. Olive remembered once having 150 pounds of gold hidden around their house.

It wasn't long before Dr. Isbell had the fever to move on. They relocated on a 9,000-acre ranch southwest of San Antonio, Texas. The Civil War chased them back to California, however, with the doctor's rifle as their only possession. This time they found their way to Ojai and moved into the abandoned Tico adobe.

Sheridan, in a speech published in a 1925 edition of *The Ojai*, described Tico's old home as being among a group of adobes "a stone's throw from the packing house," which was on the west side of what is now Bryant Street. He said that a man named Nacho Rodriguez once told him that he was born in one of the adobes 77 years before. Sheridan said that the Isbells ran a dairy business from the Tico adobe when they lived there.

Thomas Bard once found Dr. Isbell suffering from two broken legs after having fallen from a moving wagon. Bard took the couple into his Creek Road home and, while her husband rested and healed, Olive cooked and cared for him and Mr. Bard.

The Isbells eventually settled in Santa Paula where, in 1924, the community posthumously honored Olive by naming a school for her. Dr. Isbell died in 1886 and Olive passed away thirteen years later. Both are buried in the Santa Paula Cemetery.

The Founding of Nordhoff

The first assemblage of Easterners to the valley came in search of oil. The next distinct group to come were pioneers seeking better health.

Lorenzo Dow Roberts arrived with bronchitis so bad he could barely speak above a whisper. He weighed a mere 124 pounds. In less than a year, he had gained over forty pounds and could be heard shouting, they say, from a mile away. Roberts' experience so enthused him that he decided to share this mecca of health restoration with others.

VCHS
Lorenzo Dow Roberts.

On July 26, 1873, he staked out a section of his fifty-five acre farm in the vicinity of Park Road on what is now Grand Avenue, with the intentions of developing a town. He planned to call his town *Ojai*. He divided his land into150-foot lots. To entice settlers, Roberts promised to give away every other lot.

In the fall of 1873, the *Ventura Signal* ran several long articles extolling Ojai's wonders. "Ojai would make an excellent sanitarium," the editor wrote, and he listed the abundance of lumber, favorable climate and close proximity to a seaport as some of the reasons.

Royes Gaylord Surdam, an ambitious Ventura businessman who dabbled in real estate, read about Ojai with interest. Early in 1874, he purchased 1,606 acres west of Roberts for the sum of $7,974. He is credited with starting the first large-scale subdivision promotion in Ventura County. Where wildlife roamed through lavish vegetation, Surdam envisioned a public square, a fountain, an academy and a chapel. He drew a map including all of these embellishments and he advertised heavily.

Roberts' ads appeared in the *Ventura Signal* alongside Surdam's. But Surdam's advertisements were even more far-reaching. He mailed detailed brochures to Eastern doctors suggesting that they send their incurable patients to his town where the remarkable climate would heal them. Formerly known as *White Oak Flats*, Surdam now planned to call the place *Bardstown*, after his friend and the former custodian of the land, Thomas Bard. This idea made Bard uncomfortable, however, and he discouraged it.

Surdam advertised a free parcel of land to anyone willing to build a hotel on it. Abram Blumberg, a lawyer who had recently moved from Iowa to Los Angeles, accepted the offer and began construction in the northern portion of what is now Libbey Park.

The January 17, 1874 issue of the *Ventura Signal* announced that the new village would be named *Topa Topa*. A week later, the newspaper reported that the name had been changed to *Nordhoff*.

Blumberg tells this story about the naming of the town in an 1887 issue of *The Ojai*, "Surdam, my wife and myself were discussing a name. Surdam suggested *Topa Topa* and finally my wife said, 'Why not name the town for the man whose description of the county caused us to come here?' And so we adopted her suggestion and named the town *Nordhoff*."

Blumberg (erroneously) believed that *Topa Topa* meant *gopher gopher* in the Chumash language and said, "If you look upon the Topa Topa mountains and give your imagination a very wide range, you will see the outline of two gophers –

Berry family collection
Abram Blumberg.

one chasing the other. From this stretch of imagination, the Indians named the mountain." (See Chapter One for Chumash word meanings.)

According to Inez Blumberg Berry, her mother, Catharine Blumberg, had reason to honor Charles Nordhoff. She said that Catharine was sickly and spent a lot of time in bed. She read to overcome boredom. After reading Charles Nordhoff's book on the health benefits of California, she persuaded her husband to come here. The family lived in Los Angeles for a while and Catharine's health did not improve. After coming to the Ojai Valley, however, she regained her health within a year.

On April 11, 1874, Blumberg's Nordhoff Hotel opened with a gala ball. Some say that 300 people attended the affair. The *Ventura Signal*, however, lists just seventy names of partygoers including, Thomas Bard, Robert Ayers, William Pirie, George Gilbert, Thomas Clark, Sol and Ed Sheridan, George H. Suhren, Lafayette Herbert and Ed Lucas. Some guests traveled from as far away as Santa Barbara to attend this lavish promotional banquet and dance.

Mr. Surdam, the founder of the town, was king. After a $3.25-a-plate dinner, Surdam explained his plans for the development of Nordhoff and he offered land outside the proposed town limits at $6.25 per acre.

Royes Gaylord Surdam

Royes Gaylord Surdam was born in Duchess County, New York, in 1835. He received his education in Illinois and came to California in 1854 and to San Buenaventura in 1866. A man of varied business interests, Surdam is credited with erecting the first warehouse in Ventura, which was used to store grain and petroleum. He, reportedly, shipped oil to San Francisco to be used in preparation of the timbers for the famous Palace Hotel. Some historians believe him to have been the county's first brick maker. He started the first packing house in San Buenaventura and built the first fruit dryer there. In 1872, Surdam entered the sheep business in Las Posas with Thomas Bard.

Although Surdam was involved in many enterprises, he was never considered a very successful man, particularly where his development of Nordhoff was concerned. Families moved in, but made their homes in the outlying wilderness of the valley – showing little interest in Surdam's town acreage.

Even *he* didn't live in his town. Surdam maintained his headquarters at the Santa Clara House Hotel in San Buenaventura.

He deeply believed in Nordhoff, however. In fact, he offered half of his worldly goods to anyone who could discover a case of uncured asthma in the valley.

Within a few months, however, Surdam sold his interest in Nordhoff to John Montgomery. Surdam went on to plan the first county fair in September, 1877. This event was actually a variation of an annual Mexican rodeo called San Miguel Day. In earlier years, Mexicans celebrated this event with a big fiesta, bullfights, cockfights and horse races. Surdam held a facsimile of the traditional ball in Spear's Hall, one of the town's earliest saloons which was situated on the southeast corner of Main and Palm Streets in Ventura.

A pavilion held local exhibits and participants raced horses on a one-mile track near the beach. In 1891, Hueneme hosted the county fair. Shortly after that, it was dropped and was not revived until the county acquired Seaside Park along the beach in West Ventura, around 1914.

Myrtle Shepherd Frances was a little girl living in San Buenaventura when she knew Colonel Surdam (as he liked to be called). She described him as a "grizzled old bachelor," who had a twinkle in his blue eyes and always wore a black, wide-brimmed hat. She remembered him letting children put their hands inside his coat pockets in search of the inevitable peppermint candy.

According to Yda Addis Storke in her book of biographical sketches (see Bibliography), Surdam, a Royal Arch Mason and a staunch Republican, eventually moved to Bardsdale where he managed that subdivision. She wrote of Surdam, "He is a man of very generous impulses – not so much after making and hoarding money as to help his fellow men." In September of 1891, the same year that Storke's book was published, Surdam died of a presumed morphine overdose. He was 56.

John Montgomery Arrives

John Montgomery arrived in San Buenaventura from Santa Barbara during the summer of 1874 in search of a healthier environment for his ailing wife, Jacobita. He stopped at Surdam's office and viewed the maps of the embryo town. He was most eager to see this well-designed hamlet.

In Montgomery's words, "Anxious to reach the Ojai, we hurried off in a private conveyance and the seven of us alighted

Fry photo
Map of Royes Gaylord Surdam's town.

at the Blumberg Hotel. We searched in vain for the grand square, the town hall site and improvements we had seen on the map." But, alas, Surdam had not yet begun construction.

Montgomery and his family were bewildered, but not disappointed. He said, "Grander than any map painting was stamped on nature's great canvas, the dense oak forest; the perpetual play of sunshine through the foliage; the towering mountains, guardians of the rustic beauty below; and above all the balmy breath of life soothing the tender tissue of throat and lung." He goes on to say that after arriving in the Ojai Valley, his wife never had another attack of asthma.

In December of 1874, Montgomery procured 1,300 acres of Surdam's land. A short time later a man named Colonel Wiggins bought the town site, including the hotel, which, according to author, Walter Bristol was, "A small, rather flimsy affair to begin with."

Most of the names Surdam had chosen for his city streets are still with us today, with one conspicuous exception. His original chart listed the street *See Saw*. Around 1878, people spelled it *Se Sa* and a few years later, map-makers referred to that street as *Sisar*. An 1887 map shows it as *Empire Street*. By 1897, they called it *Signal*, as it is known today.

What happened to Roberts' town? According to the *Ventura Signal*, he gave up after Surdam stepped in with his bigger and better ideas and he planted 2,000 raisin grape cuttings in the area where Ojai might have been.

OVM
John Montgomery (left) and unidentified man at the entrance to Montgomery's home.

John Montgomery expressed surprise that Surdam was never properly honored. He stated in one early letter that the citizens of Nordhoff were ungrateful, "otherwise," he said, "Nordhoff would have a monumental pile of rocks in honor of Surdam, its founder, who cared for it in its infancy and gave it its first hoist in life." He continued, "Never did a fond parent extol the merits of its offspring as did Mr. Surdam the healing qualities of Nordhoff's climate."

Charles Nordhoff

Charles Nordhoff's first glimpse of Coastal California was in the line of duty with the United States Navy aboard the warship *Columbus*. He is reported to have said once that this was the least inviting land he'd ever seen. Twenty-four years later, in 1871, he took a journalistic tour of Southern California and San Buenaventura was included in his extensive itinerary. Thomas Bard, reportedly, showed him around Simi.

The New York Herald published the results of his observations, then the Harper brothers printed Nordhoff's California story in their popular magazine. A short time later, the Harpers published his material in book form under the title, *California for Health, Pleasure and Residence: A Book for Travelers and Settlers.*

Nordhoff's book aroused the interest of many Easterners. Those who missed the gold rush began to migrate in droves to tropical California where the "summers are endless." The au-thor demonstrated faith in his words by leaving his home in New Jersey for sunny California. He chose Santa Barbara as a possible home and was shocked to see the tremendous growth that had occurred since his last visit. There were not enough facilities to accommodate all who came.

San Diego Historical Society
Charles Nordhoff.

Nordhoff did not mention the Ojai Valley in the first edition of his book, but in 1882, when it was reprinted, he included this description: "The valley is famous even in California for the abundance and loveliness of its woods of evergreen oaks. It presents the appearance, in fact, of a magnificent old English park." He continues, "In the middle of the Ojai Valley lies a little hamlet, which the people have been kind enough to name after the author of this book." He says, "The air of the valley has been found especially favorable to persons with abnormally sensitive throats or lungs." And he says that Nordhoff is a "lovely sheltered nook where the frailest invalids are benefited."

According to the September 21, 1889 issue of *The Ventura Vidette*, Charles Nordhoff, his wife and three daughters visited Nordhoff that month. In 1892, he requested a subscription to the local newspaper and two years later he visited Nordhoff again. He and Mrs. Nordhoff signed the register at the Gally Cottages on April 18, 1894. On May 9, Sherman Day Thacher, founder of Thacher School, held a formal reception honoring the Nordhoffs.

Before leaving Ojai Valley, Nordhoff spoke at the Congregational Church. He impressed the audience with his knowledge of California and charmed them in his well-mannered, quiet way. He left them with his contribution to an ever-growing list of descriptive terms of Ojai by saying that the valley was a "lovely pocket in the mountains."

The Nordhoffs spent their last years between their home in Coronado and their beloved Santa Barbara.

On July 14, 1901, Charles Nordhoff died in San Francisco where he had gone to obtain treatment for diabetes. Nordhoff's grandson and namesake co-authored *Mutiny on the Bounty*.

The Valley Settlement Grows

The little settlement in the Ojai Valley had a name, a hotel and even a few residents. Next to come were local services. In 1874, Lafayette R. Herbert opened Nordhoff's first store on the north side of the dirt path now known as Ojai Avenue, opposite the western boundary of Blumberg's Nordhoff Hotel. The fifteen by thirty-foot frame structure served as department store, drug store, hardware and implement store, grocery and post office. Yet, Herbert kept relatively few items in stock. Mainly, he took orders for merchandise and livery stable owner Andy Van Curen picked up the items in San Buenaventura.

Everything came in large barrels, sacks or boxes from which shoppers scooped the amounts needed. Since nothing was packaged, the air in the small store was always heavy with the aroma of coffee, spices and leather. Herbert encouraged bartering. Typically, a farmer could obtain coal oil, calico, flour and harnesses by trading chickens, hams and eggs.

The little store quickly became a gathering place where the menfolk discussed local and world happenings and struck up acquaintances while warming themselves around the inviting wood stove. In the summer, the same men congregated on the large porch.

OVM
First store in Nordhoff, 1874.

In 1861, San Buenaventura's first postmaster, Volney Simpson, carried mail in the crown of his sombrero, calling on those for whom he had letters. Anyone who lived outside the perimeter of that town rode in to fetch their mail.

The January 3, 1874 issue of the *Ventura Signal* announced that there was a petition being circulated in Nordhoff to establish a post office. In the meantime, Andy Van Curen established a tri-weekly mail stage between Nordhoff and San Buenaventura. On March 21, 1874, it was official. Nordhoff had a post office and the newlywed Herbert was the postmaster.

Subsequent postmasters were:

Richard Jenness	1875
Addison Garland	1875 to 1876
Thomas Gilbert	1876 to 1883
Benjamin F. Brown	1883 to 1886
George Stewart	1886 to 1889
Benjamin Spencer	1889 to 1893
George Mallory	1893 to 1897
Samuel Smith	1897 to 1914

George Mallory returned to the post in the fall of 1914.

Andy Van Curen, who opened Ojai Valley's first livery stable, also served as Nordhoff's first constable. He once said, "Every town should have a jail." In the summer of 1874, according to valley pioneer, Joseph Waite, Van Curen built his home on the southwest corner of Ojai Avenue and Blanche Street where Bank of America is now and shortly thereafter he built a jail in his backyard.

He placed four-inch wide boards flat on top of one another and nailed them together by driving iron spikes one-inch apart. There were two cells, each with an iron door. The jail was windowless, but there was a six-inch square slot in each cell for air. Andy was also, the town undertaker and old-timers recall that he used the jail more to store coffins in than to house criminals.

OVM

Original Ojai jail, now at Cold Springs Tavern in Santa Barbara.

Elizabeth Thacher (Sherman Day Thacher's daughter) once said of the old wooden jail, "It was seldom used, but occasionally housed an obstreperous hoodlum or drunk shut up to consider his sins or sleep off his hangover."

In those days, citizens had little tolerance for real outlaws.

John Montgomery, in a letter published in *The Ojai Valley: Gateway to Health and Happiness*, told about one incident that wasn't soon forgotten. "With a single latch on the door we considered our houses burglarproof; and the words, 'money box' painted on an old fruit case was legal notice to the public to keep its hands off; but one morning we heard the startling news that Gilbert's store (formerly Herbert's store) had been robbed. Suspicion rested on two young strangers and half a dozen formed themselves into a vigilant committee; disguised themselves and pounced upon the suspected culprits as they lay in bed, marched them to a convenient live oak tree and tried by moral persuasion to extract that most precious essence, the truth, from a rebellious raw material." Montgomery goes on to say that it wasn't until they threw a rope over a tree limb that the culprits confessed.

The posse took the criminals to San Buenaventura and stood with them in front of a judge, only to be told that they were going to be arrested for their participation in the "moonlight circus." According to Montgomery, "The tables were turned and the conquering heroes of the morning were seen flying back to Nordhoff to take a last farewell of their families ere the interior architecture of the state's prison would engage their attention." He says that friendly intervention ultimately saved the men.

When the townspeople wanted to replace the aging constable, his feelings were hurt and he refused to let them have his jail.

In 1928, the city of Ojai petitioned the Ventura County Board of Supervisors to build a new jail. The Department of Fish and Game built one behind Libbey Park. Often referred to as a "cement box," this four-cell jail was constructed of eight inch thick, steel reinforced concrete walls. This jail, designed to hold eight prisoners, housed around 650 people in the nearly fifty years it was in use – some of them, reportedly, spending a full year in there. And no one ever escaped.

Most arrests were for crimes like writing bad checks, disturbing the peace or public intoxication. By day, prisoners worked with the city maintenance crew and at night, after dinner at a local restaurant, they were locked in the small jail. During one six month period in 1953, inmates logged 3,584 hours of labor for the city.

City officials didn't abandon the cement jail until the 1970s. Modern-day arresting officers still chuckle when remembering lawbreakers' reactions to being taken to the tiny, primitive jail. According to one officer, "There was a lot of arguing and resisting when we'd drive them down that dark, desolate road to the jail."

The police station in those days was just east of the arcade at 338 East Ojai Avenue. Because the jail was situated a good two blocks away and there were not enough officers to stand guard there, it was linked to police headquarters by an ordinary intercom system. The officer on duty was privy to whatever went on down at the jail, which sometimes included family picnics and lovers' rendezvous.

The Ojai City Jail, also known as Libbey Park Jail, still stands just south of the old Southern Pacific right-of-way behind Libbey Park. The Ojai Historic Preservation Commission is in the process of renovating it and giving it Ojai City Landmark status.

Fry Photo
Libbey Park jail.

Andy Van Curen and his wife, Esther (Horton), raised six children. She died suddenly in 1894 and Andy married Gussie Waite Corbett the following year. Andy lived until 1923.

Several years later, Mrs. Krough, who lived on the old Van Curen property, offered the old wooden jail to the city. The Kroughs had no use for it except as a storage shed for chicken feed. Unfortunately, the city wasn't in a position to take the jail and declined the gift. The jail has been preserved, however, and it stands today in a dark corner behind Cold Springs Tavern on San Marcos Pass above Santa Barbara.

Pioneer Doctors

The country doctor of a century ago held a place of considerable respect in his community. When he established a village practice, he committed himself to the entire populace – usually for the rest of his life. A country doctor rarely had competition. People relied on him despite the fact that most of his seriously ill patients died. Diagnosis was practically impossible until the disease reached advanced stages.

A good physician, however, possessed the ability to put his patients at ease and to console family members. He did the best he could and was appreciated for that. Knowledge wasn't the only thing he lacked. By today's standards, his equipment and facilities were limited and grossly inadequate. The early doctor often performed surgery in a farm kitchen. There were no antibiotics, so he sometimes had to amputate to cure an infection. Probably the most important function of the old country doctor was the bringing of new lives into the world.

OVM
Francis J. Nelson, MD, 1885.

In 1877, Dr. W.H. French came to Nordhoff to care for the valley ailing. French, a graduate of Harvard Medical School, received patients at Thomas Gilbert's store.

Dr. F.J. Nelson practiced here in 1885. He treated John Montgomery on occasion. According to Ventura County tax records for that period, Dr. Nelson owned a personal library worth $25, a watch priced at $25, a harness taxed for $25 and professional instruments valued at $25.

Doctor and Mrs. Wilson P. Kern and their sons, Peter and Frankie, lived here as early as 1887. They bought property in Nordhoff and planned to make this their home. When Dr. Kern became ill, he asked a colleague, Dr. Benjamin L. Saeger, to help him in his practice. Saeger spent the next forty years tending to the health of valley residents.

Dr. Benjamin L. Saeger

Saeger had earned his medical degree at the University of Michigan and had opened an office in Pennsylvania prior to being called to duty in Nordhoff. Alone in his practice here, he sometimes consulted with Dr. Cephas Bard in San Buenaventura.

Saeger opened the Ojai Drug Store in 1892 and began receiving his mobile patients there. His office hours were from 6-8 a.m. and 4-6 p.m.

People described Saeger as slow of motion and speech, but he was immensely reassuring to his patients and their loved ones. Everyone considered him a deeply kind man. In 1900, Dr. Saeger married Pearl McDonald and they had one son, Levan.

Dr. Saeger traveled to his patients' bedsides on horseback initially. Then he drove a horse and buggy. But most early residents remembered Doc Saeger making house calls in his Blue Streak Buick. Several years after the turn of the century Dr. Saeger sold the drug store and opened an office in his home on the northwest corner of Ventura and Santa Ana Streets. He practiced medicine until his death in 1934.

Early Cemeteries

Even though Ojai's climate and fresh dry air cured many ailing Easterners, some of them died here. In the early 1870s, a few citizens established a cemetery west of town at the current intersection of Del Norte and Cuyama Roads. A few years later, John Montgomery, whose land holdings included that parcel, deeded it to the citizens of Nordhoff for their cemetery. The graveyard contained six bodies then.

The first burial in the cemetery is thought to be 26 year-old Charles A. Weismann who died of an accidental gunshot wound in the spring of 1875. Weismann, a native of New York, was driving his wagon one day with a Colt Navy laying on the seat beside him. He ran over a stone and the pistol jolted off, hit the ground and discharged a bullet into him. He tried to run to Mr. Newby's house, which was fifty yards away, but fainted from loss of blood. He died a short time later.

Once the cemetery had been officially established as such, the townsfolk strung wire around posts to protect the cemetery from the intrusive hooves of freely grazing cattle. After every heavy rain, volunteers repaired and replaced those crude fences as the cemetery is situated in a natural stream bed. Not only did the swiftly rushing water frequently wash out fence posts, but it often carried away grave markers, as well.

Mary Gally's husband died in late 1893 and a few months later, she presented the cemetery association with a windmill along with the understanding that they would dig a well, thus provide water to "keep our city of the dead" green. Editor Leverett Mesick remarked in *The Ojai* a month later that the well had been dug but it and the windmill as yet were "unacquainted with one another." In 1905, William L. Thacher, John Wesley Heck and Edwin Baker became the first official trustees chosen in behalf of the little memorial park.

Throughout the years, there would be flurries of interest in the cemetery and groups would work to clear away the brush, trim the oaks, remove dead limbs and so forth. But there were always extended periods when the cemetery suffered from neglect and vandalism. In 1940, the 4-H Club and Future Farmers of America joined the American Legion in organizing a clean-up event. Mexican nationals from the Ojai Orange Association packing house came out in 1950 to help the Lions Club and Boy Scouts clean up the cemetery for Memorial Day services. In 1963, the city hired Ben Noren and his son to build the rock wall on the south perimeter of the cemetery and the following year, the city provided a bulletin board which listed the names of veterans buried there. It now serves as a sign to identify the Nordhoff Cemetery.

The rock wall on the east side of the cemetery was dedicated in 1994 by the Ojai Valley Garden Club, the same year the Nordhoff Cemetery became an Ojai City Historic Landmark.

Probably the biggest project ever launched on behalf of our little pioneer cemetery was Julie DelPozzo's Adopt-a-Grave program. Started in 1991 in honor of her recently deceased father, Frank George Tarcza, DelPozzo organized about 150 volunteers to care for over 250 grave sites. Volunteers repair and replace broken and missing grave markers, plant and tend flowers and clean away debris and weeds. Some of the volunteers have gone so far as to correspond with the families of the deceased.

This author's book, *Nordhoff Cemetery*, was the result of accelerated interest in our pioneer cemetery, as volunteers were hungry to know more about the pioneers whose graves they were tending.

Fry Photo
Nordhoff Cemetery.

Ours is a quaint cemetery with a country garden atmosphere. Some markers are merely native stone with the names of beloved ones scratched into them. Fading letters are barely visible on old wooden crosses. There are also large, impressive headstones which give entire families recognition. But mostly one finds simple tradition marking the resting places of those who came here to live and quietly died. Large oaks spread their limbs protectively over the graves of those who once walked this valley.

Villanova Cemetery

Father Ylla established a Catholic cemetery on Villanova Road around the turn of the century. Prior to that, valley Catholics traveled to Ventura to bury their loved ones. During the rainy season, when the roads were impassable, funerals were often delayed. Understandably, the inconvenience caused bereaved families a great deal of anxiety. Catholics abandoned the old cemetery sometime around the 1950s and vandals have destroyed all but a scant few fragmental reminders of those who rest there.

Stow Chapel

Probably as early as 1864, New Yorker, John Talcott Stow, came to California with his widowed mother, Anna, and younger brother, Frank. John supported the family by breaking horses and doing other chores for Thomas Bard during the early oil days. He later became a county supervisor.

Anna, evidently a deeply religious woman, wanted to build a chapel on a pretty spot along Creek Road, but her sons were against it. When 16 year-old Frank was thrown from a horse and killed, however, she went ahead with her idea and buried her son there. The Episcopalian Chapel was reportedly built on a section of the Larmers' ranch.

OVM
Stow Chapel.

During the 1930s, two graves were visible and most people assumed that the two Stow boys occupied them. Some historians believe that all three Stows, Mrs. John Larmer, Mrs. John Wyeth and several small children lay peacefully there. Stow Chapel is visible from North Creek Road, but it is on private property and is not open to the public.

Valley Roadways

Until 1878, there was one route into the valley – Creek Road. During the summer months, travelers bound for Nordhoff endured constant clouds of dust billowing about. The rainy season resulted in yet another inconvenience – mud. The road crossed the creek seventeen times, according to Elizabeth Thacher, who was born in Ojai around the turn of the century. This was a dangerous route to travel during the rainy season.

Yda Storke, in her 1891 book of biographical sketches, seemed to see the glass as half full with regard to the river crossings along Creek Road when she wrote, "The drive to Ojai follows an easy grade along a beautiful clear stream where trout sport and twinkle."

Blackberry vines and maidenhair fern grew in abundance along Creek Road in those days and, at certain times of the year, one would be treated to the sight of wild grapes hanging from the majestic oaks in great, purple clusters.

In 1878, Casitas Pass (Highway 150) opened and was, for several years, the main route between Santa Barbara and San Buenaventura. The supervisors thought it was worthwhile to build this road even at the estimated cost of $6,000, because the Rincon route needed $800 in repairs annually. Until Highway 101 was completed along the Rincon, Casitas Pass was a link in the great Royal Highway, El Camino Real. Roadmen marked it as such by placing a bell at the highest point along the dirt buggy road.

Although most people took the ride for granted, at least one traveler was highly impressed by the scenery along Casitas Pass and described it in an article which appeared in an 1891 issue of Nordhoff's newspaper, *The Ojai*. He told of high cliffs covered with a "network of vines, ferns, and trees." There were streams, he wrote, "leading to deep pools below silvery falls that shimmered from either side of the dirt wagon path." Others described layers of ferns hanging in the oaks and wild flowers blooming in all shades of the rainbow.

OVM
Connie Rogers Wash (standing) and her brother, Emery, and mother, Florence Halliday Rogers Gorham, in their Stutz Bearcat on Casitas Pass Road.

Prior to the construction of Highway 101 to Santa Barbara, the Rincon route, although sometimes passable, was often treacherous. Steep cliffs abutted the beach. During high tide, the waves crashed against those cliffs, making travel impossible. The sand beds were not suited to wagons carrying heavy loads. Because of the changing ocean tides, those using Rincon Beach as a thoroughfare did so usually with some delay and always with precision timing.

In 1913, a wooden causeway was built along the Rincon to Santa Barbara. Some old-timers recall the drive as better than traversing the sand, but still hazardous. It was usually slippery from the ocean spray. And the frequent water bath warped the wood, loosening nails which often found their way into the tires of unsuspecting motorists. The speed limit on the Rincon Causeway was only 15 mph.

OVM
Rincon Causeway, circa 1913.

It was during Robert Ayers' term as Ventura County Supervisor in 1884 that the Nordhoff Road (Ventura Avenue into the Ojai Valley) was built. High waters in the Ventura River during the winter of 1889-90 cut away a portion of that road just below the Casitas Crossing, however, and workers built a temporary route along the bluff. It was a steep grade making travel to and from Nordhoff treacherous and uncomfortable.

While running for Ventura County Supervisor in 1892, Kenneth P. Grant promised to reroute that portion of the road. His plan was to build a road around the hill which he called Foster's Hump on the river side to get a good, safe road without a grade. Grant's road was opened to traffic in June of 1893.

Old Creek Road, just south of the Rancho Arnaz apple barn, is the original Creek Road. Santa Ana Road, which led to the Casitas Valley, commenced directly across from the apple barn.

Sulphur Mountain Road was completed in 1892 by James B. Fox and a force of workmen.

In 1921 there were two routes to Upper Ojai: Dennison Grade and Thompson Road. After much debate and study, in 1925, Dennison Grade became the main road to the upper valley because it was an easier drive and also considered more picturesque. Hikers and residents in the upper valley have no doubt seen the remains of the old abandoned paved road.

OVM
Workers building Maricopa Highway, circa, 1930.

Weary workmen finished Highway 33 (Maricopa Highway) to Cuyama in 1933. It took 400 tons of explosives to move the mountains to make way for the road and the project reportedly took six years.

Jay Cortner family photo
Maricopa Highway through tunnel to Wheelers Springs.

Chapter Three

An Intimate Glance At Ojai Valley Circa 1879

In 1879, when Sol and Ed Sheridan published the *Ventura Signal*, they toured the county's outlying communities and wrote a series of articles featuring the people and their farms. They described Ojai Valley as being a huge white and live oak forest that was interspersed with cottonwood and sycamore trees. Moss hung pendulously from the white oaks, dangling in particularly generous clumps along Creek Road, they said, creating a most ominous effect.

Farmers had planted the fields in and around Nordhoff primarily to wheat during the early 1870s. Even under the shade of the oaks, grain grew high and thick most years. An unusually wet winter in 1878, however, damaged this crop considerably and the Sheridan brothers saw evidence of the loss all over the valley.

The Ventura Signal Visits Ojai Residents

In 1879, Thomas Gilbert ran Nordhoff's only store which was opposite the Nordhoff Hotel on Ojai Avenue. Three years earlier, Gilbert, a merchant at Chaffee and McKeeby's store in San Buenaventura, had taken an extended leave due to a serious illness. He came to Ojai Valley and its climate proved so beneficial to his health that he chose to remain here. The Andy Van Curen family, Reverend Townsend Taylor and his daughter, Sarah McFarland, lived in cottages near the store. The Nordhoff brick schoolhouse was tucked under the oaks several yards behind the store.

John Montgomery

John Montgomery lived in a tropical-style adobe house at the east edge of the small village. He was born in Liverpool, England, in 1834 and received a good education there and in France. Mr. Montgomery traveled quite extensively. While he was a merchant in Mexico, he met Jacobita Tejerina de la Fuente whose grand uncle was the author of the Constitution of the Republic of Mexico. They were married in 1863 and had four children: Antonio (Otan), Helen (Mrs. Charles Robinson), Juana, and Jacobita.

After deciding to make this valley their home, John Montgomery bought most of the town and built a house in what he considered the most desirable location. His home, at what is now 310 East Matilija Street, was considered by the Sheridans one of the most charming residences in the valley. He maintained fifty acres for his home site, planted twenty to wheat and had several acres of citrus both to the east and west of his house. He built a wind machine to raise well water, utilizing auxiliary power mostly because, as he said, "There is little wind in Ojai." The Sheridans remarked that Montgomery's home was completely under fence. A row of Italian cypress trees led the way from the front gate on Ojai Avenue at the east end of what is now the arcade, along a path to the home. Montgomery Street was named for this influential resident, who died in 1916.

Lorenzo Dow Roberts

Around 1873, Lorenzo Dow Roberts purchased fifty-five acres from A.J. Bryant, for whom Bryant Street is named. This land encompassed the area between Grand and Ojai Avenues in the vicinity of what is now Shady Lane and Park Road. Roberts' home was a neat, hospitable cottage almost hidden from view by huge pepper trees and other ornamental shrubs. A picket fence surrounded his house. Roberts had his own blacksmith shop and a twenty-two by thirty-two-foot barn on his property. The Sheridans reported that when they visited in 1879, Roberts specialized in growing peaches.

Lorenzo and Margaret Roberts' daughter, Rebecca, married James B. Fox and when Roberts died, in 1884 at the age of 67, he was buried on the Fox place in the vicinity of where Fox

Street is today. Ten years later, his body was exhumed and re-interred at the Nordhoff Cemetery where it rests in the Fox family plot.

Piries, Larmers and Reiths

The Scottish-born Piries (pronounced Peerie) lived south of Nordhoff across San Antonio Creek and east of Creek Road. Using today's directions from Ojai, one would take Ventura Street south down Creek Road about one mile to the second bridge and turn left there.

William Pirie, a machinist by trade, had come from Aberdeen, Scotland in 1856 at the age of 24 to join his two brothers in New York. He married Margaret Buchanan in 1869 and they had seven children. The Piries were lured to the county in 1873 by Reverend Bristol's pamphlet about Ventura.

They ran 400 head of sheep on their land and lived in a handsome, two-story, frame house accented by large porches and bay windows. Margaret Pirie enhanced their home with a well-filled flower garden. The Sheridans were impressed to see Pirie hoisting water from the creek and conveying it through pipes for domestic use. Pirie Street was named for this pioneer family.

John Larmer had seventy-four acres north of the San Antonio Creek along Creek Road. Larmer farmed one acre of pumpkins, thirty-five acres of wheat, two acres of alfalfa and left the rest of his land to timber. His wife, Rachel Elizabeth (White) had accompanied him to Ojai, but she died in 1877. One account says that she was buried on their ranch under an oak tree where she loved to sit and read, while another says she may have been buried in the Stow Chapel. Mrs. Larmer's body was later removed to the Nordhoff Cemetery.

John Larmer, a native of Canada, fought in the Civil War as a Union soldier in Company H, 3rd Iowa Infantry and was injured at Jackson, Mississippi. He died in an old soldiers home in 1907 at the age of 77.

John Reith's sixty-two acres joined Larmer's on the east and his and Larmer's land bordered Pirie's northern boundary. Reith grew potatoes, pumpkins and other vegetables. He built an adobe house for his family and a milk house where they made butter.

The Soule Family

Cyrus Edwin Sowles brought his family here from Sonoma in 1873 in hopes that the climate would make him a well man. He and his wife, Matilda A. (Kager), had five children: William, who met with a violent death in Nordhoff (see Chapter Nine), Earl, Nina and Zaidee, who all lived long and productive lives in the valley, and Lillian, who died in 1900 at the age of 34. None of the Sowles offspring ever married. Mr. Sowles changed the spelling of the family name to Soule sometime after coming here.

The Soule property, which encompassed 310 acres, bordered Roberts' land on the north and the Pirie's on the south. Part of this property is now Soule Park and Soule Golf Course.

The Soules had a handsome dwelling which the Sheridans noted was very neatly painted. The fact that Mr. Soule graveled his road also impressed the editors of the *Ventura Signal.* They further reported that numerous live oak trees dotted the landscape

OVM
Cyrus and Matilda Soule.

naturally and that the Soules brought in four Italian cypress trees to further adorn their yard. The Soules had about two acres planted to fruit trees including cherry, a county novelty. The barn measured forty by fifty feet including the crib and carriage shelter. Soule also planted 100 acres of wheat, twelve acres of barley and six acres of alfalfa.

Cyrus Soule died in 1890 at the age of 50.

The Robert Ayers Family

The first pioneer family to live in Ojai was that of Robert Ayers. They moved into the abandoned Tico adobe in 1868. On January, 1, 1869, Mr. Ayers purchased 304 acres in Upper Ojai from Thomas Scott through Mr. Green. Upper valley land was considered more desirable than that in the lower valley because it was flat, fertile and, although some disagree, others thought water was more abundant.

In 1872, Ayers sold that property and bought 400 acres adjoining Montgomery's on the east, Soule's on the south and reaching north to the foothills. There, he built a two-story farm house for his large family in the area of Ojai Avenue. One early pioneer remarked that the Blumberg Hotel was the only building that could be seen from the Ayers' home. Fannie (Smith) Ayers (Robert's daughter-in-law) said that the Robert Ayers' home was half mile east of Nordhoff on Ojai Avenue.

She described it as a modest two-story house with a balcony across the front and a row of cypress trees and oleander shrubs along the path to the front porch. She said there was an orchard on the right, a field where fine horses grazed on the left and a barn and granary in the back. According to Fannie Ayers', the elder Ayers home was the center of hospitality for all newcomers. She said that the fame of Mrs. Ayers' cookery spread far and wide.

In 1887, Ayers sold this land, bought 7,000 acres on the Casitas Ranch from Jose de la Riva and lived there for twelve years. This is the same property that later belonged to the Wadleighs and then to Walter and Edith Hoffman. Ayers Creek, which feeds into Lake Casitas, was named for Robert Ayers.

Robert Ayers was born in Donegal, Ireland, in 1826 and came to America in 1836 with his family. In 1848, Robert married Christiana Conner of Pennsylvania and the following year he came to California in search of gold. He did quite well in his pursuit and returned for his wife and young daughter, Agnes. The Ayers family settled in Sonoma where Robert built the Washoe Hotel eight miles from Petaluma. He ran it for fifteen years before coming to Nordhoff.

Robert and Christiana had nine children. Besides Agnes, there were Jennie, Ida, Edwin, Montgomery, John, Henry, William and Frank.

Ayers served later in his life as Ventura County Supervisor, holding office from 1884 to 1888. Christiana died in 1893 and Robert then married his sister-in-law, Elizabeth Conner. He died in 1899. Ayers Street was later named for Robert Ayers.

Frank Ayers married Fannie Smith in 1885. Nearly twenty years later, the couple bought part of the original Ayers Ranch,

OVM
Frank and Fannie Ayers' home which still stands on Grand Avenue, circa 1905.

then known as the Levy property, and moved into the home which still stands at 922 Grand Avenue. It is not known whether or not the Ayers built this house, but they lived there for about twenty years.

The Joseph Waite Family

In 1874, Joseph Waite, an asthmatic, traveled to Santa Barbara from his home in Wisconsin wanting to be able to take a full breath. Desperate for a cure, he took some advice and made his way to the Ojai Valley. "There was hardly a cow path beyond Casitas Valley," he later remarked, "and only five or six homes in all of Ojai."

OVM
Abbie and Joseph Waite, 1915.

Joseph Waite and his wife, the former Abbie P. Cory, built their home north of Ojai Avenue on the west side of what is now Gridley Road.

Mr. Waite was described as a most enterprising farmer, one who would succeed where most would fail because of his untiring industry. He reportedly had the best vineyard in the valley. He built a twenty by twenty-four-foot barn, a twenty by fourteen-foot stable and a wagon shed. The Golden West tract is approximately where the original Waite farm was located. Mr. Waite died in 1915 at the age of 81.

East End Ranchers

T.T. Wasley's eight acres adjoined Waite's land on the north. He grew wheat and had an ample barn and a nice cottage.

William S. McKee's Oak Glen Cottages, later to be known as Gally Cottages, were neatly tucked amongst the oaks and flowers on the northeast corner of Ojai Avenue and Gridley Road. (Read the history of Oak Glen in Chapter Six).

Joseph Fisher's small home sat directly opposite McKee's on the south side of Ojai Avenue. He ran a blacksmith shop there. Sometimes known as Colonel Fisher and sometimes Major Fisher, Joseph also worked in the wood and coal businesses over his lifetime. His wife and youngest daughter, Maud (age 20) were two of the earliest burials in the Nordhoff Cemetery, having been buried there within the year 1877 before it was officially established as a cemetery. His oldest daughter, Eva, died two years later.

Joseph Fisher died in 1893 at the age of 64 after being thrown from a carriage. His leg was injured so badly that it had to be amputated and he died of those injuries.

Thomas Barrows owned fifty acres north of McKee's at what later would be Grand and Gridley. His was a rustic house with a verandah and his property boasted a carriage shop, harness house and stables. He planted an orchard of fifty orange trees, 2,300 grape vines, English walnuts, apricots, olives and he had an apiary. (See a profile of the Barrows family in Chapter Ten.)

Thomas Benton Steepleton, the upper valley schoolteacher, ran the 160-acre Sunny Side Ranch along the foothills two miles east of town. He irrigated the land by ditch from a mountain spring.

Steepleton had a large home, an eighteen by thirty-two-foot barn and a seventy-foot shed which served as a granary and stables. He grew almonds, peaches, English walnuts, Mexican limes, mission grapes, oranges, Sicily lemons, apricots, apples, blackberries and strawberries. Steepleton sold his farm to Harry Fordyce in 1888. Fordyce Road was named for this owner.

Steepleton's wife, Margaret (Holley) died sometime after giving birth in 1885 and he died in 1893 at the age of 55. His grave stone at the Nordhoff Cemetery is dated incorrectly. Steepleton served in the Confederate Army in the Civil War.

A. Bronson lived above Steepleton and Irwin Barnard had a piece of property somewhere in between. Sam Gridley bought this land some time later. The Sheridans were amazed at how Bronson managed to transform a "wild spot in the foothills" into one of great beauty. He grew a variety of fruits and vegetables there and had a bee operation that included a fourteen by twenty-four-foot honey house.

Milo Cory, Mrs. Joseph (Abbie) Waite's father, grew corn and hay on his 155-acre spread. He had a most comfortable house situated just east of McKee's Oak Glen Cottages. He married Sarah in Vermont and they came to the valley in 1874. He was a Union soldier. Cory died in 1888 at the age of 67.

Dexter Munger

Dexter Samuel Munger farmed forty acres of broom straw just east of the Corys, approximately where St. Joseph's Hospital is now. He and his sons manufactured brooms and sold them door-to-door. Dexter was born in 1831 in New York and settled with his family in Shiawassee County, Michigan, where his father, Philander, pioneered the lumber business and established a town called Mungerville. After his wife, Jennie (Hall) and young daughter died, in 1876, Dexter brought his two sons, Lorenzo Burton and Seymour Dalton, to Ojai Valley.

Even though he had little use of his hand due to an injury sustained in the battle called Mine Explosion at Petersburg, Virginia, during the Civil War, Dexter is credited with inventing a gang plow that was considered superior in dry plowing. It consisted of four plows measuring nine inches each that cut three inches into the soil. Pulled by a team of four horses, it did double the work of the chisel cultivator by turning over five acres of dry land per day.

Dexter decided to return to the East around 1881, but his sons remained behind. Seymour married his neighbor Olive Cory (Abbie Waite's sister), on February 8, 1886. She died four months later of typhoid at the age of 18. Seymour stayed in the Ojai Valley for most of his life with his second wife, Julia Robison. Burton settled in Santa Paula, where there is a street named for this pioneer family. In 1894, Dexter, who had recently retired from the mercantile business, died while visiting Burton.

Munger family photo
Seymour Munger, circa 1890.

John Jones

John N. Jones held title to 310 acres of land east of Munger's. Alfilaria and burr clover grasses, thought to make excellent pasturage, were naturally abundant there.

Mr. Jones used to remark that his wife was the pioneer in their family. She came to California alone hoping to find a cure for her asthma. She lived in Ventura with the only people she knew there, the Irwin Barnards. In letters to her husband, she told about her love for California, but said nothing of her health. Someone suggested she move inland, however, and there she was completely relieved of her breathing difficulties. When Mr. Jones received the correspondence saying that his wife's asthma had improved only after she moved to Ojai, he closed his large mercantile business and joined her here in December, 1873.

C.T. Meredith's place was north of Jones, against the foothills. Mr. Meredith's orchard possessed a novelty item, a guava tree, noted by the Sheridans to be in bloom near his adobe house. Another uncommon feature of his property was the existence of several mineral springs.

F.S.S. Buckman

F.S.S. Buckman had planted 160 acres with 200 orange trees and 250 lemons which were estimated by the Sheridans to be six or seven years old. He called his place Lindercroft, possibly after a variety of orange. Buckman irrigated with water which flowed from a mountain crevice through a wooden flume. He also grew peaches, pears, apples, figs, quince and cherries. His farm was approved as a nursery outlet and he had 1,500 English walnut, 200 apricot and 10,000 small peach trees for sale.

VCHS
F.S.S. Buckman.

Mr. Buckman was one of the first teachers at the village schoolhouse and he was also the first county superintendent of schools in San Buenaventura. It is told that he sometimes had students come from school to his farm and pick strawberries which he sold commercially.

C. Howell's 160 acres joined Buckman's on the north and Charles R. Horne's property was north of Howell's.

Horne came to the Ojai Valley in 1876. Upon arrival, he purchased an acre of land on the corner of what is now Fordyce and Carne Roads. In 1890, he homesteaded 160 acres in Horn Canyon and raised hogs. A local builder, he taught carpentry for a while at the Thacher School. When Horne died in 1896 at the age of 51, he left a wife and seven children. (Historians and researchers question whether Mr. Horne spelled his name with or without an "e." It is thought that Horn Canyon was named for this man and it is spelled without the "e." The name is *Horne* on his grave marker, however, so I've chosen to use that spelling.)

Nick Walnut had about 160 acres among the chaparral and rocks south of Buckman's on what was later to be called Reeves Road. (Read more about Nick Walnut in Chapter Fourteen.)

John Hund's property had the benefit of table lands, hillsides, forest and mountain streams. The Sheridans described his as one of the most charming spots they had seen. He grew peaches, almonds and tomatoes for his own use, but his main commercial interest was in bees, of which he had 200 stands. Hund designed and built an octagon-shaped honey house that was eleven feet high and eleven feet in diameter. He glassed in the upper sections and covered the sides of the lower part with wire gauze to admit air in the extracting area while maintaining darkness. This way the bees that were accidentally carried in with the combs, saw light at the small openings which were made for their escape. Hund extracted, processed and bottled the honey on his farm.

With the accounts by the Sheridans in the *Ventura Signal* as a guideline, we can assume that there were about thirty families living in the lower Ojai Valley in 1879, or approximately 160 people. The upper valley contributed another eleven families to that number or, perhaps, fifty people.

The Henry Jackson Dennison Family

Henry Jackson Dennison had 1,015 acres which was partially in the lower valley and partly on the upper mesa. Two hundred and fifty acres of his land were under cultivation. He ran hogs, cattle and good horses. Dennison raised water by hydraulic power from a spring and conveyed it to the house, stables and corrals. He also had a small dairy operation and produced butter. The Dennisons hired the Ventura firm of Shaw and Spencer to build a two-story home on the Upper Ojai portion of their ranch at a cost of $6,000. One of the builders, B.F. Spencer, felt that his health was so much better while he was working on the Dennison house that he moved to the valley permanently.

Henry Jackson Dennison was born in Cambridge, Ohio, in 1833. He married Margaret Rapp in 1861 and they moved to Missouri, where he taught school for several years. Yda Storke tells a story in her book of biographical sketches. She says that the Dennisons were staunch Unionists and while in Missouri, Margaret made a large flag and her husband flew it from the top of the house. A large body of Union solders passed through one day and gave three cheers to the woman who made it and to the man who had the courage to fly it.

Around 1870, Henry and his father Elias, came to Ojai to explore the possibilities of settling. Both men returned to Missouri for their families, but Elias' brood refused to relocate.

The elder Dennison, however, elected to accompany his son's large family across the plains to their new home. Theirs was not a pleasant journey. Blizzards made land travel to Omaha miserable and perilous. There, they sold their teams and wagons and boarded a train for Sacramento. When the family reached Cheyenne, they encountered a torrential downpour that forced them to remain aboard the stalled train for seven days. Sacramento was also inundated and they reached San Francisco with difficulty. Storms at sea forced them to stay there for eleven more days. Finally, in 1872, the weary Dennisons arrived in San Buenaventura.

There was no wharf then; construction began later that year. The men went ashore and brought wagons into the surf. They ran small boats between the ship and the wagons, until all the family and their belongings were safely ashore.

David Mason collection
The Dennison home in Upper Ojai. H.J. and Margaret Dennison in buggy, George and Marguerite Mallory and Frank Dennison.

Henry Jackson and Margaret Dennison had ten children, some of whom were, Cora Edna, who died at the age of 19 in 1900, Schuyler, who died in 1902 at 32, Robert S. who lived to be 62, Rudolph Rapp, Junius Waldo, John Franklin and Henry.

Henry Jackson Dennison died in 1917 at the age of 84 and Margaret died five years later.

OVM

Dennison offspring: Herschel, Rapp, Emma, Waldo, Julia, Harry and Schuyler, circa 1900.

The heirs kept the ranch going and even, reportedly, added to it. A 1927 issue of *The Ojai* reported that the Dennison heirs, with 2660 acres, had the largest ranch in the valley.

Other Upper Valley Residents

Tom and Ann (Murphy) Clark owned 150 acres northeast of the Dennisons – part of which was planted to 300 fruit trees. The Sheridans found the Clark home to be especially pleasant – a two-story, cottage-style home with a beautiful view. The large porch afforded a comfortable place from which to watch the sunset. Grass carpeted the area around the home and early spring blooms added a most colorful touch. Everything on the Clark property was painted white; the house, barn, granary, fences, stables and even the windmill.

Reported to have been the third non-hispanic family to settle here, the Clarks came in 1868 from Wisconsin. According to Storke's book, Clark said there were a lot of grizzly bears when they came to the valley and they "got rid of them" through poisoning.

The Clarks had no children of their own, but they adopted a girl who they named Annie and who later married Ezra Taylor. Mr. Clark supported his family well as he was the owner of the Ventura Flour Mill and the Rose Hotel in Ventura.

Thompson family photo
Tom and Ann Clark's home in the Upper Ojai, 1911. Josephine Bullard Thompson standing in front.

Tom had two siblings, Winifred Thompson and Michael, who both joined him to live in the Ojai Valley.

Theodore Todd's place stood directly west of the Clarks. Frank White, who came to Ojai Valley in 1873 and stayed until his death in 1889, farmed it during that period.

Todd seemed destined to be a farmer despite his Connecticut upbringing, having tried farming in several states before coming to California. He served with the 44th Iowa Regiment in the Rebellion of '64 after which he married Anna Wilson of England. The couple came to Ojai in 1869.

The Proctor family and Mr. Pinkerton lived south of the Clarks and adjacent to one another. Each of those properties occupied 235 acres. Mr. Proctor had painted his cottage yellow and wrapped a neat picket fence protectively around the house. A row of pepper trees led to the area of the granary, chicken house, barn and wagon shed. In 1871, Mrs. Proctor gave birth to the first child of a pioneer family born in Ojai. Her son, George, grew up here. When he was an adult, he took a job as bookkeeper for the Ventura Wharf and Warehouse Company. George died in 1927 when a storm caused waves so large they swept away the pier that supported his office.

Mr. Pinkerton came to Ojai in 1869. His neat and cozy cottage, like that of the Proctors, faced south. The Sheridans noted that "the skillful arrangement of flowers (as were found around the bachelor Pinkerton's house) is seldom seen where there is no female hand to train them."

VCHS
John Pinkerton driving a man thought to be Charles Nordhoff. Circa 1890s.

Joseph Hobart

Joseph Hobart led a small party to the county in 1871. They fought their way through brush and oak groves until they reached the upper valley of Ojai. Hobart stayed long enough to be convinced that his asthma was cured. Then he bought the old W.S. McKee property of 442 acres, south of Clark's and bordering Dennison's on the east.

Hobart was born in Massachusetts. He had asthma as a young man and was advised to go to sea. His second voyage took him to San Francisco in 1849. He returned there in 1856, some say in search of gold. Mining was too hard on him, however, so he opened a shoe and boot business with his brother in San Francisco. He joined the San Francisco City Guards, a vigilance committee of sorts organized during the gold rush frenzy.

Hobart tried several times to live in the East, but always landed back in California. The last time he returned to San Francisco, the fog was in and breathing became difficult for him, so he traveled to Santa Barbara. He still had trouble with his asthma and decided to seek relief inland.

Mr. Hobart, "a cultured gent of extensive travel," according to the Sheridans, had a good farm planted to a variety of fruit trees including 1500 apricot trees, 1000 French prunes, 1000 almonds, apples, peaches, pears and cherries. Hobart also had his own fruit dryer and a nut huller of his own invention. Vines practically hid his neat cottage from view.

Elizabeth (Hutchinson) Hobart had planted flowers and shrubs in abundance and the Sheridans found their century plant especially interesting. Hobart also grew corn, ran forty head of cattle on his land and raised fine horses. He had two wells, one producing water at eighteen feet and the other at thirty-seven feet. Joseph Hobart, who died in 1912 at the age of 80, was known as a "staunch and decided Democrat" who had a refreshing and responsive sense of humor. The Hobarts had two daughters, Margaret and Gertrude.

Captain Richard Robinson's 440 acres adjoined the Hobarts eastern border. Unfortunately, Sol and Ed found no one home at the Robinson place when they came as reporters. They noticed that the house sat amongst a cluster of oaks and shrubs and was tastefully decorated with nature's own hues.

Captain Robinson, who spent a good portion of his life at sea, eventually settled in a home he built in Ventura where he could be near his beloved Pacific Ocean. He died in February, 1896.

Through at least 1983, members of the Robinson family still held that Upper Ojai land and continued to live in the home which was rebuilt many years ago, after a fire destroyed the original house.

Thomas Gray, a farmer first in Tennessee and later in Northern California, was thought to have had the oldest orchard in the valley in 1879. A pomegranate tree near the house received considerable attention the day the Sheridans paid Gray a visit. Mr. Gray's porch faced east, offering a view of valley and mountains together.

A.F. McClure owned over 2,000 acres at the head of the upper valley. He built a two-story house where the view was best and furnished it handsomely. He conducted water into the house from a spring 600 feet distant. McClure ran 2,250 sheep, 200 hogs and 80 head of cattle on his land.

Northwest of McClure's, among timber and grazing land, lay Bracken's 160 acres. A family named Ireland lived west of the Brackens.

In addition to the farm products listed in the proceeding accounts, everyone in the upper valley also grew grains. To save money, they combined their implements and manpower and formed a harvesting and threshing co-op. Among them they owned three headers and two threshers.

Chapter Four
The History of Our Schools

In 1869, the few residents of Ojai Valley were concerned about their children's education and they opened a school. They built the schoolhouse at the foot of the Upper Ojai Grade in the vicinity of Reeves Road at Ojai Avenue and facetiously named it Sage Brush Academy. Volunteers built the twelve by sixteen-foot structure with twelve-foot boards nailed vertically. The dozen students who enrolled on the first day of school sat at desks made of thick redwood slabs.

Henry Jackson Dennison taught at the Sage Brush Academy and we can only assume that his pupils followed the rules for schools of the day: whispering was forbidden. There was no reading of books other than the dictionary or encyclopedia. Most teachers punished naughty students by spanking them or by rapping their knuckles with a ruler.

The history of every early valley school includes stories of bear traps set nearby and the Sagebrush Academy was no exception. This was wilderness area.

The Little Brick Schoolhouse

In 1874, Andy Van Curen circulated a petition for another school that would be closer to the newly established village. As soon as school superintendent F.S.S. Buckman approved it, Abram Blumberg started making the bricks for the structure near where the main tennis courts are today in Libbey Park. A note in a July, 1874 issue of the *Ventura Signal*, states, "A brick kiln will be burned on the Ojai during the summer."

One night a mountain lion sauntered through the drying area behind Blumberg's Nordhoff Hotel and left a paw print in a brick.

Blumberg gave this keepsake to his daughter, Inez.

While the bricks were being made, the townspeople immediately erected a temporary frame schoolhouse on Matilija Street west of John Montgomery's house. Soule and Pirie offspring reported in later years that after having lessons in this crude structure for a few months, the students considered the new brick schoolhouse a "palace."

The oblong brick schoolhouse consisted of one classroom and two anterooms. It had a sixteen-foot ceiling and four windows on each side allowed sunlight in. A drum in the center of the classroom provided necessary heat. The students sat in pairs at double desks and there was a bench in front of the teacher's desk for reciting. Mrs. Joseph Steepleton, who had previously conducted a private school in her home, accepted the teaching position for the newly established Nordhoff School District.

The original wooden schoolhouse was moved to the top of the grade and became known as the Ojai School District. In about 1883, upper valley residents built a larger schoolhouse two miles east, reportedly on the boundary of Hobart's and Robinson's properties. This school operated independently until 1965. (Read more about the fascinating history of this early schoolhouse in Chapter Twelve).

Jerome Caldwell and F.S.S. Buckman were among those who taught at the little brick schoolhouse. Anna Seward taught there during 1884. She introduced calisthenics and music to the children. Agnes Howe was the teacher between 1885 and into the 1890s. Howe once claimed that the single room schoolhouse had more bats than children and she spearheaded an incentive program to rid the place of the bats.

In 1882, when enrollment reached sixty students, a brown bungalow was added to the brick school-house.

OVM
Agnes Howe, 1890.

Teachers were responsible for school maintenance. They asked the older students to sweep floors and build fires for heat. Students carried water from nearby streams or cottages and everyone drank from a pail using a community dipper. The children liked to play stick ball, pum pum pull away and marbles for keeps. There was also great interest in baseball, riding and hiking in those days, recalled Miss Howe.

Clara Smith, a well known figure in county education, taught at the village school and served as its first principal until tragedy struck in 1892. Her fiancé, Scottish-born Robert Fisher, a blacksmith by trade, died suddenly of typhoid fever on the day they were to be wed.

Clara, the daughter of community leader, Daniel Smith, first taught school in Nebraska at the age of 15. She was so devoted to education that she once walked from Nordhoff to Ventura to take a teacher's exam. Her career progressed from teaching at most local schools, as well as some outside the county, to serving as County Director of Rural Education and Assistant Superintendent of Schools. Clara Smith retired from the school system in 1935.

OVM
Clara Smith.

Teachers weren't in abundance during the early years, as was illustrated by an incident occurring in 1895. When Agnes Howe fell from a bicycle and sprained her ankle, the school closed for a week while she healed.

In 1889, 14-year-old Charlie Wolfe, son of Judge and Mrs. Irvin W. Wolfe, died at the school when he fell from a tree he was climbing. His twin sister had died at birth.

In 1893, Miss Beal's primary grades had six more students than seats. It was obvious that the community had outgrown its little brick schoolhouse.

While parents initiated plans to build a bigger and better school, others reminisced about how well the brick building had served the community. Not only had it been the fountain of education for their children for twenty years, but also a church, a meeting place and a social hall.

Every new religious group used it as a place of worship while building its church. It was the very heart and soul of the village. Within those brick walls the townsfolk held their entertainment, made new friends and cemented relationships. That is where community leaders made their decisions, some of which affect our lives today.

But progress is progress and the fact was that the town had outgrown their school and a new one was built to accommodate the education of the valley children.

After the community abandoned the old schoolhouse, the brown bungalow was moved to 570 North Montgomery Street and Ezra Taylor, who ran a machine shop in town, moved his family into the brick building. It was home to the A.E. Freeman family around 1910. Mr. Freeman, a local grocer, reportedly added the second story and began the transformation that camouflaged the original brick outer walls. G.L. Chrisman bought the Freeman home in June of 1916 and the Alton Drowns lived there during the 1920s and 30s.

In 1946, Major Richard Cannon bought the former schoolhouse and opened the Cannon School there. One year later, Mr. and Mrs. Joseph Cataldo converted the school into the Ojai Manor Hotel and began renting seven rooms. Although these owners had altered the little brick schoolhouse beyond recognition, until the 1980s, a keen eye could detect Blumberg's misshapen, aged bricks as foundation beneath the time-honored facade at 210 Matilija Street. The old bricks are still visible on the inside kitchen wall.

In the 1980s, Mary Nelson renovated the old Ojai Manor Hotel and opened it as a bed and breakfast. In 1999, the old schoolhouse, once again beautifully remodeled, has resumed as a bed and breakfast under the name, The Moon's Nest Inn.

In the meantime, the upper valley school also continued to grow. Just after the turn of the century, the Sisar School District was formed but lasted only about six years. In 1911, they formed Summit School District and in 1925, built a new brick schoolhouse. This school was adequate through 1951, when the current school buildings were built to accommodate the growing number of upper valley students. The Summit School became part of the Ojai Unified School District in 1965.

Fry photo
Ojai Manor Hotel, former brick schoolhouse at 210 E. Matilija Street, early 1980s.

Fry photo
The Moon's Nest Inn, former brick schoolhouse, 1999.

OVM
Nordhoff Grammar School, built 1895.

Growth of the Public Schools

In 1895, Edwin Senior, an Englishman whose doctor had advised him to come to California for his health and for whom San Antonio Canyon was renamed, sold some of his land to the Nordhoff School District. Contractors E.P. Zimmerman and O.N. Soderquist built a two-story, frame schoolhouse with a bell tower there on the northeast corner of Ojai Avenue and Montgomery Street. Ventura architect F P. Ward designed the structure, which consisted of four rooms and an assembly hall. The project cost $6,825. Sixty-two students enrolled in the eight grades that year.

Mrs. Mabel Pendergrass was one of the first teachers at the new wooden schoolhouse. Principals serving the district during that era included, C.L. Edgerton, Roscoe Ashcraft, W.A. Goodman, Inez Carr Sheldon and Lloyd Emmert.

By 1926, the Nordhoff Grammar School was overflowing. First grade students were moved to the Boyd Club gymnasium for their classes. Roy Wilson drew plans for a new grammar school to replace the old wooden building.

In 1927, a modern seven-room building replaced the outdated wooden schoolhouse, which was moved to the rear of the lot. The community continued to use the old building for social and youth activities. When the school district built a new auditorium in 1937, however, they ordered the old schoolhouse demolished.

In 1953, the district changed the name of the present building to Ojai Elementary School and it continued to serve the educational needs of the city until 1976, when district administrative offices relocated there.

The original bell from the early wooden schoolhouse is displayed in front of the district offices building.

Kindergarten in the Ojai Valley started in 1920 with ten pupils. Miss Clara Newman was the first teacher. Marion Knowlton (Misbeek) later taught kindergarten classes in the Woman's Clubhouse across the street from the school. Kindergarten classrooms were built at the Ojai Elementary School in 1953.

Today the 70-year-old building houses Ojai Unified School District offices, special education classes, Chaparral High School and Topa Topa Kindergarten.

Arnaz School

A handful of children living south of Nordhoff attended classes at the Arnaz Adobe in 1877. Pet Seymour was the teacher. When John Poplin bought the Arnaz ranch, in 1886, he built a

OVM
Arnaz School, built 1886.

schoolhouse about half mile south of the present site of the apple cider barn on the bank of San Antonio Creek. Another account says that the school was one mile north of the apple orchard. My father recalls his mother (Fern Watkins Munger) pointing out this as the grammar school she attended as a child.

In 1892, Ethel Robison taught at the school, which was then referred to as Ranch Number One (possibly named for Bard's Well Number One). By 1926, enrollment had grown so much that some of the students had to be moved to Laidler's grocery store in Casitas Springs for lessons. Although it once came under the jurisdiction of the Nordhoff school system, Arnaz Elementary School, now at 400 Sunset Avenue in Oak View, is part of the Ventura Unified School District.

In 1917, Mr. Nye donated a lot for a school in Casitas Springs and Mr. Hitchcock built it. It is not known where. Miss Hatti Conner was the first teacher there with forty-three students in three grades. The older children were transported by bus to the Nordhoff schoolhouse.

Santa Ana School

People of the Santa Ana Valley depended on neighbors for the social aspect of life. Their distance from Nordhoff prohibited them from becoming active in village affairs. They created their own communal atmosphere, of which their schoolhouse was the hub.

The first Santa Ana School was operational in 1878 thanks to Robinson of Robinson, Faucett and Dean Company. Robinson controlled the Santa Ana Ranch holdings after the trio's early development attempts failed and he donated an acre of land for a one-room schoolhouse. Forty pupils enrolled.

In 1923, a new school was built at the intersection of Baldwin and Dunshee Roads with boulders from Coyote Creek. Ten years later, they added indoor plumbing and another room. Until the first P.T.A. was formed, in 1949, parents raised money for school lunches, cooking utensils and playground equipment by auctioning off hay, clothing, livestock and other useful items.

In 1959, the picturesque Santa Ana School succumbed to the rising waters of manmade Lake Casitas and another school was constructed at 806 Baldwin Road. In 1980, the Ventura School District closed this school.

OVM
San Antonio School children, 1898.

San Antonio School

Residents of the valley's east end formed the San Antonio School District in 1887. One account says that the first school was on the Edward L. Wiest property, in the vicinity of where St. Joseph's Hospital is now. They held the first classes there under the oaks in what was considered to be a "howling wilderness." The parents were relieved when someone brought in an old granary structure to use as a temporary classroom.

The Friend family sold the school district the property for a proper school at what is now the southeast corner of Carne Road and Grand Avenue for $25. The first permanent schoolhouse was constructed where the tennis courts are now. It had one room and a pointed bell tower and it served until it was replaced by the present structure which Roy Wilson designed and Sam Hudiburg built in the 1920s.

Matilija Canyon School

Around 1892, children who lived west of town attended classes at a neighboring ranch while money was collected to build a school. They couldn't come up with enough money to hire a builder, so the parents constructed the school themselves. It was a rough, primitive building with newspaper covering the walls for insulation. Eighteen students enrolled in the Matilija School the first year of its existence. Frances Bella was an early teacher at this school. The first trustees were W.I. Rice, A.W. Blumberg and Joseph Cooper and the first class graduated in 1895. The graduates were Xarissa Rice, Nellie Beekman and Alice Beekman.

The school building measured sixteen by twenty-four feet. Shelves held 500 books, encyclopedias, maps and a globe. Someone donated an organ to the school, but it was never played because none of the teachers knew how.

OVM
Matilija School about 1908. Standing, (l-r), Julia Sigala, Thursa B. Cutler (teacher), Howard Bald, Lennie Soper, Alexander Lopez. Seated, Peter Lopez, Adele Lopez, Teresa Maraquin, unknown, unknown, Fred Sheldon, Jr., Joe Higuera. Bottom, Jerome Ramos, Ernesto Lopez, Frank Patrick, Vincente Ramos.

When the flood of 1914 washed the 24-year-old structure off the west bank of Matilija Creek, parents replaced it with a larger building and stocked it with over 150 books.

One teacher, Miss Myrtle Clay, taught paper cutting to the lower grades and raffia work to the older girls. The students also did gardening as part of their education. In 1918, the Matilija Canyon students abandoned their school and enrolled in the Nordhoff Grammar School.

Additional Schools

Citizens of Oak View established a school at 555 Mahoney Avenue in 1948 with 184 students.

Meiners Oaks Elementary School opened at 400 South Lomita Avenue in 1949. Maynard Lyndon of Los Angeles was the architect. The Meiners Oaks Lions Club was highly involved in the needs of the Meiners Oaks School and held fund raisers whenever the school needed a new cafetorium, additional classrooms or playground equipment.

Mira Monte School, at 1217 Loma Drive, was one of two California schools to receive an award from the American Institute of Architecture upon its completion in 1956, honoring architect Maynard Lyndon.

In 1957, Topa Topa Elementary School was ready to receive students at 916 Mountain View Drive.

Nordhoff High School

Although private high school classes were held upstairs in the frame schoolhouse as early as 1899, the first public high school wasn't a reality here until 1909. The first trustees for the Nordhoff High School District were Sherman D. Thacher, Joseph Hobart, Dr. B.L. Saeger, F.H. Sheldon and Frank P. Barrows. The first principal for the high school was Walter Bristol and he doubled as a teacher, helping Mabryn Chapman (later to become Mrs. Howard Bald).

With forty students enrolled in the public high school program, it became evident that the community needed a separate building. In 1910, they built an attractive new school of wood and stone at 703 El Paseo Road. Walter Bristol continued as principal for the following nine years.

Charles Pratt, a regular winter visitor to Nordhoff, gave the high school manual training and domestic sciences and arts buildings. Everyone considered these gifts unusual equipment for a small country school. The project cost Pratt $16,000 and was completed two months prior to the June 1917 fire which destroyed the manual arts building. Pratt generously paid the difference between the cost of replacing the building and the insurance.

By 1925, there were 115 students enrolled in Nordhoff High School. Times were simpler then. Pranks were more laughable

Nordhoff High School, circa 1910.

than harmful and crimes were generally less serious. In 1928, however, a student brought a 22 revolver to school and accidentally shot a classmate in the leg.

In 1929, when local grammar schools changed their format, Nordhoff picked up grades seven and eight and became a six-year high school.

Aside from academics, students engaged in athletics, dramatics, debating and music.

The school auditorium was built in 1938 and in 1949, Roy Wilson designed the gymnasium. The Ojai Lions Club built the cement bleachers in 1954.

In 1959, the district built the original Matilija Junior High School on Maricopa Highway. Three hundred and fifty students enrolled there in the seventh, eighth and ninth grades.

In 1966, Nordhoff and Matilija students traded schools; Nordhoff High School is now on Maricopa Highway and Matilija Junior High is on El Paseo Road.

Private Schools

The Ojai Valley has always had an abundance of private day and boarding schools. There are twenty listed in the 1999 Ojai Telephone Directory. Following are some of our oldest and most prominent private schools.

Bristol School

In 1911, Ida Belle Lamb was tutor for Charles and Philip Schuyler, the 3 and 6-year-old children of Dr. Philip and Emily Van Patten Schuyler. When Ida Belle married Robert Dennison, her sister, Olive Bristol took over as teacher for the boys and her own 7-year-old daughter, Esther.

In 1912, Walter joined his wife and they opened their home, on what is now Bristol Road at Ojai Avenue, as Bristol School. Although they accepted boys too, only girls boarded there. They began with six pupils and ten years later, thirty enrolled.

At first, the Bristol home served as the school with the sleeping porch doubling as the dorm. In 1915, James Leslie built a small school building on the edge of their property. Subsequent cottages went up with time

In 1920, Mrs. Bristol was teaching arithmetic, grammar, basketry and gardening. Mr. Bristol taught history, literature and geography to the upper grades. They hired Katherine Ball to teach French, piano and primary work and Ida Belle Dennison returned to teach chorus and drawing.

Peggy (Pascoe) Thacher's delightful reminiscences of her school days at Bristol School are captured in this author's book *A Thread to Hold: The Story of Ojai Valley School.*

Ojai Valley School

Edward (Ned) Yeomans spent most of his adult life working toward education reform. He sat on the Winnetka School Board, he lectured and he wrote about his ideas and ideals for educating this nation's children. *Shackled Youth* is the most well-known of his early writings.

He often said that his ideal would be "a school whose main subjects are music, nature study and shop work. No languages for little children and no English grammar taught to them. No arithmetic at first except what is needed for work in construction. No desks fastened to the floors, but desks that easily could be moved for the acting of ballads or poetry. No examinations; no discipline for its own sake but inner control and consideration for all working in the school and so good citizenship."

In 1920, Frank Frost contacted Ned Yeomans asking him to start a school dedicated to his principles in a climate that would be healthy for Frost's 10-year-old asthmatic son. "If you do," said Frost, "I will fund construction and underwrite the cost of the school for the first year, if needed."

In 1923, Edward Yeomans bought the Bristol's goodwill, accepted a gift of land from Edward Libbey and opened the Ojai Valley School at 723 El Paseo Road. Forty-five students in third through ninth grades enrolled in Yeoman's resident and day school – many of them from the old Bristol School. While Sam Hudiburg built Frost Hall, Yeomans rented one of Bristol's buildings for boarding students. In 1962, they opened the upper campus in Upper Ojai for high school students.

The rich history of Ojai Valley School also includes such notables as world-known storyteller, educator and long-time principal of the school, Gudrun Thorne-Thompson; Headmaster, Wallace Burr and teachers, Kitty Bragg, Cordelia Kingman, Nell Curtis, Ada Dugger, Robert Cooper, Otis Wickenhaeuser and Dok Smith. (Read more about the history of Ojai Valley School in *A Thread to Hold*, by this author).

Happy Valley School

Happy Valley School, a non-sectarian, coeducational senior high school, was a project of Dr. Annie Besant, once a world leader in the Theosophical Society. Dr. Besant believed that a new race of children were being raised in Southern California and that they would need specialized conditions in education and living. As early as 1927, carefully selected teachers taught Dr. Besant's theories to small groups in private homes in the Ojai Valley.

The current school, presently in Upper Ojai, was founded in 1946 in Meiners Oaks. In 1951, Happy Valley students planted about 100 eucalyptus trees between Meiners Oaks School and the temporary Happy Valley School. Those trees stand majestically tall today.

The emphasis at Happy Valley School is on teaching the students *how* to think not *what* to think through a flexible curriculum. The school offers a broad cultural program in which there is neither competition nor authoritarian discipline and the pupils' efforts are not graded.

Villanova

Augustinian fathers established Villanova Preparatory School for boys in 1924. Albert C. Martin was the architect for the original buildings constructed on 130 acres formerly owned by John Hobson. The school, at 12096 North Ventura Avenue, opened with thirteen pupils. John A. Howard was the first headmaster. Villanova started accepting girls in 1970.

St. Thomas Aquinas College

St. Thomas Aquinas College was founded in 1971 and moved to Highway 150, between Ojai and Santa Paula, in 1978. In 1980, the college earned accreditation by the Western Association of Schools and Colleges. Students study arts and sciences there in seminar fashion through the reading of the great books.

Monica Ros School

Monica Ros was born and educated in Sydney, Australia and her studies centered around music and small children. In 1942, she started a music appreciation class in Ojai for very young children. Many parents requested that she expand to include a nursery school curriculum. With this in mind, Ms. Ros enrolled in Washington University to prepare herself and also took classes at Teacher's College of Columbia University.

In 1943, there were twenty children enrolled in the school, some of which Ms. Ros drove to and from school herself. She retired as the director of the school in 1968, although she continued to be active. The founder died in 1991, but her school continues. Monica Ros School on McNell Road currently enrolls children from nursery school age to third grade.

World University

Dr. Benito Reyes founded the World University in 1974 on the premise that one should teach people to be human beings first and professionals second. Many of the techniques taught at the World University are rooted in Eastern religion and universal understanding, although the curriculum deals with traditional studies as well. The World University is located at 107 North Ventura Street, the site of the original Christian Church, later the First Baptist Church and then city hall.

St. Josephs Convalescent Hospital

St. Josephs Convalescent Hospital, at 2464 East Ojai Avenue, is a center of formation for young men desiring to consecrate their lives to the service of the sick and aged. The first known person to use this land was Dexter Munger. In 1876, he grew broom straw there, manufactured brooms and sold them door-to-door.

Additional Private Schools

In 1874, Mrs. Joseph Steepleton ran a school at her home half mile east of the village on Grand Avenue. Frank Girard established a school in the same location in 1918.

A teacher known as Miss Smith held classes in an outbuilding at her home on McAndrew Road from 1900 to 1911 for locals and winter visitors. Although student, Connie Rogers (Wash) named the school, The Ojai School for Girls, classes did include boys. Elizabeth Thacher attended Miss Smith's school as did her cousins, Olive, Ned and Tom Thacher.

The Thacher School

Sherman Day Thacher studied to be a lawyer and discovered that he hated it. He was without a job in 1889, when his family decided that he should take his sickly, younger brother, George, to a milder climate. Sherman, then 25, accompanied George to their brother Edward's citrus ranch in Ojai Valley.

Both brothers loved it here as it was an escape from their strict New England background – a lifestyle hampered by rigid formalities. They felt a sense of freedom here. Sherman had planned to go home, but kept putting it off. Finally he borrowed on his life insurance policy and procured George Stewart's government homestead.

This 160 acres, which abutted Edward's ranch, was covered with rocks and boulders. Sherman borrowed $4,000 from his brother, William, to build a home and to clear the land for orange trees. He then sent for his mother and sister to help care for George. The boy died a short time later, however.

The Thachers, being well-schooled, had always tutored for extra money. So it was not unusual when Mr. Farnum, a political science professor, asked Sherman to accept his nephew as a student. He wanted Henry to learn to ride a horse and to experience the out-of-doors in all its glory. Sherman agreed. He never intended to make teaching his life's work, however; he merely planned to support himself in this way until his orchard began to produce.

Others heard about Sherman's class of one pupil and requested admission for their sons. By 1890, Sherman's mini-school of the West had grown to five students. The following year he advertised for pupils and received eleven.

By 1895, the facility known as the Thacher School had accumulated a good many shacks and most of them burned to the ground that year. Sherman wasn't sure what to do then. He could rebuild the school or take his family back to Connecticut. His choice to stay proved beneficial to the Ojai Valley.

In 1896, Sherman married Eliza S. Blake and built a home for her on the school grounds. He built it without a kitchen because he had a policy that everyone, including teachers and their families, eat all of their meals in the school dining room.

"Old headmasters really ran their school," stated Anson Thacher once while discussing his father, Sherman, in a taped interview. There was strict discipline and the boys helped to make the rules. An early issue of *The Ojai* reported that students were awakened each day at 6:15 a.m. to the sound of a Chinaman ringing the rising bell. Breakfast was at 6:30, after which each boy devoted an hour to his horse – a required project. The school day began at 8:00 with gymnastics, breathing exercises, announcements and questions. At 8:20, everyone commenced recitation and study. There was a thirty minute recess at 10:20 when teachers and students played baseball.

School was considered out at 1 p.m. The boys were then allowed fifteen minutes with their horses, after which it was time for dinner. At 2 p.m., work in the laboratories and shops began and continued until 4:00. Before supper at 6:30, the students had free time to hunt, play or ride. After supper, everyone retired to the parlor for an hour of reading aloud. Sherman was a stickler for rules. He did not allow smoking in the parlor. This rule applied to everyone and, although it sometimes caused embarrassment, Sherman enforced it. The younger boys were required to retire early each evening and the headmaster insisted they shake hands with each adult before going off to bed.

Sherman was so conscientious, that upon acceptance of a student application, he would carefully memorize each requested photograph to make sure he would recognize the student on sight.

The Thacher campus expanded rapidly. New and better buildings replaced the early shacks and improvements were made to the horse facilities. In 1907, an outdoor amphitheater was created by rearranging stones already in position on the grounds. The Thacher School colors are green, symbolizing the once-abundant olive orchards and orange, representing the orange trees so familiar in the east end.

David Mason collection
Thacher School.

Thacher family photo
Sherman Day Thacher front center with arms folded. Eliza (his wife) behind him.

Death came to Sherman Day Thacher in 1931, but the school continues to follow his rigid standards for educational excellence. Eighty years after its founding the first girls were admitted as students.

Chapter Five
Early Valley Churches

History acknowledges Thomas K. Beecher as being the first preacher in Ojai Valley. According to an early account, Beecher preached under a tree in the upper valley as early as 1868. A spring, 1872 issue of the *Ventura Signal* announced that Reverend H.H. Dobbins had recently given a sermon at the original frame schoolhouse "near the Riggins place."

Townsend E. Taylor, minister for the Ventura Presbyterian Church, occasionally held services in Ojai Valley as early as 1873. Frequent travel between the two towns was exhausting, so Taylor and his daughter, Sarah McFarland, established a camp south of Ojai on Creek Road where they could rest. It was Sarah who christened the lovely oak-shaded spot, which is now a county park, Camp Comfort.

Soon, the townspeople wanted their religion on a more regular basis and they requested that Reverend Taylor establish a church for the "spiritual good and for the promotion of the best moral interest of this community." Taylor left his Ventura post and built a cottage in Nordhoff.

On January 7, 1877, he started Ojai's first regular church services with Nordhoff's brick schoolhouse doubling as a chapel. The congregation included William S. and Mary McKee, L.O. and Mary Sowles, Susana Templeton, John J. Wilder, H.J. and Margaret Dennison, Mr. and Mrs. William Pirie, John R. and Elizabeth Carr, Sarah B. McFarland, Minnie McFarland, Mr. and Mrs. A.F. McClure and John and Elizabeth Reith. McKee, McClure and Wilder served as elders.

The Presbyterian Church

The townspeople soon became anxious for a more appropriate atmosphere in which to worship and they asked William S. McKee, John Montgomery, Frank P. Barrows, Robert Gibson and Richard Robinson to select a building site.

The Los Angeles Presbytery gave the small community $500 toward a church and Charles Nordhoff is reported to have donated another $100 by mail. The community purchased a lot from Cyrus Sowles. B.F. Spencer and Charles Horne headed the construction while several townsmen helped.

Mrs. Charles Nordhoff donated the plans for the new church. While living in New Jersey, she hired architect J. Cleveland Cady, who had designed their home in Alpine, to draw up plans for a church in that community. The plans she gave for the Ojai Presbyterian Church were also Cady's design. Historian, David Mason, speculates that Cady may have given Mrs. Nordhoff two sets of plans for her to choose from for the New Jersey church and she sent the second set to the Ojai Presbyterian congregation. Mason says that Mrs. Nordhoff was upset the first time she came here to find that there was no church. He wrote in a recent article, "Mrs. Nordhoff had insisted that any respectable town must have a proper church."

Charles Nordhoff also donated a large collection of books to the Sunday school after the Presbyterian Church was built.

They finished the church, which was situated opposite Joseph Waite's home on the southeast corner of Ojai Avenue and what is now Fairway Lane, on January 6, 1884. One of the original carpenters remarked to Sherman Thacher one day while reminiscing, that it would take a lot of praying to make up for all of the swearing done while laboring on the fretwork on the church.

The belfry remained vacant for a while. However, in 1889, the mails brought a large bell to Nordhoff. Gold lettering on a wooden plaque revealed that it was donated in memory of Thomas Steele Brown, a Scot who had joined the church in 1885 and recently died. The inscription read: "This bell was given in memory of Thomas Steele Brown of Bigart, Scotland by James D. Brown and Robert G. Brown of Greenock, Scotland and Ladies Aid Society-Nordhoff, 30 August, 1889. Ring in the Christ that is to be."

Townsend Taylor resigned in 1883 and the Reverend Eugene Mills dedicated the new church. Pew rental was first on the agenda. Only those who rented pews for three months or who contributed an amount equal to three months pew rent, were eligible to vote for trustees and pastor or on church issues.

OVM
Presbyterian Church, built 1884.

The church doubled as an implement of the law. The congregation ran open trials in moral cases involving lying, cheating and other acts contrary to religious commitments. Peers of the accused often delivered harsh judgments. Local church records tell about a woman who was excommunicated from the Ojai Presbyterian Church after a lengthy and heated trial. The jury found her guilty of insinuating that her son was older than he actually was.

Subsequent pastors include:

Allen Gatch Daniels	1886 - 1889
Archibald Ogilvie	1889 - 1891
Robert Dickson	1891 - 1892
J.M. Crawford	1892 - 1896
John R. Sinclair	1896 - 1898
Thomas C. Marshall	1898 - 1903

It was during Marshall's term that the second most important event of the church occurred – the merger of the Presbyterian and the Congregational Churches.

Congregational Church

The first Congregational meeting in Nordhoff was held on October 14, 1888. Reverend C.S. Vaile was invited to serve as the Congregational pastor for twelve months and ended up staying for four years. The church began with twenty-four members and the first deacons were Captain Charles Wetherby Gelett and Thomas Barrows. G.S. Smith was a clerk and the trustees included W.I. Rice, Thomas Barrows, Dr. Wilson P. Kern, W.E.Wilsie and Frank P. Barrows. Mrs. W.P. Kern was the treasurer. In 1891, twenty men and thirty-five women belonged to the church, which was located on the southeast corner of Ojai Avenue and Ventura Street, where the Ojai Library is today.

When the Reverend Mr. Vaile left to serve the Plymouth Congregational Church of Los Angeles in 1892, F.N. Merrian took over his post. J. Milligan accepted the position in September of that same year.

The Merger of the Two Churches

In April 1900, the two churches were united and a combined committee purchased a lot on the south side of Ojai Avenue just east of Montgomery Street for $600. They moved both churches to that site. The Presbyterian building served as the church and they used the Congregational structure for Sunday school classes.

On August 5, 1900, the following Congregational members were taken into the Presbyterian Church: F. P. Barrows, Albert Barrows, Stephen Barrows, Mrs. James R. Gillett, Mr. E.A. Rich, Mrs. Elizabeth Stillwell, Philemon Weidman, Mrs. Nellie Weidman.

Adult membership in 1901 was eighty-eight and there were 163 people enrolled in the Sunday school program. The Reverend Thomas Marshall held the pastoral position for the combined church, which continued to be known as the Presbyterian Church. Marshall left in 1903 to become an Episcopal minister in Los Angeles and the Reverend C.O. Mudge became the town clergyman. An illness forced him to resign, after which he died. William Hood MacPherson, Mudge's replacement, led the

Presbyterian services until 1914, when World War I broke out in Europe and he returned to Scotland. George Marsh controlled the pulpit for the following decade.

The Thacher students belonged to the Presbyterian Church and they rode their horses an hour each week to the services. Either Sherman or his brother, William, drove the four-in-hand carrying the women including their mother, Madame Thacher. The horses didn't always stand quietly at the hitching rail; they frequently distracted the worshippers as they fought, squealed and stomped the ground.

Organized social life for young people in Nordhoff centered around the Christian Endeavor Society, which held a teen social at the Presbyterian Church once a month. There, youngsters played games and were entertained by various religious programs.

Mr. Vose was the custodian for the church. He lived on the back of the church lot where he also raised rabbits. When Vose died, Harold Rider succeeded him as custodian.

John Murdoch served as minister from 1924 through 1930 and he's credited with great dedication to the cause of building a larger church facility. In a booklet published in 1926, the authors (presumably trustees) wrote that they were concerned that strangers to Ojai might think that Protestants cared more for their schools, businesses, golf clubs, hotel and Catholic Church than their own church. They considered the little wooden church an embarrassing contrast to these newer buildings.

Edward Yeomans, founder of the Ojai Valley School, was also chairman of the building committee for a new Presbyterian Church and these words, taken from the 1926 booklet, could have been his: "The dilapidated old church must not go on advertising our indifference to religion in Ojai."

The committee commissioned plans from local architect, Austin Pierpont, Heathcote M. Woolsey of New York and Wallace Neff of Pasadena. Their ultimate choice, however, was a design by Carleton Winslow.

In 1927, Halleck Lefferts, head of the building fund committee, was authorized to purchase the Bogan property on the northeast corner of Foothill Road and Aliso Street, for $600. The committee hired the Steele brothers to build the church at a cost of $40,000. And on November 23, 1930, the congregation dedicated its grand and beautiful new church.

Agnes Brown

Mrs. Agnes (Duncan) Brown, a lady of Scottish descent, played the church organ at the Presbyterian Church for many years. She is reported to have walked two and a half miles to church every Sunday, barely having time to rest her feet before having to start pumping the old organ. Two hundred and fifty pound Stubby Fordyce often accompanied Mrs. Brown on his trumpet.

Agnes came to Nordhoff from Glasgow, Scotland around 1885 to marry Thomas Steele Brown who had come to make his fortune in America. When he became ill with consumption, he sought out the Ojai Valley and Agnes attempted to nurse him back to health. He died about four years later and Agnes decided to return to Scotland. Her brother, William Duncan, convinced her to stay here with him and the couple lived on Grand Avenue for the rest of their lives. William died in 1934 and Agnes in 1935.

Helen Baker Reynolds remembered visiting Mrs. Brown's home when she was a child. Helen described it as a "modest cottage with a small parlor that was elegant in a quaint, Victorian way and adorned with dark, old family portraits and what-nots filled with Wedgewood pieces and a handsome organ." Agnes delighted in serving tea from beautiful china and silver treasures from her native Scotland.

Agnes was a trained singer. She loved music. She walked just about everywhere she went, sometimes even the four miles to Thacher School to hear one of Mrs. Lord's music recitals, according to Reynolds. Helen remembered Mrs. Brown always stepping briskly, even when she was growing older. Agnes loved puttering in her yard and, at the time of her death, at the age of 91, her home was reported to be a "floral show place."

Nazarene Church

The original Presbyterian church building stood virtually idle until 1935, when the Nazarene congregation, which had been meeting at the Baptist Church, asked if they could use it. In 1937, Mr and Mrs. E.T. Keith, owners of the service station across the street, bought the lot and asked that the church be removed. The congregation hired J.R. Brakey, the same man who moved the church to this location, to move it to the southwest corner of Montgomery and Aliso Streets, where it still stands today.

People comparing the present day church with early photographs will note that the bell tower has been altered. This remodel reportedly occurred in 1931 when the tower was leaking in the rain.

The Nazarenes worshipped in the historic old building for fifty years. Subsequent tenants have included an antique dealer and a health club.

In 1986, the owner of the church contemplated tearing it down to put in a parking lot. The city saved the church, however, by quickly declaring the structure the first Ojai City Historic Landmark.

According to Elizabeth Thacher, the Presbyterian manse was built in 1908 with the generous assistance of Senator Thomas Bard. It burned in the 1917 fire. Early church records were also burned when George Mallory's home went up in flames. The Presbyterian manse was rebuilt in 1918 at the corner of Rincon Road and Foothill (now El Paseo Road) by the firm of Mead and Requa for $9,068. The Marshes were the first to occupy the new manse. The last to occupy the manse were Mr. and Mrs. William W. Gearhart (1952 - 1963). The old manse currently houses L'Auberge Restaurant.

The Holiness Church

The Reverend Mr. Couch first held Holiness Church services here in private homes as early as1885. The congregation erected their church four years later at the southeast corner of Topa Topa and Ventura Streets. In 1937, the original church, which seated only sixty-five people, was razed and the new church built. Now they could welcome as many as 200 to Sunday services. W.J. and Catherine Craig served as pastors. This church still stands and is now home to the Wesleyan congregation.

A Holiness Church was built in Oak View Gardens (now Oak View) in 1928.

In 1930, the Ojai Holiness Church put up tents on the corner of Encinal Avenue and El Roblar Drive in Meiners Oaks where they held revival meetings.

The Christian Church

The Christian Church assembly of twenty-three persons first met in the brick schoolhouse in June, 1892 and then Philip K.

Miller and his son, Clark, donated a lot at the southwest corner of Matilija and Ventura Streets where the congregation built their church.

There was no formal pastor for the Christian Church, so the congregation selected Thomas Jefferson Robison and his east end neighbor, John Jones, as deacons. In April 1893, a difference of opinion developed regarding the use of musical instruments in church – with some believing that music was contrary to scriptural teachings. Since no agreement could be reached, the objectors, including Mr. Robison, left the congregation and the music played on.

Thomas Jefferson Robison, born in Bloomington, Indiana in 1838, had married a Tennessee native, Laura Douglas at the age of 28 and settled in Ellis County, Texas. The Robisons had six children; James Marlon, Julia (who married Seymour Munger) and her twin Cynthia Ella (Caldwell), Anna Marion (McGlinchey), Ethel and Clara (Davenport).

After the birth of their last child in Texas, the Robisons decided to move to Azusa, California, seeking a milder climate. It wasn't long, however, before they landed back in Texas. T.J. struck out once again to California, but this time he made the trip alone. In May of 1886, he arrived in Nordhoff. The following July he purchased 115 acres from Mr. Jones for $4,002.50 and brought his family out four months later.

The Robison property was bordered on the east by what is now Carne Road and on the west by John Jones' land. The north and south boundaries were marked by Grand and Ojai Avenues. In 1890, Robison sold twenty acres at the northeast corner of his property to Essington Gibson, Mrs. Joseph Waite's grandfather, for $1,300. Gibson descendants still reside on that property. Robison sold off another twenty-eight acres to John Carne for $5,750 in 1892 and in 1894, he let the remainder of his land go to John C. Wright and William Turner for $10,875.

Robison and his wife, Laura, moved to Los Angeles County and eight years later T.J. died in Perris, California. Laura passed away in Ventura County on December 18, 1932, at the age of 93.

The Catholic Church

On May 27, 1905, the first cornerstone for the first Catholic Church in Ojai was laid. There is some discrepancy, however, as to whether Fr. E. Ylla or Fr. Thomas Cain did the honors.

Reportedly, four to five hundred people attended the ceremony, after which the George Bald family served a celebration dinner.

The Catholics built their frame chapel under the name of St. Thomas Aquinas (angelic doctor). Supervisor Tom Clark gave the lot and the pews and he donated to the building fund. Mr. Bracken of Upper Ojai presented the congregation with a bell. T.J. King was the first priest in the little chapel that served the valley Catholics until the 1917 fire destroyed it. Fr. Ylla's home was also lost in the fire, for he lived in the rectory.

For the following year and a half, the Catholics celebrated Mass in the Isis Theater while raising money for a new church and parish hall. Edward Drummond Libbey donated $1,000 to the building fund and put in another $5,000 for the outside wall and walkway.

David Mason collection
Original Catholic Church, built in 1905 and burned in 1917.

The new church was designed by the firm of Mead and Requa and built by E.E. Smith on the same site as the original church, 130 West Ojai Avenue. The first service in the new church was held in February of 1919.

In 1923, the parish hall and rectory were given over to the Augustinian Order as part of an agreement to found a Catholic boarding school. Fr. Howard was headmaster.

David Mason collection
Catholic Church, built in 1919.

In 1943, Fr. Edwin Dickinson tore down the rectory and parish hall and it was rebuilt in 1951 by Fr. Holland.

The St. Thomas Aquinas Parochial School and Convent, at 210 Canada Street, was built in 1955.

The new St. Thomas Church at 185 St. Thomas Drive in Meiners Oaks was built in the 1960s and in 1993, the original little church was sold to the city. The final mass there was in December of 1992.

The historic Catholic Church now houses the Ojai Valley Museum and the Ojai Valley Chamber of Commerce.

First Baptist Church

Minister George W. Archer held the first Baptist Church services in 1909. He served the Baptist community for three years. Frank Kelly was the second to officiate for the Baptists, generously working for two years without pay as a donation to the building fund. The Baptist congregation bought the Christian Church building at the southwest corner of Ventura and Matilija Streets and used it until its destruction in the fierce 1917 fire. It was rebuilt in 1918.

In a recent "Remembering When" column in the *Ojai Valley News*, historian, David Mason tells a story about the first Sunday in the new church building. He says, "The church was filled to capacity. It was a typical hot summer Sunday morning and the building was quite fresh and new." The varnish on the pews was fresh and new, too, says Mason. As the story goes, when churchgoers attempted to stand and sing that morning, they found themselves stuck to the seats.

OVM
First Baptist Church.

According to Mason, the old bell from the original Presbyterian Church was moved to the Baptist Church

In 1949, the Baptist Church underwent a major renovation which was completed in 1951.

In his article, Mason says that the membership was active in Ojai. He tells about one popular annual event in which the congregation would create a nativity using live animals including camels. According to Mason, the main street was closed and throngs of onlookers watched as church members reenacted the Christmas story – Mary and Joseph making their way up Ojai Avenue and even stopping at the Oaks Hotel where they were turned away. They then made their way to a rustic stable that had been constructed across the street.

In 1964, Baptists built a modern church at 930 Grand Avenue and the police station and city hall moved into the old church

David Mason collection
Live Nativity of First Baptist Church .

building. In 1976, city hall moved to the renovated Hobson estate at 401 S. Ventura Street and they built a new police station at 402 S. Ventura Street in 1978-79. The World University currently occupies the former church building.

Liberal Catholic Church

The first church built in Meiners Oaks was the Liberal Catholic Church. Members of the Liberal Catholic Guild were meeting in homes as early as 1927 in the Ojai Valley until a lot was purchased and architect, John Roine designed a church for them. The church took several months to complete, as members of the congregation built it in their spare time. In December, 1929, the new church opened in the vicinity of 140 North Encinal Avenue, approximately half block north of El Roblar with services by Reverend Frank Kilbourne, publisher of *The Ojai* during the thirties and forties.

The church was built of redwood, measured thirty by fifty feet and seated 100 people. The congregation met from October through May, closing the church during the hot summer months.

In 1949, the church was moved to a site just east of the Gally Cottages on Ojai Avenue near Gridley where it still stands next to the modern Liberal Catholic Church. The original church is used as a social hall.

Fry photo
Original Liberal Catholic Church, built in Meiners Oaks, 1929.

Church of Christ

The second church to be built in Meiners Oaks was George Biggers' Church of Christ. This congregation started meeting at the Meiners Oaks Community Hall in the 1930s. In the early 1940s, George Biggers bought a lot on the southwest corner of El Roblar Drive and Pueblo Avenue and built a church there. Biggers reportedly kept costs down by using recycled wood from the recently demolished Labor Temple on Oak Street in Ventura. According to his son, Ron, Biggers did most of the construction work himself with help from anyone who happened to be around. He opened the church July 14, 1944.

Biggers, a lay preacher, earned his living mainly with bees. He caught his first swarm outside the schoolhouse in Santa Paula when he was only 8. By the time he was 9, he had thirty hives, according to his son. Some may recall Biggers appearing on the television program, *Ripley's Believe It or Not* in 1952 wearing a beard of live bees.

His ability to handle bees was a fascination to local children and one Meiners Oaks old-timer recalls Biggers telling the children that getting along with animals and insects is simply a matter of not showing fear.

Fry Photo
Church of Christ, built in Meiners Oaks, 1944.

Former neighborhood kids also recall with fondness, Biggers' church being the center of activity for children in the community. Few people knew, however, that Biggers had a passion for helping others build churches. According to his son, he often went off to help folks in other communities to start churches like he did in Meiners Oaks.

Chapter Six
Ojai Valley Hotels and Resorts

John Montgomery remarked, upon first seeing Nordhoff, that it was odd for a place with only ten inhabitants to have a hotel. What Montgomery didn't know was that Ojai Valley would become one of the key resorts of the west.

Nordhoff Hotel

In 1877, C.P. Wiggins purchased the townsite, including the twenty by sixty-foot Nordhoff Hotel. He added the west wing and hard-finished the frame and fabric building at a cost of $5,000. Wiggins advertised in the *Ventura Free Press* that his hotel had a bar complete with wines, liquors and cigars.

Wiggins, a tall, slim man of 50, was not very well liked. Some considered him to be arrogant. Walter Bristol, in his book, *The Story of Ojai Valley*, said, "He treated his guests as though they owed him an apology and the offense could not be condoned by their silent submission to a heavy board bill. Consequently, he soon had the house all to himself."

In 1878, John Montgomery bought the hotel and shortly after that Mrs. E.P. Kinney, of San Francisco, approached Montgomery to discuss opening a young ladies academy there. She convinced the new owner that her idea had merit and soon she was busy circulating brochures. Her leaflets detailed the school curriculum and the strict rules and guaranteed the moral safety of the girls who enrolled there.

Montgomery talked about the young ladies seminary in an 1887 interview. He said, "The school continued for six months and on its closing, the building was changed again into a hotel."

According to Montgomery, Mrs. S.C. Gridley managed the hotel for a while and in 1879, he sold it to Frank P. Barrows, who changed the name to Ojai Valley House. By that time there were twenty rooms with a handsome parlor and large dining room. After a satisfying meal at the hotel, guests could sit on the expansive porch and visit, take a walk along a shaded walkway or play a friendly game of croquet.

OVM
Ojai Inn, 1990. Formerly Blumberg's Nordhoff Hotel.

Montgomery said that Barrows kept the hotel for three years and then sold it to Mr. Arundell. Records show that James Huntington ran the Ojai Valley House in 1880. Eight years later Mr. Gardner bought the hotel and built the east portion. J.J. Burke of Canada and Mr. McKinley, a tubercular bank clerk from Philadelphia, managed the place in 1891.

Yda Storke, in her book of biographical sketches, wrote that "The structure, which first was made of light scantling covered with cloth, by 1891 had developed into quite a sightly hostelry – the nucleus of a thrifty little village." She said that at that time, Nordhoff was made up of some 300 inhabitants, "many of whom are recuperated invalids from nearly every state in the union."

In 1892, the inn was known as Hotel Oakdale under the management of Burke and his new partners, Mr. and Mrs. T.J. Knox. In 1894, Mrs. S.E. Wemple and Mrs. S.E. Merrill assumed proprietorship and advertised the hotel as the Ojai Valley Inn. But when George Viall took over the inn, in 1895, he put the name Hotel Oakdale back into use. People considered the 20 year-old hotel a first-class resort under Viall's proprietorship. Mrs. O.W. Raddick took over the hotel in 1897 and ran it for ten years as Hotel Oakdale.

Around 1900, J.J. Burke, C.E. Bigelow, H.W. Forster, W.L. Thacher, G.W. Mallory, A.A. Garland, John Suess, B.F. Spencer and F.W. Hubby started the Ojai Improvement Company for the purpose of investing in real estate. They purchased the hotel and a large area of land surrounding it and in 1910, they hired F.S. Beaman to run it. It was during that period that the place become known as the Ojai Inn.

Joe Linnel was the last person to run the Ojai Inn. His stint began around 1911 and ended when Edward Drummond Libbey ordered the hotel demolished as part of his town beautification plan. (Read this story in Chapter Eleven.)

There has been much speculation throughout the years as to exactly where the old hotel stood. Local historian, David Mason is probably close when he says, "The front door was in the center of the building where the fountain in Libbey Park is today."

Gally Cottages

In the autumn of 1873, William S. McKee and his wife, Mary, camped under the oaks and pondered where to erect a sanitarium for invalids. The McKees built a home on the northeast corner of what is now Ojai Avenue and Gridley Road. By fall of 1874, they opened it to the public as Oak Glen Cottages.

The McKees could attest to the valley's healing climate, for when they had settled in Upper Ojai around 1870, at least one of them was ill. Most early reports indicate that it was William. In the August 1, 1874 issue of the *Ventura Signal*, however, Mary McKee wrote of her own experiences with the valley's healing climate: "I came here four years since with a harassing cough which left me in a few months and has not returned. I feel confident if any element in the world will cure consumption, this will."

Historical accounts show Blumberg's hotel to be the first in the valley. In an 1887 interview, however, Abram Blumberg said that when he came here, the only site for accommodations for travelers was a small hotel with a shed roof on the site of the

Oak Glen Cottages. Perhaps the McKees were taking in paying guests earlier than originally thought.

In one of Mary Gally's delightful reminiscences, she said that when an Eastern family would fall in love with the valley, McKee would let them build themselves a cottage on his property. He served them meals for a certain number of months and when they left for their Eastern home, their cottage would become his. Jesse Mason, in his *History of Santa Barbara and Ventura County*, reports that the McKees could accommodate fifty guests in the cottages and as many as may come with tents.

Throughout the early years, the healthy, the curious and the ailing trickled steadily into Ojai Valley – many of them lodging at the Oak Glen Cottages. When Casitas Pass opened, in 1878, people literally flocked from Santa Barbara and points beyond, quickly filling the McKee's facility.

Gally family photo
Gally stage at Gally Cottages, 1887.

It was a congenial place. The elaborately adorned main building included a comfortable parlor where guests could visit with one another and a dining room. McKee hard-finished the cottages throughout. According to his ads, McKee promised "all of the conveniences of home."

Oak Glen grounds, including ample stable and barn space, encompassed ninety-five acres, of which forty-two were under cultivation. McKee built more facilities as he saw the need and had the money. Nearly ten years after he opened the cottages, McKee sold them to a man named Benjamin Gally and moved his family to Casitas where they opened a nursery.

Benjamin W. Gally (pronounced Gawly), born in 1852, had planned to become a banker in his home town of Wheeling, West Virginia. When his health began to fail, he came to California instead. Immediately upon purchasing McKee's health resort, he erected four new buildings. He then bought two stage coaches and hired drivers to make scheduled runs daily to Ventura and weekly to Santa Barbara. This investment assured Gally of even more business, for his drivers would convey travelers not to the center of town, where they could walk to the nearest hotel, but to the front path of Oak Glen Cottages.

Gally family photo
Benjamin Gally, circa 1885.

In 1885, Mr. Gally traveled to Jefferson City, Missouri where he married his sweetheart, Mary Davison, and brought her to Nordhoff. Though her husband had tried, there was no way to prepare Mary for what she would encounter out West.

The newlywed Gallys arrived in Nordhoff June 5, 1885. Mary was shocked at the abundance of weeds in the valley and that the houses were "no larger than chicken coops." Mary lost all hope upon learning that she had to sleep on the ground floor and later she revealed that the sight of the huge mountains had frightened her. She thought they would surely fall on her by morning. Despite these unfamiliar aspects of the valley, Mary remained to help her new husband in his business.

Soon after settling in, the Gallys staged a hunting contest at Oak Glen Cottages. By evening, local hunters and hotel guests heaped their furred and feathered trophies on a pool table to be judged. Gin Quin Soo, head cook at the resort, prepared a feast of the game and a party ensued. There was some question as to whether small birds qualified for contest points. They were considered fit to eat, however, and Soo cooked them in hollowed-out potato skins. The Gallys served the first ice cream in the valley that night, despite the cook's conviction that no one would survive eating it.

Mr. Gally died suddenly in 1893 at the age of 41 and Mary continued to run the popular resort under its new name, Gally Cottages. In 1900, Mary advertised that Gally Cottages offered billiards, tennis, croquet and golf.

Golf was first played in Ojai in January, 1899, at Gally Cottages. With the advice of Easterners who knew the game, Mary developed the course over a forty-acre section north of the cottages to Grand Avenue where the number and placement of trees made this a particularly attractive course. The greens were oiled sand bunkers and hazards were fences put up across the fairways. It was only green when it rained.

By July, Mary decided that Nordhoff was ready for

Gally family photo
Mary Gally, early 1900s.

a golf tournament. All golfers were to comply with special rules to compensate for some unusual obstacles. If a ball landed on a stone, it was to be dropped behind the stone without penalty. If the ball rolled into a squirrel hole, the golfer dropped it behind the hole. If it was unrecoverable, another ball could be used without penalty. The course consisted of six holes and those who wanted to play eighteen holes simply went around it three times.

Golf, being new to most of Nordhoff, caused great curiosity.

A crowd of onlookers followed the players throughout the tournament. Several ladies wore high-heeled shoes that day, leaving deep imprints in the greens. From then on, Mary urged women to wear flat shoes on the golf course.

Most contestants in that early tournament were, reportedly, too embarrassed over their scores to allow them to be published in the local newspaper. *The Ojai* reported, however, that Miss Bell won both of the ladies' events. She played six holes

Gally family photo
Golf at the Gally Cottages

using fifty strokes and hit the ball 104 yards and one foot to win the driving contest. Truston Morris, a Thacher School student, shot twelve holes in sixty-three strokes and drove his ball 105 yards, two feet and six inches. Louis Haggen drove 120 yards and he tied with Mr. Hubby for second place with seventy-four strokes.

After Mary's sons were grown, her faithful employee, Soo, returned to China. She had other Chinese workers on her property, however. She tells the story of one. "I had a laundry back of the barn, managed by a Chinaman. This seemed to be the clubhouse of all Chinese in the Valley. Then I found out he was selling whiskey so I turned him out and destroyed the building."

Mary Gally died in 1953, at the age of 98, after sixty-eight years in Ojai.

Gally family photo
The Gally's cook, Gin Quin Soo.

Foothills Hotel

The Ojai Improvement Company commissioned S.M. Jesley to design the Foothills Hotel and it was completed in 1903 one mile north of town on Foothill (then known as Foothills) Road. The original edifice was of wood, standing three stories high. They lavishly decorated the fifty guest chambers with fine furniture from the East. This, the plushest of local hotels, operated only in the winter and catered almost exclusively to fashionable Easterners. In fact, after the hotel was established, the management asked all new applicants for references before issuing them reservations. By 1906, the hotel was too small, so California-style bungalows were built south of the main building to accommodate more guests.

David Mason collection
Original Foothills Hotel, built in 1903.

In early advertising pamphlets, the management proudly claimed that the cooks used no canned vegetables or cold storage poultry. They fed their chickens clean food, served only Jersey milk and cream from their own dairy and piped clear water directly from a tunnel in the mountains from 1,500 feet above habitation. Riding, golf and tennis were the featured activities.

This beautiful hotel fell victim to the 1917 fire and the war prevented reconstruction for a couple of years. In July of 1919, they started rebuilding. A contractor named Hill rebuilt the new hotel at a cost of $125,000. James C. Leslie was the contractor for a building to house the workers.

The new two-story hotel was stucco. The first floor contained the lobby, dining room and billiard room, with the west wing housing the kitchen and laundry facilities. Guest rooms, each with a bath, were upstairs. Mr. Henry W. Morse managed the hotel for a number of years. On the off season, according to Gerard and Perkins in their book, *Ojai The Beautiful,* he ran the Harbor View Hotel in Edgarton, Massachusetts. J.J. Lopez, was the gardener. He used a horse-drawn lawn mower on the hotel golf course, always putting leather shoes on the horse so as not to track the greens.

The new hotel opened February 16, 1920. The following year, more people were turned away than were served. The Foothills was considered one of the best hotels in the state. In 1926, James Leslie was commissioned to build more cottages to accommodate more of those who wanted to and could afford to come.

During the next decade, the effects of the Depression drove the once-thriving hotel into extinction. It sat majestic, but vacant. In 1942, ninety-five boys from the California Prep School facility in Covina moved into the Foothills Hotel to resume their studies. After they had abandoned the building, in May, 1955, the United Synagogue of America bought thirty-seven of the original 160 acres and established Camp Ramah, an educational camp for Jewish youths. When they needed more space, Camp Ramah moved to the old El Rancho Rinconada Orchid Ranch on Fairview Road.

In 1976, the Foothills Hotel was demolished to make way for the construction of private homes. The old golf course is now Del Oro Estates. At least one original cottage remains. It is a private home.

Pierpont Cottages

In 1893, Dr. and Mrs. Ernest Pierpont left Chicago, looking forward to their California retirement. Word of mouth led them to Nordhoff, where they occupied the two-story stone house across from Gally Cottages. Theodore Woolsey, a graduate of Yale and friend of the Thachers had designed this home for his family six years earlier.

A short time later, Dr. Pierpont bought forty acres on what is now Thacher Road where he built a comfortable residence and planted almonds. The almonds didn't do well, so he pulled them out and replaced them with lemons. The climate was too cold for lemons and he replanted the ground to orange trees – some of which remain today.

Upon their arrival to California, Dr. and Mrs. Pierpont had deposited their life savings in an Oakland bank. After just becoming happily situated in Ojai Valley, they were devastated to learn that the bank had failed and all their money was lost. Dr. Pierpont reluctantly left his well-earned retirement and attempted to return to medicine. He later remarked that there was plenty of need here, but this was a poor community and few could pay for his services.

The Thacher family encouraged the Pierponts to open their large residence to visiting parents of Thacher School students. They agreed to try it. The Pierponts were obviously filling a need and very soon it became necessary for them to expand. The doctor, wanting to keep building costs down, enlisted the help of his orange pickers. Sam Hudiburg, previously known as the fastest orange picker in the valley, developed a reputation as a very good carpenter, thanks to the experience he gained at the Pierponts.

The Pierpont Cottages, originally known as Overlook, became a thriving winter resort. Pierpont advertised his ranch as having accommodations for "first class patronage." He also felt it important to mention that the place was 200 feet higher than Nordhoff and that it had perfect drainage. Another enticement, he thought, was the indoor plumbing. His was, reportedly, the first in the valley and while the cottages were under construction, people often rode out to his home on Sunday afternoons just to view this curiosity.

Dr. Pierpont passed away in 1905 and his widow continued to run the cottages. Three years later, she asked the famous architect for Hearst Castle, Julia Morgan, to design a home for her of native stone and their former residence became the main building for the hotel complex. Mrs. Pierpont eventually gave the resort to the oldest of her two sons. In order to present the other with something of equal value, she built the Pierpont Inn on San Jon Road in Ventura.

The Pierponts' Ojai guests enjoyed playing tennis, making their own music and walking along the beautiful garden paths, but horseback riding was probably the most popular activity of all. Realizing this, Margaret Clark Hunt started a horse rental business for tourists in 1908. Each morning, for nearly forty years, she and her employees led strings of horses to the major hotels and guided equestrian excursions into the back country. Mrs. Hunt, an excellent and highly respected horsewoman, also ran the Thacher School horse program until her death in 1946.

OVM

Margaret (Clark) Hunt on her show horse, 1939.

Guests to Pierpont Cottages over the years included Lucretia Garfield, widow of President Garfield and later Wendell Wilkie who arrived to rest prior to nomination to presidency against Franklin D. Roosevelt.

Pierpont Cottages operated as such until 1940. The property looks much as it did many yeas ago. The cottages however, are now rented as homes.

The Oaks

Edward Drummond Libby organized the Ojai Hotel Company for the sole purpose of developing a much needed year-round hotel. Richard S. Requa drew up the plans and Robert Winfield built the hotel at a cost of $50,000. Mr. Libby wanted to call the hotel *The Ojai Tavern*. So many people objected, however, that he offered a prize to the person who could come up with an acceptable name. *Libbey Inn* was among the most popular titles, but the winning entry was the *El Roblar Hotel*, and so it became.

Frank Barrington, described as a huge man who was well liked by everyone, managed the inn when it opened in 1920. Six years later he bought the hotel and enlarged it. When Mr. Barrington died, in 1942, his widow continued to operate the hotel. Most mornings she could be seen in the numerous El Roblar gardens picking stocks, snaps and sweet peas which she artistically arranged on the dining tables daily.

The food was considered to be excellent and early residents remember caravans of cars coming from Santa Barbara, Oxnard and even further away to deliver ladies to the El Roblar Hotel for luncheon.

Alexander Cromwell of San Francisco bought the hotel in 1950. He and the subsequent five owners executed many physical changes to the premises during the following eight years. The pool was built in 1951 and they added the bar in 1952. I recently heard the current co-owner, Don Cluff talk about an unusual feature of The Oaks. He said there's a room directly above the bar with padded benches encircling a window of one-way glass in the floor. Cluff speculates that, in the early days, people were hired to watch the bar tender pour the drinks.

In 1953, the name of the hotel was changed to The Oaks. The following year, Jessie Arms Botke painted her famous flamingo mural on the east wall of the ballroom.

The Oaks at Ojai, located at 122 East Ojai Avenue, is now a thriving health spa, following the trend of successful businesses of the past by catering to wealthy visitors in search of better health.

What happened to the Botke painting? Spa owner, Sheila Cluff, concerned about the effects of the temperature and conditions in what is now the spa exercise room, conducted some research in hopes of finding a way to preserve it. Today the mural hangs at the Irvine Medical Center art gallery and a photograph of the painting decorates the wall where the mural once hung.

Ojai Valley Inn

Edward Drummond Libbey envisioned here a country club with an eighteen-hole golf course. As the philanthropist's last gift to Ojai, he ordered it built. George C. Thomas, Jr., designed a nine-hole course and William F. Bell built it. Thomas followed two principles in its construction. He thought that the average golfer should enjoy their round without too great a penalty and that the course should afford enough challenge so that the low-handicapper had to play fine golf in order to make par. Mr. Thomas said that nature built the course and he simply placed the traps to conform with the contour of the land.

In 1924, Libbey asked his grounds crew to plant oaks from the golf links to the main highway.

Wallace Neff of Pasadena designed the inn. The California

Architectural Board awarded him a certificate of honor for this work, recognizing him for a structure "in perfect harmony with its surroundings."

David Mason collection
Original building at the Ojai Valley Inn.

The club was very small during the 1920s. It was a private club where dinner was served only by special arrangement. Teens from well-to-do families often spent their evenings there playing records on an old crank Victrola until the Depression closed the inn in 1932.

It reopened in 1935 with some new embellishments. Architect/builder, Austin Pierpont and interior designer, Mrs. F.A. Hennessey, teamed up to build and decorate twenty-five additional rooms. The dining room and patio were also built at this time.

Seven years later, during World War II, the Ojai Valley Inn became a military camp. Officers moved into the hotel rooms and they put up wooden prefab barracks on the golf course for the enlisted men. The official name for the army camp was Camp Lah We Lah His, which was Indian for *The Strong, The Brave.* There were reportedly 1,000 men stationed at this military training camp, creating a virtual community there. To accommodate the troops, they built streets through the camp and named each of them.

Two years later, the camp became a rest and recuperation

facility for the navy and they renamed the facility, Camp Oak. It's reported that the navy built two swimming pools for their use.

Munger family photo
Julia Munger at the military camp, Ojai Valley Inn

U.S. Navy
Camp Oak

Citizens of the valley were highly involved with the servicemen – often inviting them to dinner and offering them rides.

A local USO was opened in the old Brennan's Electric store, presumably east of the Bank of America building. In 1943, more room was needed and the USO moved into the Boyd Club and the Red Cross took over Brennan's Electric.

When the military men left, the government auctioned off the barracks and some of them landed in the Ojai Valley. At least two of them are now being used as homes in Meiners Oaks – one on North Encinal Street and one on East El Roblar.

The inn reopened in 1947 with Don Burger as manager. The military attempted to restore the golf course before leaving, but neglected to reestablish two original holes – numbers two and five. Although, they expanded the course to an eighteen hole course in 1947, these two holes were not part of the course until 1999 when they were rebuilt.

In 1957, Ray Reitzel signed on as tennis pro and a short time later, the pool, riding trails and stables were added.

Presently, the inn's hotel rooms and bungalows accommodate hundreds of people all year round. The attractive gift shops, sophisticated dining and numerous available activities make it practically unnecessary for guests to leave this beautiful spot during their stay. The favorite aspect of many is the inn's patio dining area and the spectacular view it affords. The Ojai Valley Inn is on Country Club Drive.

Overflow Facilities

As time passed, a flurry of people rushed to our charming, quiet countryside, its fame growing with each stagecoach load. Most years, accommodations were never quite adequate and residents saw an opportunity to make extra money by opening their homes to tourists. Some pitched tents in their yards and refurbished old outsheds to handle the hotel overflow.

Glenwood Retreat opened in 1887 with Mr. J. N. Jones as proprietor. He could take up to ten boarders at his ranch home, just east of where St. Joseph's Hospital is now on Ojai Avenue. His neighbor, John Carne, converted part of his twenty-seven room Victorian house, on what is now Carne Road and Ojai Avenue, into the Bonito House Hotel. In 1896, he advertised that his hotel had ten rooms to let. Deleitosso Ranch was between Jones' and Carne's places and proprietor J.C. Wright welcomed overnight guests there in 1896. This is presumably the old, two-story Robison home.

According to the *Ventura Free Press*, T.J. Knox opened the Live Oak Cottages in 1888. They were described as being at the center of Nordhoff. In 1891, Live Oak Villa was advertised as a "home-like house." Mrs. A.R. McDonnell and Mrs. Annie Clark ran the ten-room Live Oak Villa in 1896. Mrs. H.C. Stauffer took over the Villa in 1898 and Mr. Eason managed the place in 1899. In 1919, Joe Linnel was running a place called Ojai Inn which was reportedly on the "adjoining corner to El Roblar Hotel."

This author was confused as to where the Live Oak Villa was located until I saw a 1925 issue of *The Ojai*, wherein there's a story about Tom Clark's home, then on the southeast corner of Signal and Matilija Streets. The editor said that this home was known for a number of years as Oak Cottage and was a popular boarding house originally built by T.J. Knox and run by Mrs. Knox.

According to the newspaper, the second story of this home was removed in 1924, the rooms were enlarged and the outside was stuccoed. Tom Clark reportedly built a wall around his home after someone plowed into the house with a car.

The wall, which still stands around what is now a parking lot, was constructed of stone from the original court house built in 1874 at 120 East Santa Clara Street in Ventura.

Joe and Inez (Blumberg) Berry opened Berry Villa in 1906 at the present site of the post office parking lot on south Signal Street. The accommodations featured separate cottages, gas lights and cold water in the rooms. Hiram L. Watkins left his apricot orchard in Oak View to run the villa during 1911 and 1912.

Long-time resident, Ann Yant recalled that Berry Villa was a "real nice place." She said that her father, Joe Linnel, ran the Berry Villa for a while in conjunction with the old Ojai Inn.

Mary Scott provided tents and cottages and advertised her place, Los Nidos, as a sanitarium for outdoor life from 1905-1908.

In 1910, Seymour and Julia (Robison) Munger left the hotel they were running in Moorpark and returned to Nordhoff where they had met twenty years earlier. They built a two-story house on the northwest corner of what is now Fox and Willow Streets, near the train depot and opened it as a boarding house. Julia and her daughters, Ruby and Marion, served their guests three full-course meals each day always including fresh biscuits.

Sometime after the boarding house closed, the top story was

removed, but the house still stands. Seymour died in 1941 and Julia continued living in the house practically until her death in 1964 at the age of 96.

Cottages Among the Flowers

Even people who have lived for quite a while in Ojai wonder about the Cottages Among the Flowers on West Aliso Street. Huge, shapely oaks cast deep shadows on a handful of tiny wooden cottages there. A local architect named Harold Burket designed the Welsh-style cottages in 1925. Apparently the construction was considered quite modern for the time. Some say the cottages were a matter of pride to Ojai because they had centrally-located, electric refrigeration systems built into the laundry rooms. In the 1920s and 30s a profusion of flowers grew over the nearly three acres of ground; hence the place name, which is still painted on the sign in front of the cottages.

Famous Resorts of the Matilija Canyon

In 1839, Raphael Lopez built an adobe home at the mouth of Matilija Canyon using bricks of sun-dried mud mixed with straw. Old tales reveal that the Lopez adobe was known as a fortress against fierce natives and a trading post for the peaceful Matilija tribe.

OVM
Pop Soper carrying the mail from Ojai to Matilija Canyon Resorts around the turn of the century.

Members of the Lopez family occupied the adobe for over a century. During that time, they welcomed the occasional mountain wanderer by offering him provisions and a place to pause. Long after the Lopez family vacated their old home, a modern house was built there, incorporating the token remains of the original adobe within it. Technically, this is the oldest inhabited adobe in Ventura County. It is a private home, however, and is not open to the public.

To passersby, the history of the adobe is invisible. People don't give the place, which is west of the highway, a second glance. They often notice Bodee's, the small bar nearby to the east of the road, however, and wonder about its origin.

Hiram Imboden Cromer opened Bodee's in 1939. In 1952, his establishment caught fire and burned to the ground with him inside. Friends helped his wife rebuild the place and Bodee's bar is still operating sixty years after its beginning.

Ojala

A few miles up the highway is a dirt road that crosses the river and leads to Ojala. This old resort is no longer open to the public, but the story behind its conception is rather interesting.

In 1875, Philander Wallace Soper and his wife, Sara Elizabeth, homesteaded 160 acres of land in the Matilija Canyon. Soper made coffins for a living. He also managed John Meiners' ranch for many years. Their son, Clarence Anthony and his twin, Clara, were born on Soper's ranch in 1881.

When he grew to manhood, Clarence took a job on the railroad. Seventeen years later a doctor told him he would soon die. He became despondent, gave up his job and packed into the local backcountry where he lived in seclusion and waited to die.

After a year, however, he felt better and returned to civilization. In 1916, he bought some acreage from his father's estate and opened a guest camp there five years later. Jack Dempsey (World Heavyweight Boxing Champion from 1919-1926) visited the resort. He suggested that Soper could rake in more money if he would fix up a ring and charge a buck a head for all who wanted to watch the boxer train for his bout with Gene Tunney. Pop, as Clarence was known, liked the idea and in 1925, he opened a fight training camp.

Dempsey used to trot from Soper's to Ojai and walk back. While they were building the tunnels on Maricopa Highway,

Dempsey would sometimes go up there and swing the huge hammer which was used to break big rocks. Once he got hit in the face by a rock and his trainer put a stop to this form of exercise.

Besides Dempsey, Gene Tunney, (World Heavyweight Champion from 1926-1928) trained at Soper's, as did Tony Chavez, Bob Nestell, Roscoe Scally, Jimmy Webster, Jackie Wilson, Jimmy Casino and Ray Brown.

In 1929, Pop sold part of the ranch to Rick and Eugenia Everett who established a religious artists' colony known as Ojala. Ojala means *hope* or *promise* in Spanish. They built the pool in 1949 and opened it to the public shortly after. They also rented cabins to vacationers for many years. Pop Soper, who himself boxed professionally for a short time, died in 1957 at the age of 76.

Matilija Hot Springs

North of the old Soper place is what is now known as Matilija Hot Springs. It was not the first resort by this name, however.

In 1872, J.W. Wilcox discovered some hot springs in Matilija Canyon. He homesteaded the property and then sold it to R.M. Brown, who built a road and invited guests there. Brown advertised his resort as *San Buenaventura Springs*. According to his *Ventura Signal* ad, in September 1873, a first-class cook prepared the meals and an attendant was provided for each bath house. "No pain shall be spared," the ad promised, "to make an invalid comfortable." Brown advertised good beds, a well-stocked library and great scenery. A man known as Captain Gardner bought the springs around 1877 and erected cottages, calling the resort *Matilija Hot Springs*. Mr. Wilcoxen and his daughter, Mrs. Vicker, took over the springs shortly before the flood of 1884 destroyed it. They continued to maintain a home there, but never again opened it to the public.

In 1887, Abram Blumberg homesteaded some land about two miles below the original Matilija Hot Springs. He pitched tents, built cottages, established a store and dining room and opened the resort, *Ojai Hot Springs*. Mr. Blumberg widely advertised his "village for the sick." He claimed that the 104-degree sulphur springs contained many healing properties. *The Fountain of Life Springs*, he said, was tonic in effect and the spring called *Mother Eve* was an alternative and cathartic.

His hot mineral baths were considered the finest known. He claimed they cured these dread diseases; rheumatism (a disease of the joints and muscles), catarrh (inflammation of nose and throat), erysipelas (inflammation of the skin), dyspepsia (indigestion), chronic diarrhea, sore eyes, liver and kidney complaints, cancer, syphilis and all sorts of blood and skin diseases. He encouraged people to drink the water and to bathe in it. Mary Gally even attempted to boil an egg in it once.

By 1893, Blumberg could accommodate 100 guests at Ojai Hot Springs. He ran a daily stage to Nordhoff to fetch patrons bound for his health resort. He delivered spring water, too. Mr. Mesick, *The Ojai* editor, was one of his best customers. Mesick had a "cranky liver," but once he began a regular program using Blumberg's curative water, he felt quite a lot better. Blumberg shipped Matilija water as far away as New York.

Abram Wheeler Blumberg had been educated as a lawyer. He moved his family from Iowa to Los Angeles in 1872 in hopes that his wife's health would improve. Blumberg and Catharine Elizabeth Van Curen (Andy Van Curen's sister) had been married for thirteen years by then. Part of her ill health was, no doubt, a result of the loss of their 2 year-old daughter, Izora, who lay buried in Boon County, Iowa. The Blumbergs had four living children: Wheeler, Inez, Birdsel Ward and Irene May.

Catharine died at the age of 47 in 1890. Three years later Abram married Ella Ranard, daughter of D.A. Sackett of Ventura. They divorced in 1895 and in 1898, he married Mrs. F.H. Roberts of Santa Monica and promptly separated from her because he thought she was a bigamist.

During his later years, Abram ventured out and learned to ride a two-wheeler. He became quite fond of the sport. In 1899, in Los Angeles, however, he fell from his bicycle and died of the injuries at the age of 63. Another report said that he died after being struck by an electric car while riding his bicycle.

In 1901, The Blumberg heirs sold the resort, then known as Matilija Hot Springs to S. P. Creasinger of Los Angeles. He spent $50,000 to improve the resort by adding a pool and electric lighting, but he went bankrupt. Sim Meyers took over in 1904 and ran it for ten years, dropping a reported $100,000 into the resort. Joe Linnel ran the springs between 1920 and 1938. In 1947, Ventura County acquired the 60 year-old resort when it purchased land for the Matilija Dam project. Various individuals managed the resort off and on throughout the subsequent fifty years offering therapeutic massages and hot mineral bathing.

Many locals recall taking Red Cross swimming lessons there and attending swimming parties with their family and friends during the late 1940s through the 1970s. One could have a picnic on the bank overlooking the creek and there was a wonderful little store where children loved to buy candy treats.

Lyon's Springs

Deeper in the canyon beyond Matilija was another resort – once a thriving vacation spot. Newcomers and natives under 60, however, may never have heard of Lyon's Springs. In 1871, when Robert Lyon became ill, he took leave of his position as auditor and recorder in Douglas County, Nevada, and bought a home on Ventura Avenue in Ventura. His next door neighbor, Mr. Chilson, knew that Lyon's health was failing and related a story to him about some curative springs in the mountains. Chilson said he accidentally stumbled upon the springs and that only he and some Mexican cowboys knew about them. He camped there once and noticed an improvement in his own health. Chilson agreed to lead Lyon along the rugged route to the springs.

After a short stay, Lyon felt so much better that he returned for his family. He hired an experienced guide named Mr. Morman to lead the four of them to the wilderness spot. They camped at the Lopez adobe the first night and secured some horses and gear there. In an article she wrote about her life several years later, Lyon's daughter, Belle, said that this was the first horseback ride for her and her sister.

The family grew fond of the rustic retreat and built a house there. People were in the habit of naming their homes then and the Lyons called theirs *Cliff Glen*. They lived in the mountains for six months at a time, spending the reminder of the year on Ventura Avenue. Mr. Lyon's condition worsened and when he became an invalid, according to an article by Belle Lyon, six of his friends carried him up and down the treacherous mountainside in a rocking chair.

After the original Matilija Hot Springs resort, which was above Cliff Glen, was destroyed by flood waters and the owners decided not to rebuild, several former guests, who were aware of the Lyon's location, wrote begging the family to find a place to tuck them in for a few weeks. The idea of boarders didn't much appeal to the Lyons, but the mortgage forced the issue and in 1888, they opened Cliff Glen to visitors. Robert Lyon died in

1889 and his widow, Gertrude, and her two daughters continued to run the resort.

They advertised the "health and pleasure resort" as being at the 1,321-foot elevation level, where the climate was delightful and the scenery beautiful. Mrs. Lyon provided "camper's homes" measuring ten by twelve feet. These cabins had "good floors, shake roofs, doors and siding of heavy, dark blue duck." The furnished huts rented for $2.00 per week. Bedding, extra cots, cooking utensils and so forth could be secured on the premises at reasonable rates. Gertrude established Live Oak Park for campers who had their own tents and they paid an extra $1.00 for baths, towels and water.

The butcher wagon called upon vacationers three times per week, or guests could dine on Mrs. Lyon's good home cooking, "of which there was always plenty." Resort goers enjoyed lawn tennis and croquet. There was a dance pavilion and even a darkroom, "fitted up for the Kodaker." Ads assured anglers that, within a stone's throw, they would find a large mountain stream "filled with speckled trout." One resort guest claimed that she watched a man catch 105 fish in one evening.

The postal department granted a post office for Cliff Glen in 1906, but not under the original name. Officials pointed out that there were already too many towns using the names Cliff and Glen and so the resort became known as *Lyons Springs*.

The property passed out of the Lyon family's hands during the Depression, but succeeding proprietors kept Lyons Springs alive and thriving until the advent of Matilija Dam. Project heads ordered the resort demolished as it was in the area soon to be a lake. Some old-timers say, however, that the water in Matilija Lake never reached the resort site.

Wheeler Hot Springs

Wheeler Blumberg once shot a deer and it fell close to a bubbling sulphur spring. He visualized a resort there and, in 1888, he homesteaded the wilderness property, opening it to the public three years later. Wheeler built a twenty-four by forty-foot cement swimming bath and filled it with hot sulphur water for his guests.

Wheeler, Abram Blumberg's oldest son, married Rose Anna Goodrich. Wheeler died in 1907 and the Blumberg's son-in-law, Webb Wilcox managed Wheeler Springs until 1935.

Twenty-two-year-old Webb Wilcox came to the county from

Illinois in 1903 and later married Wheeler and Rose Anna's daughter, Etta. In 1935, he established Wilcox Cottages and a post office on the east side of Highway 33 across from Wheeler's. In 1948, when George Fleegle was postmaster, *Ripley's Believe It Or Not* featured the six by seven-foot building as the smallest post office in the United States. It served eighty families.

Jay Cortner family photo
Webb and Etta (Blumberg) Wilcox on their wedding day, 1905.

Until 1933, there was no road to Wheelers. The stage had to go through Matilija Hot Springs, over the hill and through what is now Matilija Lake bed. Arthur Waite remembered when they carried resort patrons by Stanley Steamer. The driver met the train and took passengers up the canyon along old Rice Road. They had to cross the river and always took that opportunity to throw out the hose and pump the tank full of water.

Jay Cortner family photo
Wheelers auto stage.

Jay Cortner family photo
Wheelers Plunge.

Sam Sklar ran Wheelers resort in 1953. He had big ideas for the spa, which included building a 400-room hotel there. He also bought a hotel at the corner of Grand Avenue and Montgomery Street and planned to run it in connection with the resort. He wanted to schedule a bus between the village hotel, which is now Grey Gables Retired Teachers Home, and the resort in the mountains. This didn't work out, however, and a couple of years later Art Linkletter bought Wheelers.

Just prior to the devastating 1969 floods, Evelyn and Frank Landucci purchased the 78-year-old resort. Because of the flood damage, they spent immensely more time and money at Wheelers than they expected to. The result was Casa Landucci, an Italian dinner house where many people, including celebrities, came from near and far to dine.

Lathrop's and Pine Mountain Lodge

Herbert Lathrop ran a popular hunting and recreational resort in the Sespe until 1914, when he was shot and killed.

Floyd Perrit, a friend of Lathrop's and a pitcher for the Los Angeles Nine, was hunting one morning with a 30-30 ball rifle when he saw movement in the shrubs. What Perrit thought was a mountain lion, was in reality Lathrop checking his traps.

Margaret Hunt and Andy Van Curen rode up to bring the body back. They laid the body on a stretcher and six Mexican men took turns carrying it over the mountain trails to Nordhoff.

It wasn't easy dealing with a death or a serious illness occurring in the backcountry then. During the same year, Sespe old timer, 80-year-old Ramon Ortega fell 200 feet to his death while riding in the area of Potrero Seco near Santa Barbara. His nephew, long-time forest ranger, Jacinto Reyes, and a group of volunteers rode Ortega out on horseback. They reportedly placed the body on a pack mule and put boards around it to support it in a sitting position. Then they tied a rope to the body leaving both ends free. One rider held the rope in front and another held the rope in back to keep the body from swaying. They reportedly rode thirty miles by rugged trail to Wheelers in this manner.

OVM
Herb Lathrop.

OVM. Erle Stanley Gardner took the photo.
Bill Herbert and Howard Bald at Pine Mountain Lodge around 1914.

Jay Cortner family photo
Lathrop's Lodge.

Around 1895, twenty Ojaians subscribed to a fund to build a hunting lodge at Pine Mountain. Essington Gibson and his son, James, built the chimney. The sixteen by twenty-foot hewn log structure, known as Pine Mountain Lodge, bunked an even dozen men.

While Lathrop's Lodge (a privately owned ranch) still stands near Rose Valley, the Pine Mountain Lodge burned during one of the forest fires and was never rebuilt. Hikers and riders will see the old rock chimney standing alone east of Haddock.

Chapter Seven
The Boom of the Eighties

Increasing interest in the valley spurred many real estate inquiries. A few land owners noticed this and realized that there was a shortage of property. That concept started the boom of 1887.

The first evidence of a land boom came when a piece of property worth $40 sold for $300. The purchaser then resold it for a profit. This madness went on all over the valley.

Some citizens were worried about the effects of such a boom and they wrote newspaper editorials stating their desire for permanent residents, not land promoters and "real estate tycoons." They made it clear that they expected to live the remainder of their days in Nordhoff and did not wish to see "a wild spirit of real estate development here." They warned, "We want permanent settlers, not speculators."

Although the boom of 1887 lasted for just three months, the valley would never be the same again. Things were quiet and pleasant here before the land frenzy. Modest dwellings housed hard-working families – mostly farmers. That changed when a more sophisticated group of people migrated to the valley. They came with fancier possessions, new ideas and rules designed to exclude some. The terms, "uppity" and "stuck up" became part of the everyday language and envy invaded the peaceful little valley. The community was growing and being altered in the name of progress.

Valley Ranches and Residents Circa 1890

Things changed rapidly in the valley during those early years. Some of the large ranches of the 1870s had been reduced to hundreds of small parcels twenty years later. Many people developed virgin land. This section describes some of the alterations that occurred during that period. Our tour begins in the Matilija Canyon, which can be reached by taking Highway 33 north from Ojai.

Matilija Canyon Ranches

In 1890, F.M. Lopez tended the land at the mouth of the canyon on which his ancestors had built the family adobe many years before. J. Logan Kennedy's Faun Hill Ranch was north of Lopez and west of Matilija Creek. It was considered one of the prettiest and healthiest home sites in California. Kennedy had twenty acres of oranges, lemons and prunes. Kennedy was a boyhood friend of Thomas Bard's.

Fred Sheldon's property, east of Kennedy's, was known as the Hello Ranch, where his principal activity was bee-keeping. He also had citrus trees. Sheldon's father, Charles, was a carriage maker. He brought his family to the county in 1887 and opened a blacksmith shop in Ventura. Although Fred helped his dad in the business, he preferred farming and soon bought the eighty acres that he called home. Elmer Friend now owns that prime citrus land

On up the canyon, beyond Sheldon's place, were the resorts described in Chapter Six.

West Valley Ranches

Following the rutted, dusty horse path back down to the canyon floor in 1890, you would first approach John Meiners' Cherry Acres Rancho situated amid an 800-acre oak forest. This is now Meiners Oaks (read about the development of Meiners Oaks in Chapter Thirteen).

El Nido, meaning The Nest in Spanish, owned by W.I. Rice, was west of Meiners' in the Ventura River bottom. Rice Road is named for this large landholder. Mr. Hall's land was east of Meiners at Los Cerritos in the vicinity of what is now the West Hills development along Rancho Drive.

The Maricopa Highway shopping complex is on the western boundary of the 342 acres Kenneth P. Grant owned. Grant was thought to be an unusually generous man. In 1892, he began subdividing his land. He claimed that his property was worth

$200 an acre but he sold it for $100 because, he said, "It is a shame for men to hold more land than they can make use of while honest, deserving, poor men are compelled to do without simply because they haven't money enough to buy large tracts."

William Kerfoot bought a parcel in the southwest corner of Grant's acreage and this is where Krotona Theosophical Society is now.

Henry K. Winchester and E. William Dean were absentee landowners of 360 acres northeast of Grant's. This is now part of the beautiful Arbolada residential area. James McKee held a long, narrow section of real estate next to Winchester and Dean. McKee Street, southeast of Del Oro Drive, marks the approximate center of his land.

Camouflaged by chaparral in the foothills behind Hall's 187 acres lay B.F. McDonald's Hopernell Ranch. (This is the present site of Camp Ramah on Fairview Road). His nearest neighbor to the east, in the 1890s, was F.F.J. Millard who established his home, Gold Fern Ranch, in the brush at the end of the little trail now known as Foothill Road. Millard's wife liked to trap wild animals and make their skins into buggy robes and coats.

Captain Gelett

Captain Charles Wetherby Gelett's land was situated between Millard's and Winchester/Dean's in the Stewart Basin. His home was on the north side of Matilija Street between Signal and Ventura Streets.

Gelett came from Kingston, Massachusetts in 1887 with diseased lungs but soon became what people described as "hale and hardy" for a man in his 70s. In fact, he was considered a walking advertisement for Ojai's healing power as he hadn't had so much as a cold since coming here.

It was reported in the newspaper that on his 78th birthday, in order to show how sprightly he was, Gelett jumped up in the air and cracked his heels together not once, but twice before alighting. He was also known as a man without fear or caution. In 1895, at the age of 82, Captain Gelett, who was reportedly driving too fast along Creek Road, was thrown from his buggy and killed. His wife, Jane (Russell) lived to celebrate her 95th birthday in the valley.

In the Foothills

J.C. Daly owned an undetermined number of acres in the foothills to the east of Millard, plus ninety-five acres north of Grand in the vicinity of what is presently North Daly Road and Drown Street. Louis Spader's Bella Vista was tucked into the foothills behind Nordhoff. His closest neighbor to the east was Sam C. Gridley, who owned the Gridmoor Ranch beyond north Gridley Road. Mr. Gridley, for whom Gridley Road is named, came to the valley in 1876 and planted raisin grapes. He built a thirteen-room, two-story stone and shingle home for his family, Margaret, who died of consumption in 1886 at the age of 43 and their children. After Margaret's death, Gridley married Ella C. Roberts.

Village Properties

Meanwhile back in the village: Lotta Deline owned a lot on South Ventura Street. Andy Van Curen had a few acres west of Deline's. People now live in homes there on San Antonio Street and Crestview Drive. K.P. Grant owned the corner of Ventura and Santa Ana Streets, where now stands the police station. Edwin Senior held title to the southwest corner of that intersection, where Ojai City Hall is today. Reverend Vaile lovingly called his home on South Signal Street, directly behind Libbey Park and east of Grant's lot, Buena Vista. J.B. Fox possessed quite a bit of land in the area now known as Fox Street. Adjacent to Fox and west of Bryant Street, I. J. Hudiburg had twenty-two acres.

Judge Irvin W. Wolfe held twenty-eight acres between Lion and Signal Streets. Thomas Barrows owned a piece of property to the east of that in the vicinity of Buena Vista Street, directly west of Daly's town acreage. George Stewart owned land on Summer and Eucalyptus Streets.

The Edwin Baker Family

During this period, the Baker family lived in John Montgomery's old home at what is now 310 Matilija Street. The old adobe had a new look by then because Mr. Baker had covered the exterior with wood siding.

Edwin Baker had brought his family to Ojai Valley in 1886 hoping to retire in better health. He had made his money in various business ventures in Walla Walla, Washington. Mr.

Baker's youngest daughter, Helen (Reynolds), later wrote a delightful story about her family and their life in Nordhoff. In her *Family Album* she portrayed her father as a very practical man, not one to spend unnecessarily. When he considered more space in the home essential, for instance, instead of building entire rooms, he added little alcoves.

Mr. Baker liked to fish and hunt. He was an amateur photographer and converted one of his outbuildings into a darkroom. Most people considered the Bakers well-to-do.

The Bakers adhered to the etiquette for people of leisure. The ladies took afternoon naps after which they dressed and went calling. Afternoon calls were formal. Helen Baker Reynolds relates that the more special the outing, the more petticoats one wore. "To be really grand," she said, "one had to rustle." A lady caller, according to Helen, "wore a good dress, well corseted, of course; a flowered or beribboned hat set high on the pompadour and very tight, white kid gloves."

A large part of her mother's calling time was reserved for the sick and aged. She went bearing flowers from her garden or homemade preserves from the cellar. The Bakers traditionally accepted callers on Monday. Mrs. Reynolds, although too young to participate, recalls that her mother and older sisters usually served their guests tea and a chocolate drink frothy with whipped cream.

Sarah (Miller) Baker was a self-taught woman whose love of learning continued throughout her life. Although she only completed four grades of school, she had a passion for learning and became extraordinarily well educated in world history and in several languages. When she was 80, she took up Greek.

She also loved music and always made sure there was plenty of music and religion in the household. In fact, she often played hymns on the organ in the morning to announce that breakfast was being prepared. The huge meals in the Baker home were prepared by their Chinese help Esing. He also did the family laundry in the outside wash house and the ironing. Mrs. Baker and her daughters took care of the routine housecleaning.

Her mother, Mary French, came to live with the Baker family in 1902. Helen describes her grandmother as a tiny, gnome-like woman who was so stooped she was almost bent double. She had a spinal deformity brought on by years of overwork. Helen remembered her having "sad, anxious gray eyes and gray hair parted in the middle and drawn back into a small tight knot." Mrs. French was almost deaf.

Her days were filled with knitting string wash clothes, gathering eucalyptus bark to be used for fireplace kindling and helping the cook, Esing, in the kitchen whenever he would allow it. Helen remembered her as a worrier. "Anytime anyone from the family drove out with horse and buggy, she would station herself at the sitting room window and engage in silent but concentrated anxiety while watching for their return."

During the weekday, Mrs. French wore a calico apron and she always changed just before supper into one of white percale. Outside the house, she wore a sun bonnet.

Mrs. French cast the first ballot of her life at the age of 84 in the presidential election of 1912. The event had such meaning to her that she was the first one to the polls that day in Nordhoff.

From a child's standpoint of life in the valley in those days, Helen Baker Reynolds shares this, "Something exciting and wonderful was always going on, especially outdoors – currying the horses, gathering eggs, cutting alfalfa with the scythe, storing persimmons or pears in the cellar, stacking hay in the barn… Best and most exciting of all," she said, "was irrigating the orchard. What a thrill of delight to hear the engine in the windmill house come to life with coughing and wheezing, a sign that soon water would be feeling its way down the ditches between the orchard trees, making streams delightful for wading."

The Clausens bought the Baker's house in the 1930s and turned it into a funeral home. The property is currently still owned by the Clausen family and, as of this writing, houses a quilt shop called Heartwarmers Mercantile.

East End Ranches

Joseph Waite owned fifty-four acres just east of the Nordhoff Grammar School and including what is now lower Drown Street to Grand Avenue. Waite Street, just off Drown, is named for this pioneer family. A. Levy held the fifty acres east of Waite, and D.A. Smith had forty acres bordering Levy's eastern boundary. Combined, these two parcels included what is now Shady Lane and Sarzotti Park. This is the same land that once belonged to L.D. Roberts and it probably included part of the old Ayers ranch, too.

The Gally Cottages encompassed seventy acres of the

126

northeast corner of Gridley and Ojai Avenue. Reverend A. Daniels owned fourteen acres at the far northeast corner of that property on Grand with the San Antonio River running along its east section.

When following the river north, just across Grand, one would have found C.A. Sayre's Sylvania Apiary backed up to what is now known as Orange Road.

T. Wasely, as in the 1870s still owned the eighty acres running the entire length of Gridley Road north from Grand Avenue and across from the Waites.

On the northwest corner of Gridley and Grand lived John G. Smith, originally of Santa Barbara. He called his place Fairoaks. He had recently purchased this ten-acre ranch from Thomas Barrows for $2,450.

C.E. Bigelow of La Laggia lived directly across Ojai Avenue from the Gallys in the rock house Theodore Woosley had built. T.C.H. Smith had a small parcel behind Bigelow's called Alder Bar. Michael Clark, supervisor Tom Clark's father, owned fifteen acres where he and his wife had raised their children, south of Ojai Avenue and just west of what is now the Ojai Lumber Company.

The Soules called their ranch Sunny Slope. It's now known as Soule Park and Soule Golf Course

The acreage immediately east of Gally Cottages belonged to the Cory family in the 1890s. East of Cory's was Los Olivas – Hugh MacMillan's olive orchard, which Seymour D. Munger had first planted in the 1880s. Gorham Road now divides these two parcels.

Ed Wiest owned the old Munger place in the early 1900s. In later years, it was known as the Lombardy Ranch and is now St. Joseph's Health and Retirement Center. Wiest's old home has been incorporated into the facility.

Harry Fordyce's place was

OVM

Mr. and Mrs. Harry Fordyce.

north of Cory's. Adjacent to the olive orchard was J. N. Jones' twenty-eight acres and further east lay John C. Wright and William H. Turner's seventy acres. John Wright and his brother-in-law, Mr. Turner, bought their land from T. J. Robison and Mr. Wright moved into the Robison house.

The next ranch, known as Bonito, was owned by a wealthy Chicago man, John Carne. He had bought the ranch from Thomas Jefferson Robison. Carne, a prominent real estate dealer, first visited Ojai Hot Springs for liver treatments. After his wife died, he brought five of his seven children here: Katie, Inez, Marion, Lucy and Charlie. Carne had architect W. T. Richardson design a huge two-story, twenty-seven room home for his family, and John Heck built it in 1894. Carne sold his home to A.G. Poplin in 1912. It reportedly burned to the ground in 1952.

Essington Gibson, Mrs. Waite's grandfather, lived directly north of Carne on the Keystone Ranch. Gibson had also purchased his land from Robison. Gibson was a mason by profession. Jack Ross Bennett's place, Lismore, was located between Carne and McNell Roads south of Grand and was flanked on the north by the San Antonio School, Thomas McNell's twenty acres, Emily Stephenson's eight acres and William Friend's five acres.

Margaret Walter family photo
Bennett's Lismore Orchards on Carne Road next to San Antonio School.
Pictured: Hattie, Anita, David and J. R. Bennett.

Jack Bennett

Jack R. Bennett was born in Ireland in 1845. As an adult, he went to work for a cousin in Quebec. He became a merchant, taking clothing to Labrador and bringing back fish and oil. He later worked at a saw mill in Mendocino and then he established a dairy business in San Francisco.

A bout with catarrh brought Bennett to Nordhoff in 1887 where he purchased sixty-one acres and became a farmer. A December, 1889 issue of *The Ojai* states that Bennett was getting ready to build a house on his property at the cost of $2,500. They named their ranch, Lismore presumably after a castle in Ireland. The Bennett's main crops were prunes, almonds, olives and raisin grapes.

Bennett married Hattie (Harriet Elizabeth) Greenleif of Canada. They had five children, John, Lillian (Carne), Stuart, David and Anita. Their son, John, died in 1918, of pneumonia while serving in the armed forces in Washington DC. He was 26. At the time of his death, according to family members, John was engaged to marry Mary Gally's niece, Margarette Davison.

Margaret Walter family photo
Bennett family, 1895: (l-r) Stuart, Hattie, David, Lillian, Jack, Anita, John (Jack) R. Bennett.

South of Bennett was Thomas Krutz' land. Patria Encina (oak of the native land), on what is now Reeves Road, was owned by Rynerson and Leach. Nick Walnut's winery was a few miles east of Rynerson's place. The Pierponts built Overlook or Pierpont Cottages, on what later became Thacher Road and near what is now McNell Road. Farther east on Thacher Road was Sherman Thacher's school. More of Thomas Krutz's land, later to be called the Topa Topa Ranch, adjoined Sherman's on the south.

Upper Valley Ranches

Upper valley residents didn't seem to succumb as easily as the lower valley people to the temptation of making a profit selling off parcels of their land. Or perhaps newcomers weren't interested in living so far from the village. For whatever reason, very few real estate transactions had taken place in Upper Ojai.

Thompson family photo
Thomas and Winifred (Clark)
Thompson

Thompson family photo
Emma Bullard's house on Bryant Street before the turn of the century.
(l-r) Josephine 19, (later married John Thompson); Emma; John Josselyn, 14 (Mrs. Bullard's brother); Eva 11; Ira 15; Ted 21 and Louise 6 (married Fred Burnell).

130

Thomas Thompson

Thomas F. and Winifred (Clark) Thompson brought their family to the lower valley and settled on eighty-three acres in the area where the Siete Robles tract and Ojai Lumber are today. Around 1878, Thompson sold fifteen acres of his land to his brother-in-law, Michael Hugh Clark, and built him a large house west of his own home. A few years later, Thompson traded his ranch to Theodore Todd and moved to the upper valley next door to another brother-in-law, Tom Clark. Thompson ran cattle on his ranch and had a winery.

NEWSPAPERS, LIBRARIES AND TRAINS

With an increase in valley residents, came the need for more services. It was time for Nordhoff to have a newspaper, for instance.

John H. Bradley of Santa Barbara established the county's first newspaper, *Ventura Signal,* in 1871. Early Signal editors seemed to take seriously their responsibility to the entire readership. They faithfully devoted column space to the happenings in each community. Approximately every fourth issue carried Ojai Valley tidbits – informing readers about someone building a home in Ojai, giving the time and place of Reverend Taylor's next church meeting or telling who was harvesting what produce on which farm.

J.M. Scanland began the first local newspaper on December 10, 1887. Regrettably, it hasn't been possible to locate copies of his *Ojai Valley View.* It seems that Scanland's ideas were unpopular with most of the citizens. Apparently he went so far as to publicly downgrade Nordhoff as a resort and he soon left and bought a winter home in Baja, California. In 1890, R.E. and R.G. Curran (father and son) bought the paper and published it under the title *Recurrant.* Reporter Sam Garner covered the valley news for a short time after the Currans gave up. R.G. Curran remained in the publishing business in Los Angeles for many years.

On October 27, 1891, Leverett M. Mesick started *The Ojai.* Ernest Allinson once told a story about a conversation his father, Daniel W. Allinson, the Reverend Vaile from the Congregational Church and Mr. Mesick had about naming the new newspaper.

Evidently, Vaile suggested the name, "Ojai Retreat" and Mesick rather liked the idea, until Allinson objected. He said, "Not retreat. The idea is to advance." And so the newspaper became simply, *The Ojai*.

Mesick published the small tabloid every Saturday, selling it for a nickel a copy. As is customary, he wrote a message to his readers in the first issue expressing his views and his ambitions for the paper.

"The degree of the paper's usefulness depends upon the quantity of its financial and moral support. It is a mirror," he said, "that reflects the conditions of public affairs and the progress its people have made and are making." Mesick promised to keep its columns clean so that the paper might be, "freely admitted into the sacred precincts of every home. It will be an educator, aiming to tell the truth in an entertaining manner," he said. And then he predicted this. "It will not be long before every acre of land in the valley will represent the home of a prosperous, happy and law-abiding family."

It seems that people either couldn't or wouldn't take Mesick's initial financial plea seriously, because in1894 he printed this statement. "*The Ojai* has been complimented by press, pulpit and people as being the best country newspaper in California. Words like these are gratifying, but they won't pay the bills. To produce a paper requires work and money. To produce the best country paper requires much more work and money."

He continued, "During the last two years, the editor has been compelled to keep his son out of school to set type in the office. The editor came for his health and is compelled to work day and night, which isn't good for his health. The editor's wife must forego social pleasures to work long hours."

He asked the community for advice and remittance. His request must not have been answered to his satisfaction, however, because in November, 1895, Mesick sold *The Ojai* to Sherman Thacher for $500 and moved to Santa Barbara, where he started the *El Barbareno,* a high-class, illustrated weekly.

Sherman moved the printing press to Thacher School and the boys, who had been reporting school happenings on one page of *The Ojai*, published the entire paper for six months. Thacher felt strongly that the valley needed a newspaper and he thought the experience would be of good educational value for the boys.

Even though his pupils did benefit from the newspaper business, Mr. Thacher was soon anxious to locate a responsible person to take it over. He wanted his boys to return full attention to their studies. So it was that in 1896 Thacher gratefully sold *The Ojai* to Randolph Freeman.

F.W. Train took over the paper three years later. When Train became ill with typhoid, however, Freeman returned to the press until 1901, when he was succeeded by C.E. Bundy as editor. In 1903 Richard Barry called the editorial shots from *The Ojai* office, then located on the southwest corner of Signal Street and Ojai Avenue.

In 1904, B. Overall, C. Grant, P. Pierpont, E. Wheeland, and W. Bayard Cutting, Jr., rallied to keep the little paper on its feet. C.F. McCutchen was the editor/publisher in 1908, but died during the year and his brother, J.L. McCutchen took over. He wrote an editorial stating, "Remember that when the local news is short, you might have committed suicide, gotten married, quarreled with your neighbor, stolen chickens, let your team run away or a hundred other things to make local items."

The Ojai relied heavily on the locals for news. It seems that before anyone left the valley they first reported to the current editor their destination, reasons for the trip, estimated time of arrival, when they would return and so forth; all of which was printed in the next issue. They must have been hard up for news when they ran this pronouncement, "The kittens that died last week are still dead."

The Ojai's content shifted with each new editor. Those who found the locals unnewsworthy concentrated their efforts on bringing word from Santa Barbara, Ventura and even places beyond.

Early obituary headings, although once read with the solemnity with which they were intended, cause chuckles in these times. The following are typical epitaphs from the past:

Mr. So and So answers the summons.
Mr. So and So is entering the larger life.
Mr. So and So crosses the great divide.
Mr. So and So answers the final call.
Mr. So and So departs this life.
Mr. So and So passes to the great beyond.
Mr. So and So is toted up thar.

Headings like these accompanied death notices:

The grim reaper claims another.
Another old-timer joins the silent majority of pioneers.
Death musters out another veteran.
Life's journey ends.

Movie ads occupied a great deal of newspaper space in the 1920s, very often filling an entire page. In the 1930s the paper focused on local plays. It wasn't until 1947 that sports became newsworthy. Were these noticeable shifts in reporting indicative of what was important to the community at the time? Or did they reflect the interest of the current editor? Perhaps the answer lies somewhere in between.

The Ojai continued despite the lack of continuity at the helm. Most publishers stayed on for less than three years. Of them, Frank Kilbourne showed the most stamina, running the newspaper from 1932 -1947 when Morgan Coe bought it. There is speculation that Kilbourne also managed *The Ojai* for owner Annie Besant during the late 1920s. H.W. and C.W. Klamser bought the paper in 1952 and began producing it in its present format in 1956.

The first location of *The Ojai* is unknown. An office was reportedly opened on the southwest corner of Signal Street and Ojai Avenue in 1894. In 1914 the building was moved to south Signal by a team of mules to make room for J.J. Burke's movie theater. Around 1920, *The Ojai* moved into the arcade east of the pool hall and it stayed there until the late 1950s.

Newspapers in Competition

In February, 1949, C.J. (Bob) Andrews, who once worked for *The Ojai* and Kenneth Prairie started *The Ojai Valley News* in competition with *The Ojai*. They sold their paper to Malcom Edwards and Cleve Webber one year later.

In 1958, J. Frank Knebel bought *The Ojai* and the *Ojai Valley News* merging the two, and included a small fledgling newspaper, *The Oaks Gazette*. He called this publication *The Ojai Valley News and Oaks Gazette*. He bought the property at 1016 West Ojai Avenue and built a new plant there.

On November 19, 1959, Faye and Charles Hill distributed the first copy of *The Ojai Press*. The following year marked the birth of *The Oaks Sentinel*. Neither of these young newspapers could get a foothold in the community. Rather than see a newspaper monopoly by *The Ojai Valley News and Oaks Gazette*, a publication they thought to reflect the interest of just a few, a group of over 100 people calling themselves the Voice of the Valley pitched in to support the floundering papers. They felt that the valley needed an alternative source of information, so they combined the two fledgling publications and established the *Press Sentinel* in competition with the 67 year-old newspaper. They were so dedicated to this project that volunteers put out the paper each week without fail for two years.

In April, 1962, Fred Volz applied to purchase *The Ojai Valley News*. Reassured by his solid credential, the Voice of the Valley sold him its interest in the *Press Sentinel* and, feeling secure about Mr. Volz's abilities and views, they went back to their former pursuits.

The Ojai Valley News, now a bi-weekly country newspaper operated by Ren Adam, is located in the industrial center on Bryant Street.

Libraries

Just after Mesick started *The Ojai*, a local resident advertised that he would loan books from his private collection to "knowledge-seeking young men" on Saturday nights. During the same year, Frank P. Barrows publicly requested donations of books and magazines for a small reading corner in the Congregational Church, which was open to all citizens Monday and Wednesday afternoons. Barrows urged the community to establish a free circulating library.

The Ojai Club (the town council of the time) accepted the challenge and formed a library committee. As their first order of business, they reviewed finances and promptly appointed Mrs. J.K. Newton to the position of chief fund raiser. She organized a candy sale which netted $10.65.

On April 21, 1893, the library committee held a well-attended garden party under the oaks at the Woolsey ranch near Gridley Road. Volunteers sold ice cream, cake, lemonade and candy from artfully decorated booths under colorful Japanese lanterns. An orchestra, including Professor E.T. Carter, R.F. Rollins, Earl Soule, C.W. Robinson, Maggie Pirie and Mrs. C.W. Robinson, entertained at the gathering. Sherman Thacher furnished authentic Chinese music by persuading two of his school employees, Hung and Hing, to play songs from their native land. Mrs. Newton collected $80 for the library fund that day.

George Thacher Memorial Library

A few weeks later, Sherman Thacher provided a better financial solution. He announced that he and his family would give $500 toward the free public library in memory of his brother, George. The committee enthusiastically agreed to his two stipulations: proper housing for the books and that the library would be known as the George Thacher Memorial Library.

Fry photo
Theodore Woolsey built this home of wood and native stone for his family in 1887.

Frank Barrows presented the town with a lease on a lot 100 feet south of Ojai Avenue east of Stewart Creek on what is now South Montgomery Street. Members of the Congregational Church voted to give $100 of the $500 needed for the building. With this as incentive, the community quickly raised the rest.

A lecture series was held. One could attend the entire series for $1 or hear a single lecture for just 25 cents. The speakers included Rev. J.R. Sinclair (pastor for the Presbyterian Church),

Edward S. and Sherman D. Thacher and Mr. S. Bessel.

John Wesley Heck built the sixteen by sixteen-foot library, and since people enjoyed having porches in those days, he built one for the library. A board of commissioners governed the library, among them Edwin F. Baker, Mrs. J.K. Newton, Benjamin W. Gally, Mrs. Frank Barrows, Mrs. W.I. Rice, Edward Thacher, Joseph Hobart, Professor John Murray and Sherman Thacher. Mrs. Newton agreed to be the first librarian.

A kerosene stove provided library patrons with heat, replaced many years later by a wood-burner and finally a gas radiator. Lighting was supplied by two kerosene lanterns at first, later by gasoline lamps. Electricity was installed in 1913.

David Mason collection
Original Ojai library, built in 1893.

Mrs. Newton worked at the library for less than a year and then Gertrude Hobart took over her position for a short time. Lillian Soule served as librarian in 1895. When she died five years later, her sister, Zaidee, took her place.

In 1908, it was evident that expansion would soon be necessary, so they moved the library to an adjoining lot which some say was half on the site where the Art Center is today, at 113 South Montgomery Street and half where the original old fire station (now Masserella Pottery) is. Two years later, while Clara Smith was librarian, they enlarged the building.

Eliza Higgins and Ethel Freeman served as librarians during

1910 and 1911, then Frances Wilson took over for two years. Belle Lyon worked for the library between 1913 and 1916. The little country library continued to grow until it was beyond what local finances could support. So on January 7, 1916, just before Lottie Busch began her two-year stint as librarian, the board negotiated an affiliation with the Ventura system. The county accepted financial responsibility for the staff, while the local board continued paying the water bills, handling repairs and maintaining the grounds.

New Library Building

During Edward Libbey's massive village face lift in 1917, there was talk of a new library – one more in harmony with the Spanish flavor of the town. Libbey suggested building the library on the southeast corner of Ventura Street and Ojai Avenue. Ironically, that is where the Congregational Church had housed the first library over thirty years earlier.

Ima Busch took over the librarian's job from her sister Lottie in 1918, and the following year Zaidee Soule resumed the job. In April, 1927, the Ojai Improvement Company, controlled by the Libbey estate, launched a campaign to raise money for a new library. The most generous donors were listed as: Mrs. Thomas Bard, N.W. Blanchard, Jr., Sarah E. Blanchard, Walter W. Bristol, R.H. Cooke, Roger C. Edwards, Mrs. E.P. Foster, Mabel Isenberg, J. Krishnamurti, H.S. and Alice Nixon, the law firm of Sheridan, Orr, Drapeau and Gardner (Erle Stanley), S.D. Thacher, Mabel C. Gage, Franklin Perkins, A.S. Dodge, Edward Yeomans and Charles Pratt. They raised nearly $20,000 in one month's time.

The committee selected the site Libbey had recommended before his death and those in charge of his estate gave the $10,000 lot to the library committee. The trustees named to the new board were: Walter W. Bristol, Mrs. F.A. Hennessey, A.E. McAndrews, Frank Mead, Franklin H. Perkins and Sherman D. Thacher.

Architect Carleton M. Winslow designed the new library and Sam Hudiburg headed up construction. By April 15, 1928, the new library was formally open. George Noble turned the old library building into a cabinet shop. Ten years later it was moved to the corner of Lion and Aliso streets. The old frame library served as the Boy Scout clubhouse for many years and then it became home to the Girl Scouts. The old library is currently privately owned by descendants of the Daniel Smith family who originally donated that lot to the city.

In 1944, Zaidee Soule retired after a combined total of over thirty years as librarian. Mrs. Joe Waite was the new librarian. Mrs. Viola Berrey took the librarian job in 1950 through 1963. Her husband was Lester V. Berrey, a writer who was considered a leading authority on slang. He wrote, *The American Thesaurus of Slang*.

In 1958, the Ventura County Free Library system accepted total responsibility for the Ojai Library. The $500 reserve, still in the local library fund, was used to buy a roof-top cooler.

Up until that period, the library's staff had left the grounds to nature. Native shrubs and trees crowded around the structure. Maintenance included trimming, watering and raking up debris. And then the Ojai Valley Garden Club built the charming patio at the library entrance and have, for many years, maintained attractive planters there.

Sometimes statistics can give an interesting perspective on a community. In 1916, 4,600 books were circulated throughout the valley. The library had 5,000 volumes on hand in 1928. During the Depression years, when money was tight, the emphasis was on free entertainment like reading. During 1932, for example the library posted a circulation figure of 25,989, but by 1936 circulation had dropped to 19,441. There were 10,000 books in the library by 1949.

The 1979 book count was 50,000 volumes. This may sound like a lot of books for a small town, but the great influx of people, the emphasis on education (apparent in the number of excellent private schools here) and the circulation statistics made it obvious that our library was again too small. The library needed more space and more books to properly sustain, entertain and educate this community.

A group organized under the name of Friends of the Library attempted to raise $50,000 through community activities to supplement the already promised county funds. Within a matter of months, they reached their quota and a beautiful new wing opened in the summer of 1981.

Because of Ventura County Supervisor, J.K. Ken MacDonald's support for this project, his peers asked that the new wing be known as the J.K. Ken MacDonald Annex.

Enter the Southern Pacific Railroad

The train chugged into San Buenaventura for the first time in 1887 and that is when our county seat became known as Ventura. Employees couldn't fit enough letters on the Southern Pacific timetable to spell the old name, so they suggested it be shortened.

It was a long, dusty stage ride to Nordhoff from Ventura and some felt that the discomfort and inconvenience kept certain people out of the valley. "When the train comes," Leverett Mesick editorialized in 1891, "it will bring a better class of people. They will come and stay and bring their libraries. An invalid can recline in an upholstered seat within the observation car and be whirled over hill and vale to his destination, instead of (having to endure) a tedious ride by stage coach."

Local promoters thought a railroad would be of great economic interest to the valley. Not only would it bring tourists and new residents, but it would provide a more convenient and reasonable means of transporting local crops. In 1891, a few prominent citizens, who had earlier met in private, called an open meeting to discuss the railroad. Desiring a large attendance, they published a notice in Mesick's paper and distributed posters all over the valley.

Judge S.A. Sheppard chaired the meeting at the Nordhoff schoolhouse and W.E. Wilsie kept the minutes. Sheppard heard the report of the previously established railroad survey committee, suggesting that the tracks end where Nordhoff commenced. Joseph Hobart predicted that the center of town would move east with growth and that the tracks should be extended.

The main result of this meeting was the appointment of a committee to secure right-of-way along the proposed train route from Nordhoff to Ventura. Chosen were, J.P. Wykoff, J.J. Burke, K.P. Grant, Judge Sheppard and Dr. Pierpont.

There was little public mention of the train issue until about a year later when a large audience gathered again to discuss the Ventura-Ojai Railroad. Joseph Hobart presided at the meeting. Judge W.H. Wilde stated the objective and George Stewart kept an account of the proceedings. The big problem was money.

W.S. Chaffee suggested that people put their hands deep into their pockets and bring out whatever they could. They appointed a "good committee of citizens" to ascertain ways that Ojai people could help bring the train to Nordhoff. J.C. Daly, Edward Thacher, J.P. Wykoff, Judge Wolfe and J.R. Bennett all agreed to serve on this committee.

J. Logan Kennedy, A.W. Blumberg and W.I. Rice were appointed to canvas the Santa Ana and Matilija areas and H.J. Dennison, Robert Gibson and Thomas Gray would talk to people in Upper Ojai. In an effort to determine the resources available in Ojai Valley, they distributed questionnaires asking property owners their financial status. Some resented this invasion of their privacy, however, and those in charge felt embarrassed about pressuring people to return the queries.

A few weeks later at a committee meeting, Sherman Thacher asked that each man there determine what he could afford for the project. It surprised everyone that these thirteen men pledged over $3,250 – one-sixth of the sum needed to bring a railroad to Ojai Valley. This seemed encouragement enough to seriously continue the project.

In 1893, Mrs. Soule let it be known that there already was a railroad in the valley, for she had a short-line on her property that ran from the drying field to the sulphuring house. Joseph Hobart announced that he too had a railroad like the Soules' and he had built his two years earlier.

Mr. Freeman, *The Ojai* editor, wrote that the coming of the train might encourage someone to tap the immense asphalt and gypsum deposits and oil wells in the valley and perhaps find a stone quarry. He speculated that it would also increase the population.

Finally in August, 1897, several men and ninety-five mules came to build the sixteen-mile Nordhoff spur. They set up camp at the Goodyear Ranch (Rancho Arnaz). After seven months of their labor, on March 12, 1898, the first train rolled into Nordhoff. A large committee invited everyone to a basket social to celebrate the coming of the first train, which carried prominent people from Los Angeles, Santa Barbara and Ventura. The train arrived to the loud blare of trumpets. The Ojai Band played as the crowd cheered, and white-clad horsemen were on hand to maintain the peace. Someone stated that day that the sound of the train was strangely out of place in this quiet grove of oaks. Although newspapers reported that the Ventura Band played that day, the photograph indicates that the Ojai Band was also on hand to melodiously greet the train.

In 1898, employees of the Ventura River and Ojai Valley Railroad erected a depot just east of South Fox Street and west of Bryant Street. Originally the depot had a waiting room and an agent's office. When Southern Pacific took it over in July, 1899, they added a freight warehouse and platforms.

David Mason collection
The Ojai Band celebrating the first train to Nordhoff in March of 1898.

The train from Ventura stopped for passengers at Weldon (probably on Ventura Avenue), La Cross (near Rancho Arnaz) and Tico (at Highway 33). Next the train stopped at the Wells Fargo office at Grant's Station, which was also known as Matilija Junction at Highways 150 and 33. This is where the Matilija and Wheelers stage drivers met their resort guests. The last stop was the depot. There were always from five to twenty passengers aboard. Sometimes the engineer would spend the night at Nordhoff. On such occasions the railroad company hired Joe Berry to guard the locomotive while it was otherwise unattended.

Before chugging into Nordhoff, the engineer routinely blew his train whistle to alert the townsfolk that he was on his way to the Fox Street depot.

The train created enormous excitement throughout the village. Almost everyone dropped what he or she was doing to meet it and see who or what it carried into Nordhoff. Practically everything anyone used came by train in those early years.

Howard Bald, according to a *Historical Society Quarterly* published by the Ventura County Historical Society, said that the train's arrival was "a popular source of entertainment on long summer evenings for certain men, boys and dogs."

Boyd Henry driving the Nordhoff Taxi. Tom Clark standing. Southern Pacific train depot in background.

Up until then, people depended almost totally on the horse for their transportation and the advent of the train didn't alter that fact to a noticeable degree right away. There were still plenty of horses around when the train came to Nordhoff. Because horses were unaccustomed to the sight and sound of such a large machine, they frequently created excitement at the depot. But while the train terrified most horses, others accepted it passively. Here's one account:

Two little girls in town delighted in driving the family buggy to the depot to meet their father when he returned from work by train. Every afternoon, upon hearing the whistle, the sisters rushed out, jumped into the buggy and coaxed their old mare to "git along" to the station. One day the younger sister was a little late and when she dashed out of the house, the horse and buggy were already gone. She was slightly upset that her sister had left without her. Later, however, her father arrived home alone in the rig. It seems that the mare was also conditioned to the sound of the whistle and, when neither of the girls showed up to drive her, she took it upon herself to keep the appointment at the station.

The Nordhoff line followed a fairly loose schedule, with the train usually making two trips daily. During harvest, however, the train came as many as six times a day.

It wasn't unusual for the train to pick up the occasional passenger at an unauthorized stop. And certain engineers were known sometimes to stall the engine at Mirror Lake in Mira Monte and hunt ducks while passengers watched from the windows.

By 1949, the automobile had taken away most of the train passenger business and the Southern Pacific came into Ojai only for the orange harvest. For years, members of the Southern California Railway Club made Ojai a regular stop on their annual spring trip through California. They experienced Ojai by train for the last time in May, 1955, just before the Southern Pacific Company phased out the steam engine and dismantled the water tower. In 1958, the Fox Street depot was closed for good, and after the 1969 floods, the remains of the tracks were removed.

The old railroad right-of-way is now a walking, cycling and riding path. (Read more about this in Chapter Nineteen).

EARLY ARCHITECTS AND BUILDERS

No town can be built without designers and craftsmen. The following offers a glimpse into some of Nordhoff's architects and builders.

Builders

John Heck built the Carne home and the original wood-frame library.

Ed P. Zimmerman built the two-story frame schoolhouse in 1895 and was an inspiration and mentor to local apprentice builders.

Canadian, **James Charles Leslie** came to Ojai in 1889. He first operated an apiary on a ranch north of Fordyce Road. He learned the building trade by working alongside early builder, E.P. Zimmerman and went on to build the central building of the Pierpont Cottages, some of the Thacher School buildings, cottages at the Foothills Hotel, the Boyd Club, General Penney's home and the Kings Daughter's Clubhouse.

According to his granddaughter, Harriet Kennedy, Leslie once planted 3,000 eucalyptus trees on his property in hopes of using the wood for building. His plan didn't work out, though, as the wood was too soft.

Samuel Judson Hudiburg was born in Santa Paula and went to school in Ojai. He learned the carpenter trade from James Leslie and worked for him from 1906 -1919 when he went into contracting himself. Hudiburg is credited with building the current Ojai Library; the art center; Mrs. Pierpont's home, which was designed by Julia Morgan; the original Thacher School library; Frost Hall at Ojai Valley School; Grey Gables; Orchid Town and about 90 homes in the valley and Santa Barbara, including the homes of Frank Frost, George Mosle (now the Hitching Post Clubhouse) and the Gorhams (at Whale Rock Ranch). He was also the contractor overseeing the building at Star Camp in Meiners Oaks.

In 1928, Hudiburg agreed to build a mountain lodge of native stone at Piedre Blanca for George C. Kimball. Frank Noren did the stonework. The men had to pack the building materials, consisting of cement, doors, timbers and so forth, fifteen miles by horseback from Wheelers. On one such trip, there was an accident. Three pack horses, in Hudiburg's train were killed when they fell from the trail. Natcho Ramos, the packer, had to cut the ropes of those who fell to save the others. The horses belonged to Margaret Hunt.

Hudiburg was a charter member of the Masonic Lodge and, in fact, built the Masonic Lodge in Ojai. He married Pearl Wood, chief operator at the telephone building. Bill Ash took over his business when he retired.

Robert Winfield moved to Los Angeles from Ohio in 1907. He came to Ojai at the request of Richard Requa and Frank Mead to build the arcade, post office and pergola and he came back to build the El Roblar Hotel. Winfield later settled in Ojai. He built many homes in the valley, including the Hobson home, the original Royal Oaks Dairy ranch house (now in the Persimmon Hill development), Blakely's Photography Studio (now Local Hero Bookstore) and the Catholic Church (now the Ojai Museum and Chamber of Commerce).

In a newspaper interview, Winfield talks about the homes he built without so much as a drawing to guide him. He said, for example, "The first time the Hobson home was on paper was when someone came along and took a picture of it."

P.K. Miller built John Meiners house which still stands

behind the Ranch House Restaurant on Lomita.

B.F. Spencer built the Dennison's large home in Upper Ojai and with Charles Horne, headed up construction for the Presbyterian Church in 1884.

Architects

S. M. Jesley designed the Boyd Club, the original Nordhoff fountain and the first Foothills Hotel.

Austin Pierpont, a local resident, came into the architectural profession in the early 1920s. He designed the second phase of the Ojai Valley Inn, including twenty-five rooms, the dining room and patio, Ojai Art Center, Friend's gas station at the corner of Fox and Ojai Avenue, the bulletin board at the post office and, with Roy C. Wilson, he designed the Ojai Festivals Bowl in Libbey Park.

Carleton Winslow, who studied at the Chicago Art Institute, was the architect for the current Ojai Library and the current Ojai Presbyterian Church.

Roy C. Wilson designed the new Ojai Elementary School (now housing the district offices), the current San Antonio Schoolhouse, the Matilija Junior High School gymnasium, Foster Park Bowl, Bill Baker's Bakery (George Noble was the builder) and, with the assistance of Mrs. Ramelli, the Ramelli house on the hill near Rancho Arnaz.

Wallace Neff designed the original Ojai Valley Inn clubhouse for which he was awarded a certificate of honor by the American Institute of Architects.

Zelma Wilson was a prominent architect in the Ojai Valley for many years and she designed or participated in designing the following: the remodel for the Ojai City Hall (the original Hobson estate), the U.S. Forest Service building, St. Andrews Episcopal Church, Oak Grove primary and secondary schools, the Anson Thacher Humanities building at Thacher School, Ojai Valley Racquet and Swim Club, a bridge on Creek Road, Meditation Mount and she was involved with the redevelopment project in downtown Ojai when the city transformed a back alley eyesore into a pleasing plaza. Five of her structures received American Institute of Architecture Honor Awards. In 1983, Zelma Wilson became a Fellow of the American Institute of Architects.

Chapter Eight
A Community Develops

Ojai Club

Although Ojai Valley came under the jurisdiction of the Ventura County Board of Supervisors, we had no localized government here until October 1892, when citizens formed the Ojai Club.

Sherman Thacher said to an attentive group, one Saturday at the Nordhoff schoolhouse, "There is work in this valley for an improvement club." He asked John Murray to read a list of things that such an organization could accomplish. Murray explained that a club of this sort would further the interests of Ojai Valley citizens. It would promote friendly debates on political and economic matters of national and local concern and accomplish valley improvements such as adding sidewalks and a town hall. He suggested promoting lectures and other entertainment to raise money for these projects.

There was a growing tendency toward what Sherman Thacher called "rowdiness and lawlessness" in the valley. He wanted the frequent abuse of the Chinese and deliberate destruction of property stopped and he thought the Ojai Club could help preserve law and order by cooperating with authorities in such matters. It was also to be a social club. Murray invited everyone to join at a fee of 50 cents.

The club formed these committees: Club Management – Mrs. E. Pierpont, Reverend J.M. Crawford and J.C. Anderson; Debates – Miss Clara Smith, Mrs. Lillian Mesick, Reverend J. Milligan, William Soule, George Straley and John Murray; Village and Valley Improvements – Mrs. B.W. Gally, Mrs. W.I. Rice, Reverend J.M. Crawford, General Smith, Edward S.

Thacher and Dr. Ernest Pierpont; Social – Mrs. Rynerson, Mrs. Spader, Miss Hobart, Mrs. Milligan, Mr. Bronson and Mr. Senior; Music – Miss Soule and Vernon Gelett; Library – Mrs. J.K. Newton, Miss Dickson, Mrs. Frank P. Barrows and Professor John Murray; Horticulture – W.E. Wilsie, Joseph Hobart, W.J. Hall and J.R. Bennett. In 1893, members of the Ojai Club formed an advertising committee designed to lure people into the valley.

The Ojai Club persuaded the Ventura County Board of Supervisors to pay shovelers to spread gravel on Ojai Avenue. In return, valley citizens agreed to furnish teams and men under the supervision of Watts Haydock to haul gravel from San Antonio Creek.

Under the auspices of the Ojai Club, its president, Sherman Thacher, inspected local slaughterhouses. His findings were favorable, but he suggested regular inspection tours to safeguard public health.

Members of the Ojai Club later discussed a new schoolhouse and it was under their regime that it became a reality – thus providing the valley with a larger town hall. In 1899, stray dogs created a nuisance in the village and the Ojai Club hired Fred Ortega as pound master. His log indicates that his main duties involved rounding up stray cattle and loose horses.

The Ojai Club didn't formally disband at the turn of the century, but its membership grew less active, its leadership weakened and it soon became ineffective as a community force.

Committee of Fifteen

In 1903, nine people founded the Ojai Citizens League which set up a vigilance group known as the Committee of Fifteen. The first committee members were Tom S. Clark, H.W. Forster, A.A. Garland, Charlie E. Gibson, Thomas L. Gray, Sam C. Gridley, Joseph Hobart, George W. Mallory, A.E. McAndrews, C.O. Mudge, Benjamin L. Saeger, S.L. Smith, P.W. Soper, Earl E. Soule and Sherman D. Thacher.

Committee members gathered signatures of those wishing to back the new organization by passing petitions around the community. The document read, "We, the undersigned, hereby become members of the Ojai Citizens League for the purpose of cooperating with the Committee of Fifteen in promoting these objectives without incurring any legal obligations." In return, the committee pledged to enforce the law, preserve order and promote good citizenship. They claimed no political affiliations and were simply a group of Ojai men responding to popular demand to act for the citizens of Ojai in matters connected with the public good.

Walter Bristol, in his book, *The Story of the Ojai Valley,* said, "The work of the Committee was that of vigilantes in a mild way. No gallows was erected on which to hang miscreants, but they did have a struggle to stay the illegal sale of liquor in the community. In their rather infrequent meetings the Committee discussed a variety of matters connected with the welfare of the valley."

The Committee of Fifteen established a dumping ground which cleaned up the town considerably. They also appointed the valley's first health officer and sanitary committee. They renovated the cemetery, planned ways to preserve the trees along Creek Road and worked to keep the wooden sidewalks in good repair.

A county law had been passed around 1900 that banned the sale of liquor in rural areas, but contrary to it, one saloon in Nordhoff continued to operate. The Committee of Fifteen raised money, engaged a detective, held conferences and, with the help of the district attorney, closed the saloon. The next year a club member triumphantly noted that there was less drinking and disorder in Nordhoff than ever before.

In 1904, eighty-five citizens attended a meeting during which they discussed what sort of trees to plant along Ojai Avenue. Gum, palm, umbrella and acacias were all considered, but Joseph Hobart's "wit and eloquence" according to *The Ojai* "turned the majority of the voters in favor of the pepper tree."

Nordhoff Board of Trade

In 1906, the Nordhoff Board of Trade had come into being, taking the place of the Committee of Fifteen, with forty members. It advertised Ojai as a resort hoping that by enticing more people here they would sell more land, get better railroad service, roads and bridges and there would be increased trade and industry.

The first board of directors included E.S. Thacher, H. Waldo Forster, C.E. Gibson, E.F. Baker, W.C. Hendrickson, Joseph Hobart, F.P. Barrows, Dr. Saeger and J.J. Burke.

Members of the Nordhoff Board of Trade were serious about drawing the world to Ojai Valley. A committee prepared booklets to send out all over the nation telling of their wonderful town. They also urged the community to write letters to the Southern Pacific Railroad Company requesting upgraded service.

Ojai Valley Civic League

In 1912, Frank Weir started the Ojai Valley Civic League. He wanted to set up an office in Los Angeles to direct people to Ojai but couldn't collect enough money. When the ailing Mr. Weir died, the club also perished.

Weir, a Canadian native, came to Ojai in 1905. In Montreal, he studied the arts and law. He practiced law in Montreal. He was married and had three children, all who died within their first five years. He also studied journalism and published a book called, *The Law and Practice of Banking Corporations.* Weir moved to Alaska and mined for five years before moving here for his health.

During the seven years he was in the valley, he was an active citizen, although not very well. He died at the age of 53.

Ojai Valley Men's League/Chamber of Commerce

On April 24, 1914, in order to develop Edward Libbey's town improvement ideas, village leaders organized the Ojai Valley Men's League. They obtained more street lighting and a street cleaning system. They collected $374 toward street paving and they pushed for incorporation.

In 1927, The Ojai Valley Men's League became the Ojai Valley Chamber of Commerce, with Walter Bristol serving as the first president. Anson Thacher was president in 1938 and then Charles T. Butler headed the chamber post.

When the chamber went defunct, Bob Andrews encouraged the establishment of the Ojai Jaycees and they filled the void until the 1950s when the Chamber of Commerce made a comeback.

Ojai Lions Club

The Ojai Lions Club was formed in 1927 with Bill Hendrickson, president. The Lions Club may have been instrumental in building an airfield near the Y in the late 1920s, early '30s, where Maricopa Highway meets Ojai Avenue. They were the group discussing it as a possibility as early as 1928.

In 1944, the Lion's Club constructed a Roll of Honor listing the names of all the men and women in the valley who were serving in the armed forces. There were 392 names on the redwood plaque. Those servicemen who died, were indicated in gold letters. The Honor Roll stood between the Boyd Club (which served as the USO then) and the Bank on Ojai Avenue. The plaque was designed by Austin Pierpont and constructed by William Ash and Jack Tulleys. Matt Chepin did the stone work and Eugenia Everett cut the wood emblem. Another account of this project said that Owen E. MacBride was involved in carving the seal.

In 1947, the Lions Club took down the original wooden Honor Roll, as the weather had affected it and they replaced it with an engraved bronze plaque listing just those who died serving their country. This plaque was unveiled on Memorial Day, 1947 and still stands at the entrance to the parking lot east of Libbey Park.

OVM
Daniel and Angelina (Eddy) Smith standing outside their home, Hard Scrabble Ranch, in 1910.

Profiles of Leaders

Daniel Smith

Our Ventura County Supervisor in 1896, Daniel Smith, had brought his family here in 1882 hoping to regain his health. He first purchased forty acres from Ed Ayers half mile east of

Nordhoff and later built the family home on land he bought on Foothill Road.

In 1891, he helped organize the People's Lumber Company and continued as director until his death. The former People's business office was where the Emporium Coffee Parlor is now at 108 South Montgomery.

Mr. Smith and his wife, Angelina, had six children: Clara (a well-known educator), Fannie (Mrs. Frank Ayers), Winnie (who died young), Elred, Elroy and Ira (long-time local resident Vivian Noren's father and Janice Prairie's grandfather). Daniel Smith died in 1931 at the age of 86.

Tom Clark

Thomas S. Clark, who served as Ventura County Supervisor from 1904 to 1936, was born in Lafayette County, Wisconsin, to Michael Hugh and Margaret Clark in 1865. When Tom was 13, his father, Michael, left his family to join an older brother, also named Tom, who had established a good home for himself and his wife, Ann, in the Upper Ojai. Michael Clark's brother-in-law, Thomas Thompson, sold him part of his property a mile and a half east of Nordhoff and even provided a house. Clark/Thompson descendants are certain that Thompson built the house, but aren't sure if he built it expressly for Michael Clark. Once settled, Clark sent for his family.

Besides Tom, the Clarks had six other children: Robert, (a county sheriff), Margaret (famed for her extensive knowledge of horsemanship), Hugh, William, Emma and Catherine (Mrs. George Bald). The family home still stands next to Ojai Lumber Company at 1884 East Ojai Avenue.

Tom was also a superb horseman, an ability that aided him in landing a job as driver for the Nordhoff/Santa Barbara stage. In 1894, Tom married Ella Bakman. They had nine children: Dortha (Roberts), Jack, Richard (who died in the influenza epidemic of 1918), Margaret, Elizabeth, Thomas, Louise, Hortense and Edward.

While supervisor, Tom Clark was in charge of roads and he was one of the main proponents of building highway 33 to Bakersfield. According to one descendent, his sister, Margaret (known in the family as, Peg) was against the project because she thought that allowing easy access to the back country she loved so much, would spoil it.

Tom Clark, his Ojai Livery Stable in background.

Tom opened a livery stable at the northeast corner of Ojai Avenue and Signal Street in 1895 and ran this business until 1917. He advertised fine carriages and dependable horses for rent. Even though he had several employees, Tom always drove on the more difficult trips. When others hesitated trying the swollen, treacherous waters that hampered travel to and from Nordhoff in winter, for instance, Tom made the necessary trek. He rescued many stranded travelers and was always the one who came through with the mail, even in the worst kind of storm. When Ella died, Tom married Ida Clayton Bramble. The Clarks lived in an old house on the southeast corner of Signal and Matilija Streets for many years. This is now a parking lot. The wall around the parking lot, however, is the one Clark built of stones from an old court house in Ventura. (See details in Chapter Six). Tom Clark died in 1940.

Sheriff Bob Clark

Robert Emmet Clark, Tom's brother, was born on August 25, 1876, in Wisconsin. He became known as a master stage driver, but he is also credited with keeping a heavy hand on the law.

Redheaded Clark, when young, was adventurous and joined every rumble he could find. He even tried to join Teddy Roosevelt's Roughriders, but, according to a descendant, started too late. The war was over before he got there to help out.

Clark met his wife-to-be when he drove her and her sister to the Matilija resort. Three months later, Robert Clark and Alice Burnett eloped. He was 30 and she only 20. They had ten children.

According to Clark's granddaughter, Pat Clark-Doerner, his wife thought that driving a stage was too dangerous and she talked him into leaving that business. Around 1905, he was appointed as a United States Ranger by President Theodore Roosevelt and became widely known for his part in breaking up an early cattle rustling ring in Castaic.

Although he was exceedingly familiar with the back country, he didn't much like the forest service job. It was hard work and he was gone all the time. In 1913, he retired from the service and decided to do ranch work. He bought a ranch in the Santa Ana Valley and became a farmer. Clark-Doerner says, however, that everything that could go wrong did go wrong for Clark, the farmer. She says that a drought killed their crops, their pigs got cholera, their cows got into the alfalfa and died of bloat and they lost a beloved child.

In 1922, after much prodding from friends and acquaintances, Bob Clark ran for sheriff and won by a landslide. He held the position for the next eleven years.

Valley old-timers recall Clark's passion for locating illegal liquor. He reportedly visited local farms and tore their wineries apart in search of bootleg liquor. Once he ruined a "perfectly good crock of pickles," I'm told, by stirring it to see if liquor bottles were hidden within the brine.

Keeping the peace wasn't all that was expected of a sheriff in those days. He was a public servant, after all, and a neighbor. It wasn't unusual for people to call on Mr. Clark to run errands. Mrs. Fraser of Creek Road once asked the sheriff to pick up her child's repaired shoes from Ventura and drop them in her mailbox on his way home. And he did, tooting his horn before leaving to let her know he had completed his mission.

In 1933, Bob Clark became United States Marshal and he held that position for the following sixteen years.

According to his granddaughter, Bob Clark was not a highly educated man in the traditional sense, having only reached the third grade at San Antonio School. He loved learning, however, and obtained a good deal of education from Colonel Bigelow, a man with an extensive library who lived in the old Woolsey house. As an adult, Clark eventually moved his own family into the landmark Woolsey house.

Mr. Clark died in 1956 at the age of 79.

Justices of the Peace

The old-time justice of the peace was an honorable position held locally by just seven men over a span of fifty years.

1872............ W.D. Hobson
1874............ P.V. McCarty
1878............ C.D. Bradshaw
1887............ James McKee
1905............ I.W. Wolfe
1915............ Harrison Wilson
1922............ Boyd E. Gabbert

Judge James McKee

In 1887, 50 year-old Indiana native, James McKee came to Nordhoff from Iowa for his health. He was promptly elected Justice of the Peace, an office he held until his death. He often said that it was "not easy to act as umpire where everyone knows you." His was an informal court; he tried cases in his home and even under an oak tree in his yard.

OVM
Judge James McKee, Justice of the Peace, 1887-1905.

McKee, a former educator, joined the military when the war broke out. As first duty sergeant with Company F of the 68th Indiana Infantry, he participated in the Battle of Munsfordville and was taken prisoner. He was released and remained in the service until 1865. When the war was over, he went back to teaching and became principal at Napoleon School until 1875. Experiencing failing health, McKee went to Maquoketa City,

Iowa and worked in agriculture for a while before coming to California.

Once here, McKee worked as a pharmacist at Saeger's drug store. McKee and Nancy Eaton were married in 1857. They had four children, one of whom died in childhood. The McKee's living children were Clarence, Sarah and Ellen (Mrs. John Linder). When Nancy died in 1894, McKee married Marie Louise Holt. McKee Street, which is off North Canada Street, is named for Judge McKee.

Judge Irvin W. Wolfe

Judge Irvin William Wolfe was born in 1844. He moved his family here from Ohio in 1882 because his wife suffered from tuberculosis.

He was a patriotic man with great respect for those who died while serving their country – having himself been shot while fighting in the Civil War. He reportedly lost an earlobe in the incident. Wolfe liked to brag that he enlisted when he was just 17. He served as a Union soldier with the 22nd Ohio Infantry, Company H. He was wounded in the battle of Chancellorsville while storming the lookout and was honorably discharged in 1865. Wolfe always observed Memorial Day by planning a yearly program to honor the war dead. He would lead a parade to the cemetery and ceremoniously decorate each war veteran's grave.

VCHS
Judge Irvin W. Wolfe, Justice of the Peace 1905-1915.

Wolfe married Philena Eddy in 1867 and they had four children, Frank (a photographer), Nellie (Pelter) and twins, Charlie and Jessie. (Jessie died at birth and Charlie died when he was 14 after falling from a tree on the school grounds.)

Wolfe served as Justice of Peace for ten years. In 1910, his son, Frank, reportedly built the Judge a courthouse. The Wolfes built a home, in the vicinity of 216 and 218 Aliso Street and it burned in the 1917 fire. There is a cement building still standing on that property, however, with the words, "Wolfe, 1908" above the door. This was presumably Frank Wolfe's photographic studio. According to descendants, the Aliso Street property was Frank Wolfe's and Judge Wolfe built the two-story house at 308 North Signal Street around the turn of the century for his own home.

Philena Wolfe died at the age of 46 in 1890. Although her grave marker states that her name is Philenia, family members have confirmed that it is Philena. Angelina (Mrs. Daniel) Smith was Philena's sister.

In 1915, when Judge Wolfe died, all of Nordhoff's business district closed and the entire population participated in the funeral procession which Thomas Bard lead through the village.

The Organizations Diversify

Grange

The first recorded community organization in the valley, outside of the church and school, was the Grange, founded in 1875 by twenty farmers to discuss farm questions, purchase staples in large quantities and socialize. As the only local united force at the time, the Grange members also put Creek Road in good repair after a damaging rain.

The original roster included C.E. Sowles (Soule), William Pirie, Thomas G. Gray, H.J. Dennison, Joseph Hobart, E.W. Whittmore, George Waters, John Reith, Lorenzo Dow Roberts, R.M. White, J.B. Goddard, Orsin Sowles, H.P. McClean, Robert Ayers, Theodore Todd and T.B. Steepleton. They used a small building on Robert Ayers' property to store bulk coffee, rice, flour, soap, etc. for members to buy on Grange day.

The present Ojai Valley Grange #659 was established in 1937. They dedicated their meeting place, at 381 Cruzero Street, in 1950.

Literary Clubs

Political debates, lectures and study sessions sustained the Ojai Republican Club in 1892. Joseph Hobart headed the club and William Soule, J.W. Heck, I.W. Wolfe and Walter Haydock were among the early members.

The Fortnightly Club was the primary literary group in Ojai, established in 1893. In 1900, eleven people gathered in the name of Chautauqua Circle. Mrs. Edwin Baker took over as president and her daughter, Edith, agreed to be secretary. This group developed a course of systematic study of history, literature, science and art.

A group of single adults founded the Ojai Journey Club in 1904 and its members read and studied great literature together.

The Misses Ednah Baker and Clara Smith started the

Thompson Family photo
Memorial Day in Ojai, 1908. First row (seated l-r), unknown, Esther Waite, Lizzie Soper, Marjorie Houk, Margaret Clark, Tony Bailey. Second row, Alice Soper, Ruth Kincher, Helen Baker, Ann Robertson, Annie Freeman, Ann Linnell, Lena Soper, Thelma Kimball, Elsie Gibson. Third row, Byron Bray, unknown, Arthur Waite, Walter Houk, Jack Clark, Ray LeValley, unknown, Thad Timms, George Timms, Harold Edgerton, Bill Reilly. Fourth row, Emily McKee, Dolly Soper, Nelson Cota, Joe Edgerton, Elmer Freeman, Roy Berry, Elizabeth Kincher, Joe Waite, Linnie Gibson, Dortha Clark, Clara Smith, Edythe Reilly. Fifth row (without band), Dan Smith, unknown, unknown, Olive Cota, Mary Freeman, P.W. Soper, Ruth Soper, Unknown, I. W. Wolfe. Sixth row, Jennie Miller, Evelyn Herbert, Mrs. Harry Fordyce, C.L. Edgerton (teacher), Mrs. Freeman, Abbie Cota, Nina Freeman, Edna Baker, Orpha Wolfe. Band, Bennie Houk (drummer), Levi Bray, Bert Conrey, Selwyn Beaman, ____Wurm, Charles Baker, Frank Spencer, Jim Fordyce, Charles Stutsman, Howard Gally (by flag), unknown, Claude Gallentine, JimThompson, John Thompson, Jack Bennett, Boyd Henry, Harry Dennison.

Shakespeare Club in 1909. They invited just twenty members into the Baker home for the purpose of studying Shakespeare. Later they expanded their interest and membership.

Kings Daughters

For the Presbyterians, with little else to serve them for entertainment, the church quickly became the social center of the valley. Women members handled the light duties of maintaining their gathering place. As time passed, these dedicated women took it upon themselves to fill other needs of the church-going community.

In October, 1899, Reverend Thomas Marshall organized this willing workforce and named them the Kings Daughters, an auxiliary of the church.

The first president of the club was Joseph Hobart's daughter, Gertrude. She was known as a "powerhouse" and ably maintained the head position for quite some time. Under her leadership, the Kings Daughters sponsored domestic training in the schools for girls and carpentry classes for boys. They became the village welcoming committee and offered a warm hand of friendship to strangers.

In 1906, the twenty-two members of the Kings Daughters aided San Francisco earthquake victims by collecting basic articles to send the needy. Benevolence was their theme in 1910. "This is a prosperous and happy valley," one of the members stated, "but occasionally there is a need to lift a heavy load from weak shoulders." The Kings Daughters were there to do it.

They raised money to purchase spectacles for the aged, donated equipment to local schools and became active in village improvements. Once they bought a street sweeper and sponsored school boys to clean city streets on a weekly basis. This organization was the first to protest roadside billboards in the valley.

Ojai Woman's Club

In 1911, Mrs. Pierpont Ginn searched for an organization worthy of her late husband's legacy. Finally, she chose to build a clubhouse for the Kings Daughters. Mrs. Ginn did some of the architectural work on this project and James C. Leslie was the builder.

Four years later the Kings Daughters became the Ojai Valley Woman's Club and Mrs. Frank Beaman was its first president.

She held this position for the following fourteen years.

The clubhouse, located at 441 East Ojai Avenue, has always been shared with the community. It served as headquarters for distribution of supplies during the 1917 fire and became a nurses' home during the influenza epidemic of 1918. The women turned their clubhouse over to the Red Cross during the war. Six congregations held services there while they built their churches and it housed kindergarten classes during the 1940s.

David Mason collection
Kings Daughters Clubhouse, now Ojai Valley Woman's Clubhouse, built in 1911.

In 1937, Mrs. A.L. Drown began an offshoot of the club which she called the Pioneer Section. It was open to anyone who had been a resident of Ventura County for twenty-five years or more. Together they gathered and documented historical data from those who had actually lived it. There were people still living who had witnessed the first train into Ojai, for example. Some were around when Abram Blumberg made the bricks for the first village schoolhouse. There may have been people here then who prospected during the big local gold rush. It wasn't too late to capture the elusive history of the valley.

Mrs. Drown was one of those who had experienced much of Ojai's history. She lived in one of the oldest building in town – the former brick schoolhouse. Her husband, Alton, a New Yorker, had moved to Santa Paula in 1886 where he and a partner opened a livery and team stable under the firm name of Davis and Drown. In 1912, he sold the business and bought farm land in Upper Ojai. He set out apricots, pears, almonds and prunes on his 250-acre parcel. He became successful over the years and was one of the first to subdivide lower valley land for housing when he laid out the Drown tract.

In 1951, the Ojai Valley Woman's Club came to the rescue of bored children by providing a "stay-at-home-camp" to occupy and entertain the children. The Ojai Valley Woman's Club still meets in its clubhouse. The members' prime concerns are still children, underprivileged residents, conservation causes and community beautification.

The Woman's Clubhouse is an Ojai Historic Landmark.

The Boyd Club

In 1902, Jack Boyd, a student at Thacher, suffered an attack of rheumatic fever and died. His parents wanted to establish a memorial for him at the school, but Sherman Thacher insisted, "Our boys have too much already." He suggested that they finance a clubhouse for the village instead. They donated $2,500 for a community clubhouse. Mr. Thacher raised the remainder of the money and asked S.M. Jesley to design it. They bought a lot from the Ojai Improvement Company and built the Boyd Center at what is now 307 East Ojai Avenue. This structure provided a meeting place where men could discuss town problems, have entertainment and lectures and play games. Mr. Thacher's intentions were to foster good companionship among the men of the valley, as well as provide recreation and refreshment for them. This, in the beginning, was a private club, owned by its members. Dues, in 1927, was $1.10 per month.

The Boyd Club has a long history of involvement in tragic as well as joyful times. The center doubled as a hospital for seriously ill patients during the 1918 Spanish flu epidemic. The community helped in this crisis by donating food, beds and money as well as travel services. During that time, everyone was required to wear a flu mask whenever outside their homes. Of the thirty-nine patients admitted to the temporary hospital, thirty-five were discharges, one was sent to the county hospital and three, including Tom Clark's son, Dick, died.

The clubhouse served as a disaster center during the floods of 1937-38. The USO took it over in 1942-45 and it housed at least ten clubs over the years. The building was moved to its present location, Sarzotti Park on Park Road, in February of 1957, to make room for the new Bank of America building. Eventually the Boyd Club became part of the Ojai Recreation Department and it is currently used for offices, a meeting place and game room.

Frank Achelpohl was the first custodian for the Boyd Club. Joseph Poole took over the job in 1916.

Munger family collection.
Boyd Clubhouse

The Red Cross

The local Red Cross had its beginning in 1917, when Mrs. George Cooksey, a Bostonian who wintered here, encouraged its establishment. She asked John L. Clymer, director of the Pacific division of the American Red Cross, to form a chapter here. The local Red Cross sustained the firefighters during the 1917 fire. This organization presently offers first aid classes and instruction in CPR. It supports a disaster action team and, through a yearly summer program, has taught hundreds of children to swim.

Ojai Valley Garden Club

In 1924, a woman named Mrs. Osgood began asking questions about gardening in Ojai. She wanted to know how to preserve plants indigenous to the valley. The more involved she became, the more ambitious were her goals. In 1926, she wanted to plant a memorial avenue honoring local boys who had been killed in the first World War. She initiated a campaign to protect the beautiful native oaks and soon others began showing an interest in her botanical crusades.

Fifty-four women and one man established the original Ojai Valley Garden Club. Their objective? "Ojai is beautiful and we are going to work to make it still more beautiful."

In 1926, they hung a bulletin board and posted notices of interest to gardeners and conservationists at the post office. Then they arranged fresh flowers there. This quaint practice continues today. There is some speculation that Mrs. Austin Pierpont initiated the post office garden club bulletin board and her husband designed it.

The same year, members of the garden club agreed to carry out Osgood's ideas for a memorial planting. Starting at the west end of Ojai Avenue near the Y, they planted 118 live oak trees, placing them in alphabetical order reflecting either the names of their purchasers or the soldiers represented. Some of the families who participated were: Barringtons, Boardmans, Bennetts, Bards, Clarks, Hobarts, Isenbergs, Mrs. Frank Frost, Emery Rogers, Esther and Elmer Van Curen, Walter Hobson, Jose Lopez, Mrs. Helen Meiners, Ernest Pierpont, John Carne and the Thachers.

Irate over destructive acts toward trees, garden club members wrote in a newspaper editorial, "Why don't people realize that trees were not intended as a place on which to tack notices and mailboxes?" In 1938, they fought to save the trees at the corner of Signal and Oak Streets and at Ventura and Eucalyptus Streets. This was not their first, nor was it to be their last battle on behalf of native trees.

Although the Ojai Woman's Club was the first organization to decry billboards, the garden club can take credit for the initial charge to prevent unsightly, overbearing advertising signs in Ojai.

It was garden club members who designed and planted the triangle at the Maricopa shopping center. They perform landscaping at school yards and parks. They replace fallen trees and they turn eyesores into adornments.

In 1928, garden club members discussed adopting a flower as an emblem for the valley. A cactus was suggested. It wasn't until 1964, that the Matilija poppy was selected as the official city flower.

Masonic Lodge

The Masonic Lodge opened in 1927. The Masons formed in Ojai in January of 1926 with fifty members and built the lodge on Mallory Way the following year. Sam Hudiburg was the builder. They also constructed cottages around the Masonic Lodge as a money making project. During the Depression, the cottages were sold and some were moved off the property. One of the original Masonic Court cottages now stands at the southwest corner of Gridley and Grand Avenues. The Masonic Hall was extensively remodeled in 1941.

Early Youth Organizations

Around 1892, boys could join a drill team of sorts and become known as cadets. The Boys Brigade wore uniforms and marched together up and down the streets of Nordhoff. This group is considered the forerunner of the Boy Scouts in Ojai.

David Mason collection
Masonic Court, built in 1927 on Mallory Way.

The original charter for Boy Scouts of America, Troop 501 is dated May, 1929 with the Ojai Lions Club as the sponsor. The Ventura County BSA started in 1921. There are currently six troops in Ojai.

In 1919, Mrs. Cecil Hathaway, principal of the grammar school, started the first Campfire Girls organization here.

A Juvenile Grange for children 5 to 14 was started in 1945.

In 1952, hot rod clubs were popular and in 1956, a Police Boys Club came to Ojai. The Pet Masters Club of 1958 kept children involved with animals. A highlight of this organization was an occasional pet parade. In 1960, the Jaycees started a teen club.

There were two clubs that stand out in the history of youth organizations, however.

Panther Club

Doug Jordan coached a youth baseball team and when the 1944 season was over, the boys had grown quite close and didn't want to disband. So Doug helped them organize a club in his grocery store in the arcade. They decided to pattern this organization after the Lions Club and become involved in civic matters. They also wanted to hold social events for young people.

Any boy between the ages of 15 and 21, who wanted to be of service to the community, was eligible to join the Panthers. They kept the arcade lights burning, promoted a "shop in Ojai" campaign and sponsored baseball teams for younger boys.

In 1948, the Panthers incorporated as a national organization, making Ojai their headquarters. Alan Rains was the head Panther in 1949 and in 1951, Jerry Clausen led the club. It's estimated that around 500 boys were members during the ten-year period the Panther Club was active.

Topa Topa Club

In 1945, 158 boys and girls between the ages of 13 and 19 formed the Topa Topa Club. The men no longer used the old Boyd Club building, so the Topa Topa Club took it over and renamed it Teen Town. They supported the clubhouse by holding various fund raising events – taking total responsibility for maintaining the premises.

In 1948, the Topa Topa Club ran an employment agency. The following year, funds ran dangerously low and the teens tried desperately to raise the money needed to keep Teen Town open. When the community was unable or unwilling to come to their aid, they wrote letters to Hollywood stars who either lived in the valley or visited often. All of this effort was to no avail, however, for later that year they reluctantly gave up Teen Town.

Other Valley Organizations

Ojai Valley Jaycees

In 1948, C.H. (Bob) Andrews saw a need for youthful leadership relating to community improvement. The Chamber of Commerce was defunct and downtown was shabby and unkempt. The need for a new approach to civic tasks was evident and Andrews founded the Ojai Valley Jaycees on that premise.

Their first project was to paint an air marker to direct planes to the airport in Mira Monte. The Jaycees were the first to decorate Ojai at Christmas time. They held a soap box derby for youngsters. In 1952, they spearheaded a promotion to shop locally and, to further entice shoppers, they repaired the arcade.

Altrusa Club

The Ojai Altrusa Club originated in December, 1956. This organization is composed of women who hold executive positions in business, own or operate their own enterprises or are in professional fields. Membership in the Altrusa Club is by invitation only. Although these community-minded women serve in a number of ways, their most recent outstanding gifts were the post office chimes and funds for their upkeep.

The valley's first YMCA was started by Frank Peleg Barrows in 1910.

A Parent-Teacher Association was established in 1917 with Mattie Miller presiding. The fire that year drew people's attention toward more urgent matters, however, and the PTA was dropped until 1921, when twenty members joined and elected Mrs. C.C. Orr as their president.

In 1925, some valley homemakers established the Rest-a-Bit Club. Once a month these ladies simply took time out from their chores and got together to rest a bit. That same year, Mrs. F.A. Hennessey and Mrs. Morgan Barnes started the Needlework Guild of America to assist the needy and clothe the poor.

Ray Craft established a Better Business Bureau in 1931.

The American Legion was meeting at the high school cafeteria in 1938 and moved to the new Camp Comfort meeting hall later that year. According to the club historian, the first American Legion building was on Bryant Street. In 1954, they met where the Firebird building is now on East Ojai Avenue. They currently meet at 821 East Ojai Avenue.

Fred Linder started the Ojai Valley Disaster Committee to help flood and fire victims in 1941.

The first Rotary Club in Ojai began in 1948.

In 1952, Guy McCombs directed the Ojai Civil Defense. That same year Mrs. Laurie Eakin presided over the first Oak View Women's Club meeting.

Herbert J. Finch established the Ground Observer Corps in 1957. In 1958 the Ojai Search and Rescue Team was established.

Chapter Nine
As the Century Turns

By the turn of the century there were 1,100 people settled in the valley. What was Ojai like then? Had the population growth marred this unique vale? Did its charm wane with the increase in residents? According to newspaper accounts, this was hardly the case. Visitors found this to be a refreshing place. People still praised Nordhoff for the healing power of the sunlight and dry air. The unmatched beauty held sojourners in awe, as nature's blossoms continually dappled the hillsides. Lush grass filled vast fields, seasonally changing from green to golden. It was impossible to see all of the village at once for the abundance of trees. People said that one could not take this valley for granted.

Mr. Mesick's first issue of *The Ojai* carried this statement under the heading: "for the good of mankind by telling of the greatest sanitarium for throat and lung troubles in the known world... the famous Ojai Valley."

At first, Ojai attracted mostly the afflicted. In the 1890s many of the ailing visitors were also rich. And ten years later people both healthy and wealthy were claiming Nordhoff as their permanent or part-time home. Some of them built expensive residences here while others became regular guests – causing local resorts to flourish. For a time, Ojai was home to and host to the very rich and those who catered to them.

The new century ushered in all variety of change to accommodate the growing populace. Stricter laws, as an example, are always a necessary byproduct of expansion. One major concern was the use of liquor.

The Temperance Movement

The Woman's Christian Temperance Union (WCTU) grew out of the nationwide Woman's Temperance Crusade of 1873. The churches were the main vehicle through which Nordhoff women received information and encouragement to join their sisters' battle against overindulgence. The local WCTU struck out against the use of tobacco as well as liquor. They attempted to educate the public by staging meetings and demonstrations and pleading with abusers.

"Liquor excites the heart, hinders the digestion, disturbs the liver and stupefies the brain," preached advocates of the temperance movement. And they referred to liquor as "shame water." This comment appeared in an 1895 issue of the newspaper: "Does anyone doubt that smoking in public interferes with the freedom of others?"

Some men did their part to maintain an alcohol-free community, too. Tom Clark expressed his opinion that Nordhoff was too small to support a saloon.

In 1897, a document five feet long was presented to the Ventura Board of Supervisors against allowing a permit for a saloon in Nordhoff. It is reported that nearly every citizen in Nordhoff signed this petition. But gambling was tolerated.

Gambling Saloons in Nordhoff

C.C. Eason ran a pool hall here in 1880. In 1893, P.N. Roberts bought the billiard parlor from B.F. Pitts. Gambling was its principal business then. But as soon as Roberts took it over, there were rumors accusing him of selling hard liquor. He publicly stated that he ran a place where "refreshing temperance drinks are sold, not intoxicating drinks" and that he allowed no small boys or boisterousness within his establishment. He stated that he hoped to overcome the town prejudices.

Those who believed the whispered charges, however, made it impossible for the newcomer to earn a living here. He wanted to expand and improve his store, but the primary builder, John Heck refused to do the work. No merchant would sell to him. Edwin Senior owned the property and he asked Roberts to vacate it. The stranger was forced to move on.

In 1895, Jules Vissierre was the town barber and the proprietor of the temperance hall. When Dave Raddick took it

168

over, liquor was still not served there. It is said that anyone desiring beer or whiskey had to go to Oxnard. Then John Lagomarsino came to Nordhoff and opened a saloon.

It seems that the lawmakers decided to compromise on the liquor issue and, in 1901, according to *The Ojai,* Lagomarsino signed a local liquor agreement promising to do away with gambling, music, women, prize fighting and any other entertainment degrading to his liquor business.

Evidently he didn't totally comply because four years later the Committee of Fifteen instructed Lagomarsino to remove the handles from his slot machines. Even that wasn't good enough and on April 30, 1904, they ordered Lagomarsino not to run any saloon or even temperance hall, billiard parlor or any other "resort" in the territory covered by the ordinance which they drew up.

A Killing in Nordhoff

Nordhoff was basically a peaceful town, the main excitement being an occasional runaway horse or a staged bucking show in front of Clark's Livery Stable. In the teen years of this century, however, a killing took place in the quiet, country village.

Sid Houk ran the billiard parlor then. As the story goes, Bill Soule, Cyrus Soule's son, had lost quite a bit of money in a card game at Houk's. He was still angry about it the next day and decided to take his losses out on the proprietor. Bill knew that Sid walked home for lunch every day along Signal Street, so he waited for him.

Soule situated himself between two buildings – a bottle of wine in one hand and a gun in the other. He waited for Sid to walk past. Mr. Raddick usually relieved Houk at noon, but that day he was too ill to come in.

Soon it became obvious to Bill that Houk wasn't coming out on the street. He was pretty well liquored up as he bolted through the front door of the pool hall and began waving his gun at Sid. Earl Chrisman grabbed the barrel of the gun just as Soule squeezed the trigger and the bullet grazed Sid Houk's arm. Sid ducked behind the counter, came up with a gun of his own and killed Bill Soule on the spot.

The coroner hadn't yet arrived from Ventura by the time school was out that day and Arthur Waite remembered the sense of wonderful curiosity and horror he felt as he and his schoolmates walked slowly past the pool hall and saw the feet of the corpse just inside the doorway.

Banking Comes to Nordhoff

In 1906, Felix Ewing, Edgar Carne and J.J. Burke met in Burke's real estate office and discussed starting a bank. Judge Ewing was made president. Adolpho Camarillo was vice president and Edgar Carne was the secretary. They hired Miss Mabel Isenberg, a former employee of Collins Bank in Ventura, as their accountant.

Mr. Burke, the cashier for the new Ojai State Bank, kept the money in a small safe in his office until they installed a vault. Although its size was suitable for a while, the small space, which now houses the Ojai Realty Company at 260 East Ojai Avenue in the arcade, eventually became inadequate for a bank.

In 1910, H.R. Giddings of Ventura, using the plans drawn up by Los Angeles architect Silas R. Burns, built a new bank just east of Libbey Park on Ojai Avenue where the parking lot is today. Edward Wiest, Judge Ewing's son-in-law, was manager.

The new bank building was stately and considered by many to be out of place in this rural hamlet. Rather Roman in style with large concrete pillars in front, it certainly dressed up the main street of Nordhoff.

In 1926, *The Ojai* editor, Gerard wrote, "The Ojai bank building was the first building with any claim to beauty erected here."

Felix Ewing, a superior court judge in the early 1900s, had organized several banks. He presided over the little Ojai bank for nearly twenty years. When he died in 1926, his son-in-law E.L. Wiest was promoted from manager to president. C.O. Anderson became cashier and Mabel Isenberg was assistant cashier.

In 1927, a large organization bought the little local bank and renamed it Bank of Italy, National Trust and Savings Association, Ojai Branch. Wiest stayed on as manager. In 1928, John Lay became manager.

In 1932, V.C. Eicher became manager and in 1934, Mabel Isenberg retired from the bank after twenty-seven years of service.

In 1930, the bank became Bank of America and in 1957, a new bank building was erected just east of the original building. The Boyd Clubhouse, was moved to Sarzotti Park at that time.

170

The old Bank of America building was removed in 1960 to make room for a parking lot.

After the Bank of America moved its operation to the old Security Bank facility on the southwest corner of Blanche Street and Ojai Avenue, the former building stood empty for some time. Eventually, it was beautifully refurbished and transformed into store and restaurant space.

The Bank Robbery

In March, 1916, a local man, George Downing, in desperate need of money for his family, brazenly robbed the Ojai State Bank. First he entered the Boyd Club just east of the bank and told the custodian, Frank Achelpohl, that he wished to take a bath. Mr. Achelpohl furnished him with a towel. Once Downing had closed the shower door behind him, he jumped out the window and headed next door to the bank. Mr. Wiest had gone to lunch and the teller, Mabel Isenberg, was alone. Downing blindfolded the frightened clerk, promised not to hurt her and wrapped $3,800 in the Boyd Club towel. While being questioned later, Miss Isenberg insisted that the robber reminded her quite a lot of George Downing.

Reportedly, Downing was one of the first to show up in front of the bank after the news of the robbery got around and he even armed himself to aid in pursuit of the thief. Authorities caught up with Downing as the robber, recovered most of the money and gave him a light sentence.

What would provoke someone to rob their community bank? One clue to Downing's decision might be in the fact that his wife, Laura (Poole) had died three years earlier at the age of 36 years and left him with two small children. Maybe this was a reaction to the stress of his personal situation.

John Joseph Burke

J.J. Burke's name crops up often throughout the history of Ojai Valley. He contributed a great deal to this community and his name lives with its history.

Burke, known to his friends as Jack, was born in Canada in 1862. When he was just 25 years-old he became quite ill and his doctor told him that he would not see 30. Burke had met Edward Thacher seven years earlier in Kansas and they had kept in touch since then. When Burke wrote to tell Thacher the bad news, his friend urged him to come to Ojai, where the climate performed medical miracles.

Burke arrived with 50 cents in his pocket. He clerked in Frank Barrows' store for three months, then he rented acreage from the Soules and farmed it for a year, raising and selling fruits and vegetable. He worked in Van Curen's grocery store for a while and then took a government claim of 160 acres in Lions Canyon, which he ranched for several months.

Burke regained his health and vowed never to leave Nordhoff. He was a progressive thinker and became involved in numerous community affairs. Burke not only helped organize the Ojai Improvement Company and the Ojai State Bank, but he supported recreation and served as secretary for early tennis tournaments. He was prominent in creating the Gridley Water Company and he helped launch the Ojai Olive Mill in 1901. He built the Ojai Theater, started the Nordhoff Water and Power Company and formed the Ojai Realty Company. Once sickly, Burke died in December, 1952, at the ripe age of 90.

Services for the Community

Telephones

By 1892, there was a telephone line between the livery stable and Gally Cottages, but it wasn't until 1894 that Nordhoff had communication with Ventura by wire. Then, the San Francisco telephone directory consisted of 204 pages; the Los Angeles directory had twenty. Ventura County numbers filled one page, with only one telephone listed for Nordhoff.

They placed the single phone in Dr. Saeger's drug store, automatically making him town message-minder. Anyone requesting information from Ventura or wishing to pass something along, left a note in the doctor's office for him to relay or receive by phone. The operator, Mrs. Scott, was always happy to give the time of the next stage, announce a birth and even pass on a bit of gossip.

In 1898, Sunset Telephone and Telegraph Company put in a long distance extension to Thacher School, John Carne's home, Louis Spader's place, Gally Cottages, the John Suess Cash Store and then hired Miss Ethel Hudiburg as the operator. A one minute conversation between Ojai and San Francisco was $1.

In 1904, just a fraction of the homes and businesses in

Nordhoff had phones and in 1908 there were about a hundred. The phone company installed 445 manual dial phones here in 1929 and that's the same year that they built the Pacific Bell Telephone building on the northwest corner of Ojai Avenue and Blanche Street.

Miss Marjorie Blewett, who started working for Pacific Telephone Company in Los Angeles in 1927, moved to the Ojai exchange in 1930. Fourteen years later, the workload was more than one person could handle and Mrs. Irma Newton came to help. When Blewett retired, in 1954, Mrs. Newton took her place.

In 1958, telephone service reached 1,391 people in Ojai and the following year, people in Ojai could call Ventura toll free.

Electricity

Prior to the advent of electricity, people used kerosene and acetylene gas lanterns for lighting in their homes and businesses. In 1910, Cockly and Phillips came to town and presented an electric light demonstration. Their claim was, "Our only competition is the sun."

J.J. Burke had shown an interest in better lighting for quite some time, having installed and maintained street lamps in the village as early as 1892. The lighting exhibit was more than just a passing curiosity to him. It may have been the boost he needed to bring electricity to Nordhoff, for two years later he helped organize the Nordhoff Water and Power Company.

Charles M. Pratt, Dr. Van Patten, Judge Ewing, D.A. Smith, E.L. Wiest and J.F. Dennison held the stock. Mr. Burke was the president and M.W. Phillips served as vice president and manager. George Mallory took Dennison's place when he died. They built the plant on South Montgomery Street, installing two huge diesel engines that weighed an estimated 36,000 pounds. The old knob and screw system carried the electricity through the village.

On New Years Day in 1913 at 5:08 p.m., Ojai had electric lights for the first time. The Foothills Hotel and Mallory and Dennison's store were the first to have electricity and power was connected to the Ojai Inn a short time later. Upper Ojai didn't have electricity until 1922. In 1927, there were 365 water connections throughout the city of Ojai and 612 electric meters.

Phillips Electrical Company incorporated in 1920 and in 1928, they sold the company to Edison.

There are always some people who view anything new with

skepticism and electricity was certainly no exception. People thought it to be dangerous, unhealthful, a passing fad and not very practical. Some thought the electricity would be off most of the time and in a way they were right. Service was not continually available in those early days. It was switched on from 5 p.m. until midnight and from 4 a.m. until sunrise. There was no need to provide lighting during sleeping hours or daytime. Claude Munger remembered that the plant operator blinked the lights twice to warn residents when he was going to turn them off for the night. He also recalled the engines creating a tremendous boom that vibrated throughout the town each time the power was switched on.

The Fire Department

Fighting and preventing fires, settling quarrels and marching in parades were some of the duties of the original Nordhoff Rangers. Their territory, however, was the back country. If a ranger wasn't nearby when a fire broke out in town, which was usually the case, it was up to untrained volunteers (whoever was handy) to squelch the flames. Many homes caught fire during the early 1900s and the majority of them were traced to careless trash burning.

The village organized its first volunteer fire department in 1904 with Frank S. Beaman as the chief, Ezra Taylor was assistant chief, secretary was S.S. Barrows and C.O. Mudge was treasurer. J.F. Dennison was the foreman in charge of ladders, Tom S. Clark took command over locating and doling out axes and Mr. Lawson's duty was rounding up and distributing buckets. The fire marshals were I.W. Wolfe, S.L. Smith and J.J. Burke. Ezra Taylor and A.A. Garland were on the excuse committee.

The Committee of Fifteen authorized the new fire department to spend $200 on buckets, ladders, hoses and other fire fighting equipment and the Ojai Improvement Company gave the community another $1,500 for the fire department with which they built a fire station on the south side of Ojai Avenue just west of the Nordhoff Hotel. The little wood-frame building was described as being the size of a single garage stall. They financed the fire station and equipment after that by holding an annual firemen's ball.

During that time, the Committee of Fifteen called a town meeting to provide an opportunity for everyone to voice their

174

opinions and make suggestions to the new fire department about fire prevention. Someone suggested that the firemen check around buildings for overgrowth of dry weeds and the people also wanted someone to come down hard against the use of firecrackers. They felt that the fire department should give citizens instructions in the proper storage of coal oil and gasoline.

Another practical comment was that the firemen should take authority against those who drained their water mains at night. It seems that some people feared they weren't getting their money's worth through normal use of water, so they ran it at night just to use it up.

In the long run, the townsfolk were not terribly impressed by their firemen. The consensus was that they spent entirely too much time on the tennis courts to be effective.

The ringing of the school bell signaled a fire. Upon hearing it, the bigger boys left school to become part of the bucket brigade.

In 1910, the fire department was given a forty-gallon Badger soda and acid fire extinguisher. It included fifty feet of one-inch rubber hose which was pulled by four men in a basket on a two-wheel frame. The douser on wheels now serves to decorate the front of Fire Station 21 near Soule Golf Course on Ojai Avenue.

In 1918, J.E. Houk was the fire chief and Ed Wiest was treasurer. That's the same year that Libbey reportedly donated a 1917 Model T Ford fire truck to the fire department.

David Mason collection
Ojai Fire department, 1910. Blumberg Hotel in background.

In 1923, the city built a new firehouse just east of the Boyd Club at what is now 321 East Ojai Avenue. The street level floor had stalls for two fire trucks and the chief lived downstairs. Fire calls came into the Boyd Club and were relayed to the chief. The department had two 1917 Model T fire trucks by then – one was a hose truck and the other had two twenty-gallon soda and acid fire extinguishers, an extension ladder, an ax and a one-inch rubber fire hose. There was a gong mounted on top of the truck and a fireman pulled the rope to sound the gong for right-of-way.

OVM
Ojai's first fire truck.

There's a lapse between the time the old fire station was torn down to make way for Libbey's town beautification project and the new one was built. Some speculate that the current Coldwell Banker real estate office at the corner of West Ojai Avenue and Country Club Drive was once a garage for the city fire engines. Perhaps this was during that time: 1917 - 1923.

In 1921, Fred Linder became the fire chief. Five years later, the county took over the local department and William Bowie was made the first fire warden for this area.

In 1928, the fire company bought a new La France fire truck. In 1935, the city applied to the Works Project Administration to have a new fire station built and the following year it was operational at 109 South Montgomery Street. This fire station was in use through 1979 when the department moved to their new headquarters on East Ojai Avenue and Oak Glen. The old fire station housed the Ojai Museum for a number of years and now Frank Massarella makes his pottery there.

Major Ojai Fires

Two of the town's most devastating fires occurred in 1917. The first fire was started by campers in the Matilija Canyon in June. It reportedly killed five people and burned sixty buildings leaving 1,000 people homeless. The Foothills Hotel was destroyed as were the Baptist and Catholic Churches, Bristol School and the homes of Robertson and Van Patten on Foothill Road and Sinclair and Farnum on Fairview.

In September of the same year, a gasoline stove in Miss Elvie Peasley's store in the arcade, exploded and the resulting fire burned nearly half of the business district. Citizens tried to help by carrying merchandise from the stores and stacking it in the street. In their haste to save it, much of it was destroyed, however.

Glen Hickey, who had recently taken over the old Barrows place of business, reportedly, left his hardware store open so people could get equipment with which to fight the fire. Volunteers quickly grabbed what tools they needed, tossing money into the register. Later, when Hickey counted the cash drawer, he became convinced that there was more money in it than there should be. It was after these two fires that Edward Libbey, shocked into awareness of the inadequacy of the firefighters' equipment, gave the community a fire truck.

In 1932, an eleven day forest fire burned acres and acres of brush.

A fire, said to be the most devastating since the 1917 fire, roared toward Ojai Valley in 1948. Fifteen hundred firefighters fought this blaze that burned 30,000 acres and consumed thirteen homes. This fire started near the pool at Wheelers Resort when a butane pipe burst. Orchid Town and Cal Prep (the old Foothills Hotel) were just some of the properties that were badly scorched in that fire.

In 1985, fire terrorized the valley once again. This blaze started on an extremely hot July 1st and wasn't contained until fifteen days later. Remarkably, we lost just twelve homes. Numerous outbuildings were lost, however, and the damage to citrus was estimated at over $300,000. More than fifty of the 3,000 firefighters who came to help were injured in this blaze.

This, a suspected arson fire which started near Wheelers, prompted evacuations all over the valley as the fire, heightened each evening by strong, hot winds, threatened homes and property. This author was personally involved with evacuations and threats of evacuation every night for four. We evacuated friends along the Ventura River bank one night. We took in refuges from the Drown tract the next night and Siete Robles the night after that. One late night we were awakened by neighbors in West Hills. Our homes were being bombarded by giant, glowing embers.

When the nightmare was over, grateful citizens posted large signs all over the valley offering thanks to the firemen. Later that year, a huge boulder was placed at the Y and a plaque honoring the firefighters was attached.

The Automobile

No two people agree about who drove the first automobile into the valley. Some say it was the Waites. They had a one-cylinder, one-seater, side-winder that was as "high as a house." Others remember the first motorcar as being the Pierponts snazzy Maxwell. The Gorhams are in the running for the honor too, with their Locomobile sports car, which was just one of thirteen in a row for them. The matter of who was first may never be resolved, but we can be fairly certain that by 1906, there were four automobiles in the valley.

There was scarcely a bit of road in Ojai that didn't account for an accident between auto and horse during these early days. The state recognized this as a problem and formed the Automobile Club to establish road laws and to watch out for reckless drivers. In 1905, the speed limit on the approach to a dam, bridge, sharp curve or steep descent was four mph. Through incorporated towns, fifteen mph was the maximum speed and a driver could cruise up to twenty mph in the open country.

In 1910, local concern was directed toward better roads and stronger bridges. Bridges were often built without a middle section, having just narrow tracks for the car tires. This county reported an accident a day then. Since auto mishaps were occurring everywhere, the Automobile Club employed speed cops to make random appearances in towns to patrol and instruct drivers.

At one point, the Automobile Club considered drawing a line down the center of all state roadways. They thought that if cars traveling in opposite directions drove on one side of the road or the other, there would be fewer accidents. The cost of such a project, however, was prohibitive.

David Mason collection
Vintage autos in the Ojai Garage.

This was a learning period for lawmakers as well as for citizens. As more accidents occurred, new motor laws were introduced, including the rule that drivers must signal to turn and should stop and look before proceeding through an intersection.

The automobile does not get the credit for inventing the road accident. People managed to collide often enough when they traveled about by horse – long before the coming of the car. In 1903, George Bald, according to his son, Howard, was riding a wild horse on a dead run down the main street of Ojai when he met Wheeler Blumberg with a team and a two-seater surrey with guests bound for his resort. Howard said that Wheeler was famous for his fast driving. "Well, they collided head on," Howard continued; "the bronc went under the surrey and Dad catapulted into the front seat between Wheeler and Miss Frances Harrow, a teacher from Los Angeles. The team kept on going, leaving behind the surrey and its passengers."

When Phillip Pierpont, Dr. Pierpont's son, decided to buy an automobile, he went to Los Angeles to examine the current selection. He had no experience in operating a motorcar, so after he bought a Maxwell, the salesman drove him home.

Confident that he, too, could maneuver the machine, he asked his brother, Austin, to come along and together they set out for town. Howard Bald and Fred Houk were riding near Gally Cottages when the Pierpont car whizzed past and startled their horses. Bald became angry and vowed to "fix that snob." The two horsemen followed the Pierponts' path with the idea of settling the score.

In the meantime, Phillip was involved in a dilemma of his own. When he reached the village, he discovered that he didn't know how to stop the car. He drove through the town, turned up Signal Street to Grand Avenue and headed in the direction of his home. Upon entering the yard, he still hadn't figured out how to get the machine to stop, so he did the only thing he could – he ran into the nearest haystack.

In 1906, Edwin Baker's cousin, Frank More, made big news when he attempted to drive from Seattle to San Diego. His crew, reportedly, had to utilize levers and block and tackle often along the way to hoist the car over boulders or pull it out of the mud. It couldn't have been a pleasant trip for, in addition to that, they averaged three flat tires a day. It was a day of pride for the Bakers when the More auto rolled into their yard for all the town to see.

Enthralled by the very idea of owning one, the Baker children immediately began working on their father to purchase a car. Edwin Baker was very careful where and how he spent his money. But by 1908, he, too, could see the advantages of having a family car and he invested in a dark blue Franklin.

David Mason collection
Cars parked in front of the arcade.

This editorial appeared in a 1911 newspaper: "Never a day passes but that there aren't from six to twenty autos either stopping here or passing through. We've got the climate, we've got the water and we've got things coming our way – we are attracting attention." In 1914, there were forty-seven cars in Nordhoff, one of them Mr. Libbey's Packard.

The auto was an invention of great popularity and most people were fascinated by the machine. Some, however, could never quite accept it. Seymour Munger, for instance, wouldn't ride in an automobile, but a day finally came when it was necessary for him to do so. He took an occasional ride after that initial introduction, but always with the door open and one foot on the running board – just in case.

The Ojai carries a story about an automobile mishap incurred by the Mungers in 1926. The report says that Julia Munger was driving while Seymour had his arm out the window holding onto an oil stove which was riding on the running board. Evidently Julia drove too close to a truck and sideswiped it demolishing the stove and damaging her husband's hand in the process.

Julia and Seymour's grandson says, however, that he never knew Julia to drive and suspects that it was one of his aunts at the wheel that day.

Arthur Waite remembered a game that valley children played in which they carried a piece of paper and a pencil to write down the description of every car they saw. This didn't take up very much of their time in those days, according to Waite.

Marion (Fraser) Ring told me about the day she took her first driving test in Ojai. First she had to wait until a qualified person came to town to give her the exam. And then they drove around for a long time in search of two cars parked close enough together for her to try parallel parking.

The Auto Livery

Andy Van Curen ran a livery stable in town as early as 1873, but its location is unknown. Maddox's Livery was reported to be on the northeast corner of Signal Street and Ojai Avenue in 1887. Watts Haydock ran the livery in 1893. And in 1895 Tom Clark opened a livery stable there and ran it as such until autos became important. Then he reportedly altered the place to cater to cars instead of horses. It was during Libbey's town facelift that Tom Clark rebuilt his livery quarters using native stone.

E.A. Runkle succeeded L.C. Rounds in the Ventura/Nordhoff Stage Line late in 1916, operating the line from the Ojai Garage at the east end of town. In 1917 Runkle took over Tom Clark's modernized auto, taxi and stage line business. Runkle's ads boasted a roomy garage, a waiting room and an office with an attendant. His was an informal operation. Although he ran his twelve-passenger Studebaker on a daily schedule, the driver could stop anywhere along the route for passengers. Elizabeth Clark (Tom Clark's daughter) worked for her brother-in-law, Dr. Roberts, a dentist, in Ventura. She rode the auto-stage every day and said it was an hour trip each way.

Claude Munger (Seymour and Julia's eldest son) drove the stage until his boss found out that he was only sixteen years old. He recalls that the road from Ventura was paved only as far as Casitas Springs.

Once, on his way home from Ventura, he stopped at a watermelon patch, where Dahl's Market is now at 445 Ventura Avenue in Oak View, to try the time-honored prank of swiping a few melons. When the farmer caught up to Claude, he waved a gun and demanded payment for the melons. Claude said, "You can't bother me, I'm carrying the United States Mail." Upon hearing that, the farmer allowed the stage to pass. After thinking it over, however, he continued his pursuit. When asked later what he did when the farmer caught him, Munger answered, "What else could I do? I paid up."

Around 1919, Harry Hunt (who married Margaret Clark) bought out Runkle and opened Hunt's Auto Livery at 110 North Signal Street. Mr. Hunt rented cars for every purpose, with or without his own trained drivers, and he stored cars for hotel guests – parking each one in perfect alignment with the others and caring for them as if they were pure gold.

Joe Gholson, chauffeur for the William Ladd family of Ojai, felt that Mr. Hunt contributed more to the uniqueness of the village during that period than any other individual. Hunt owned several cars, including a seven-passenger Packard sedan, a five-passenger Chrysler Imperial and a large red truck. In 1928, he had twenty-nine cars and employed eleven drivers. His chauffeurs wore dark suits, caps and black gloves. They were trained to give their patrons as fine a service as could be found in New York or London.

Hunt did not dress the same as his employees, he generally wore a gray business suit and hat and practically always had a Roi Tan cigar clenched tightly between his teeth.

Hunt's service provided a way for Thacher and Villanova students to keep doctor and dentist appointments. Mr. Hunt's fees were probably high for the times. One could be chauffeured to Los Angeles for $40 or to Santa Barbara for $14 and to Ventura for $4. Once Hunt earned $3,750 for six weeks of his time when he drove a family to Yellowstone in their own car. Hunt reportedly sold his business to Walter Rowe and William Mallory in 1944.

When Hunt bought out Runkle and moved his business to Signal Street, just behind the original location, George and Ida Crampton opened a drugstore in the front portion (where Ojai Village Pharmacy is today). In 1924, they sold the business to R.J. Boardman, who ran it as Boardman's Drug Store until 1947.

Chapter Ten
Business in Ojai Valley

According to Yda Storke's 1891 account of the Ojai Valley, there were two hotels, two churches, two schools, two general merchandise stores, two blacksmiths, a builder, a contractor, a lumber dealer and a butcher shop.

A town can be measured by knowing what businesses prospered there and its people are better understood by knowing what businesses they supported. Here's an attempt to reconstruct the business district through the early years. Although every effort was made toward accuracy, the following is not, by any means, complete.

Businesses, Circa 1887

In 1887, Maddox Livery was on the northeast corner of Ojai Avenue and Signal Streets. Benjamin F. Maddox sold his business to Watts Haydock in 1893 and in 1894, Ed F. Arnold took it over. Tom Clark bought the business the following year and ran it for twenty years. The old horse livery was an auto livery through the 19-teens and then it became a drugstore.

Also operating along what is now the arcade in 1887, were, F.P. Barrows General Merchandise (originally Lafayette Herbert's store), a drug store, Arnold and Van Curen's Mercantile (later owned by George W. Mallory who eventually took in Frank Dennison as a partner), a meat market and Archie McDonnell's blacksmith shop.

It's speculated that Archie McDonnell's blacksmith business was where The Hub Cocktail Lounge is today at 256 East Ojai Avenue. Not only do early place descriptions indicate so, but in 1948, The Hub underwent extensive remodeling and the owners found a profusion of horseshoe nails under the flooring. It wasn't until the redevelopment of the plaza behind the arcade, that the old barn doors were removed from the building.

OVM
Archie McDonnell's blacksmith shop, circa 1890

Businesses: Early 1890s

F.P. Barrows, general merchandise
George E. Stewart, real estate
J. McKee, Justice
Robert Gibson Jr., meat market (formerly run by J.A. Gibson)
Watts Haydock Livery
J.C. Smith, blacksmith at Watts Haydock's Livery (Charles Morse and Charles Gibson took over the blacksmith business in1893 and Gibson later moved it to the southeast corner of Ojai Avenue and Signal Street. D.J. Raddick took over this business in 1911. When they removed the building to make room for the new post office in 1917, Y.L. Valencia bought the business and moved it to Topa Topa Street.)
A.R. McDonnell, blacksmith
Charles Trotter, harness and boot repair
S.L. Stuart, dentist
A.N.Soliss, Ojai Hardware
R.G. Ayala, tonsorial artist (This business was on the south side of the main street near the Nordhoff Hotel. When Ayala left, Dr. Saeger and J.J. Burke bought his business and found a

new barber for the town. The new barber was a man named Knoeller.)

People's Lumber Company (at what is now 108 South Montgomery Street.)

Businesses: 1895

John Suess, cash store

Tom Clark Livery (1895 - 1919)

F.P. Barrows, general merchandise

J.J. Burke, real estate (Ojai Realty was started by John J. Burke and B.F. Spencer. Spencer died in 1927 and Burke formed a partnership with Boyd E. Gabbert.)

Mallory and Dennison, general merchandise

Van Curen, groceries

Saeger's Drug Store (at 306 E. Ojai Avenue where Blue Sky music is now.)

Eason's Saloon

Stewart and Sheppard Real Estate

People's Lumber Company

Businesses at the Turn of the Century

Charlie Gibson's Blacksmith Shop (where the post office is today)

Orton Plumbing

Steven's Grocery

Freeman's Grocery

Nordhoff Machine Shop

Arthur Garland, general merchandise

J.B. Berry, house painting and papering

Valentine Cagniacci, barber

J.J. Burke, real estate

J.A. Hagerman, barber

Robert Wietzman, upholstery repair and chair caning

F.P. Barrows, general merchandise

Fidelis Schroff, harness maker (reportedly located at what is now 337 East Ojai Avenue)

J.B. Fox, Nordhoff Transfer, Feed and Livery (later, presumably run by A.R. McDonnell)

Green's Shaving Parlor

Tom Clark's Ojai Livery

Stores on south side of Ojai Avenue, circa 1905

Businesses in 1910

A.E. Freeman, grocery

Otto Busch, grocery

Walter E. Houk, groceries and meat (He added an ice business in 1911. George Harris bought Houk out and built a new ice plant in the arcade in 1922. Three years later, he bought the old McDonnell Transfer building on Fox street, tore it down and built a twenty-ton capacity ice plant. The building still stands and now houses Rick's Plumbing.)

Frank P. Barrows and Son, general merchandise

B.B. Cota, painter and wallpaperer

W.H. Stuart, carpenter and builder

J.J. Burke, real estate loans and fire insurance

Seymour D. Munger and **Marlon Robison,** cement pipe manufacturing

Fidelis Schroff, harness maker (He remained in this business for more than twenty years and then sold his shop to William Pierdella. This store, reportedly, later became Western Auto. In 1926, Ralph Andruss opened the first Ford dealership in the valley in the vicinity of the City Garage and Schroff's old shop. In the1940s this building was transformed into a bowling alley.)

F. Byrd, watchmaker,

F.E. Sperry, laundry

Dave J. Raddick, billiards

Harold Mathews, Ojai Bakery (He later sold his business to Clark V. Miller who sold to Mrs. Gertrude Bailey).

Lee Darnell, sweet shop, billiards and tobacco

Linder, dry goods and notions.

Selwyn S. Beaman, Ojai Garage

Charles Gibson, blacksmith, (D.J. Raddick succeeded him in 1911)

Elizabeth Stuart and Sarah Harvey, ladies and children's garments and millinery

Schuler and Wakefield French dry cleaning

R.E. Bachelor, photography

George Mallory and **J. F. Dennison,** general merchandise

T.S. Clark Livery

A.R. McDonnell Transfer (His barn was on Fox Street)

J.C. Leslie, contractor and builder

N.V. Voss, shoe repair

Mrs. L.A. Bray, millinery

Hass and Rothnier, barbers

Kincher Laundry

David Mason collection
Downtown Ojai looking east from where the post office is today. 1912.

188

The Business District After 1920

During the first quarter of the twentieth century, shopping had become immensely more convenient. A valley housewife could purchase her staples at the village market and have vegetables and meat delivered fresh to her home. Kinchers Laundry also provided free delivery service. The Kinchers' daughter usually made the house calls in a horse-drawn wagon. A Chinese man drove the vegetable cart door-to-door. Two horses pulled the flatbed meat wagon from ranch to ranch and through neighborhoods. Constance Wash, Harry Gorham's stepdaughter, recalled that the driver always tossed a hunk of ice in among the meat to keep it cool. By the time he arrived at their east end home, however, all that remained was a trail of water.

The butcher dropped the tailgate and used it as a chopping block, cutting the meat exactly to suit his customers. I am told that in those days 15 cents worth of round steak would feed a family of four with some to spare for the dog.

There must have been a very different code of ethics in business as well as in everyday life then – a trust not comparable to that of more modern times. "Folks respected the property of others," a man in his 80s told me. "All a store clerk had to do was write 'money' on his cash box and people would leave it alone."

Marion (Fraser) Ring, who grew up on Creek Road during the 1920s and '30s, said that she and her mother were shopping in Mr. Craft's grocery store once when the fire bell rang. Craft, a volunteer fireman, hastily told Mrs. Fraser to continue shopping in his absence, keep track of what she took and come in and pay him later.

But not everyone could be trusted even in those days. A rash of robberies in the downtown area, prompted merchants to pool their money and hire a night watchman. Harry Cummings was first to take the job in 1926 at $150 per month. Walker Gabbert was the next night watchman until he resigned in 1928. William Koch watched over the stores at night in 1929.

Following is historical data about some of the businesses currently in the Ojai Valley.

It was shortly after the original John Montgomery property was sold off along Ojai Avenue that a service station was built on the northwest corner of Montgomery Street and Ojai Avenue. J.R. Thurmond built the first one there in 1921.

In 1927, a service station and fruit stand were built at the bottom of the Dennison Grade on the Leach property, where Boccali's Restaurant is now. A man named Van Gordon managed it. Cecil Fisher ran a store on that site and it is not clear whether it was before or after 1927. In 1940, the store, then known as Crowder's Grocery, was replaced by a new building.

Frank Martin opened The Mysterious Inn in 1929 at 338 East Ojai Avenue, where the Ojai Valley Board of Realtors office is now. This later became the site of Ojai City Hall. The Ojai Museum took this space over in the early 1970s.

The City Garage, now the Ojai Valley Cleaners at 345 East Ojai Avenue, was established in 1921 by Chester D. Johnson. In 1930, it was sold to Frank C. and C.B. Johnson (no relation). Charles Quesnel and H.W. Butler bought it in 1933. Quesnel had been with Chester Johnson in the business from the beginning.

OVM
City Garage on the southwest corner of Montgomery Street and Ojai Avenue. Now Ojai Valley Cleaners.

Before Chester sold the business, a man came in one day to pay an old debt. He said that a year earlier, he stole $21 from Chester and he wanted to clear his conscience by paying it back.

In 1933, a unique grocery store, called the Alphabetical Store, opened in what was earlier the Triangle Market. Everything in the store was shelved alphabetically. A shopper would find cinnamon, carrots, cream and crackers in the same area, for example. Bread, bandages, beer and bologna would also be shelved together.

Austin Pierpont designed the little gas station on the southwest corner of Fox Street and Ojai Avenue for Elmer Friend in 1936.

The service station on the northwest corner of Ojai Avenue and Ventura Street was built in 1938.

The building that houses Rains 2 Apparel and Salon, at 209 East Matilija Street, was once a grocery store. Vans Market opened there in 1944. It was Car Low Market in 1954 and later Lee's Food Center.

A man named Tremaine bought the old Craft Market in the arcade in 1944. Three years later he built a new building on the northeast corner of Ojai Avenue and Canada Street. Shortly thereafter, he sold the market to Thomas "Slim" Bayless, who changed the name to Santa Cruz Market. Bayless built a new building across the street, at 131 West Ojai Avenue in 1952 and changed the name to Bayless Market. (Some say he didn't change the name until 1956). The market is now known as Starr Market.

Bert Hanson built Locker Market at 802 East Ojai Avenue in 1945.

Jim Neville and Edgar Pierce opened the Hitching Post Restaurant at Ojai Avenue and Bald Street in 1955. They advertised 19 cent hamburgers.

Ojai Valley Motors opened a car dealership at 821 West Ojai Avenue in 1955.

Profiles of Early Merchants

The Barrows Brothers

Thomas Barrows was born in 1843 and his brother, Frank Peleg, in 1850. The Barrows brothers had several things in common; they both suffered from throat and lung ailments and, when grown, they both sold Victor sewing machines in Chicago. They made pretty good money. When Thomas was 36 and his brother 29, they moved West seeking a healing climate. They arrived in Nordhoff in 1879. Frank bought the Nordhoff Hotel and changed the name to the Ojai Valley House. Later, he took over Herberts (then Gilberts) general merchandise store and ran it for several years. In 1891, Barrows was the largest store in town and he employed five clerks. Barrows store is now Rains Department Store. (Read the history of this long-running business in Chapter Seventeen.)

In 1882, Frank married Julia Smith (the daughter of S.S. Smith) and they lived in a handsome residence alongside a shaded brook on ten acres near the center of town on South Montgomery Street. Frank and Julia had three children; Albert, Stephen and Edward

Thomas bought 160 acres upon his arrival to Nordhoff and commenced raising good cattle and fine horses. Thomas married Sarah Coffin. She died during childbirth and he married Ella Cole. Thomas's children were Charlotte and David.

George Mallory

George Mallory came to the valley in 1886. He clerked in Frank Barrows' store for $30 per month before entering a partnership with Ed Ayers in the meat business in 1888. Two years later, George Mallory and Frank Dennison purchased Van Curen's dry goods store and continued it under the name of Mallory and Dennison Dry Goods for twenty-five years. An 1890 photo shows Mallory and Dennison's store just right of the Suess Grocery.

Mallory married Fannie McConnel. When she died, he married Lulu Dennison. His third wife was Mary Gally's niece, Mary Davison.

Mallory served as post master for eight years and was active in the Ojai State Bank and the Ojai Improvement Company. He was an elder in the Presbyterian Church, superintendent of the Sunday school program, a clerk for the Ojai Elementary School District and the mayor of Ojai in 1934-39. George Mallory died in 1939.

The Houk Family

Walter Houk and his wife Josepha (Carrillo), Leo Carrillo's cousin, lived in Carpinteria. Around the turn of the century their son, Fred, had a bad bout with pneumonia. When he seemed to have a difficult time recovering in the damp air near the coast, the family moved inland to Nordhoff.

To earn a living, Mr. Houk opened a grocery store just west of Signal Street on the south side of Ojai Avenue. He specialized in fresh meats and eventually dropped the grocery items altogether.

Around 1911, Houk built Nordhoff's first ice plant. Until then, they hauled ice blocks from Ventura. Since refrigeration was unheard of in those days, Mr. Houk kept his meats cool by placing ice on top of the storage chests. Having a place in town that manufactured ice was a most important step toward the health of the community.

Fred Houk used to help herd the cattle from Cuyama and the Sespe to his father's slaughterhouse on Foothill Road. When Edward Libbey began developing the Arbolada (an exclusive housing tract), he ordered the slaughterhouse moved west to Del Norte Street. He then built a lovely Spanish-style home on the old butchery site and named the cross street, appropriately, El Toro.

In 1911, Fred Houk married Ruth Jones and two years later, he built a home for her on a lot that his father had won in a poker game while on a train to Santa Barbara. Ruth lived in that home on what is now South Blanche Street, practically until her death in the late 1980s.

"There was no road then," Ruth recalled of the early days. "It stopped at the railroad tracks on the town side. I kept asking them to make the road lead from our house to town, but they said that too many crossings in a town were dangerous."

She told me that the Hobsons owned the land next to theirs. It included the site where city hall is now on Ventura and Santa Ana Streets. According to Mrs. Houk, "Their home was not as elegant then. Mrs. Hobson spent years transforming it from a simple structure to a splendid estate."

About the time the newlywed Houks were settled in, Walter sold the meat market in Ojai and bought another one in Carpinteria. He sent Fred and Ruth there to run it and they rented out their Ojai home. Later, Walter bought George Harris' meat market at 238 East Ojai Avenue (where Gracie's Antique Mall is today) and Fred ran it for the following thirty years.

Benjamin Maddox

Benjamin F. Maddox, one of eighteen children and a native of Kentucky, moved to Illinois at the age of 10. When he was of age, he enlisted in the 57th Illinois Volunteer Infantry, Company E. He was with General Sherman on his march from Atlanta to the sea.

After the war, Maddox went to Kansas, married Jennie R. Whaley and in 1874, they came to Ventura County. According to Yda Storke's book of biographical sketches, Maddox was a carpenter by trade until an accident forced him to quit and then he moved to Matilija Canyon and began raising bees.

The Maddox's had two sons and two daughters, Harry, Forrest, Lela and Eugenia.

In 1886, Maddox ran the only livery in town. By 1891, he had sixteen horses and ten conveyances.

Charles Kincher

Charles H. Kincher ran a laundry for many years in Ojai. In 1889, he married Mary Suess and they had five children including, a set of twins who died during their first year of whooping cough and a son, Earl, who had a severe case of curvature of the spine and died at the age of 8.

The Kinchers built a laundry facility on Montgomery Street in 1907.

Harry Hunt

Harry Hunt came to Nordhoff in 1900 and opened a transfer business. He hauled oranges to Ventura to be shipped by steamer to San Francisco. Hunt is reported to have brought the first motor truck into the valley in 1917. In 1919, he advertised eighteen autos for hire. W.E. Mallory and W.A. Rowe leased the Hunt building in 1944 and opened a Chevrolet agency there which they ran until 1952.

Chapter Eleven
Nordhoff Transformed

Edward Drummond Libbey

Edward Drummond Libbey initially experienced Ojai Valley in the winter of 1908 when he and his wife, Florence (Scott), came here to visit a long-time friend, Harry Sinclair, a former hardware merchant in Toledo. At Sinclair's suggestion, the wealthy glass manufacturer lodged at the plush Foothills Hotel.

Libbey was entranced by this rural mecca, so dissimilar to his hometown of Toledo. While Libbey yearned to spend all of his winters here, it is said that his wife preferred Pasadena. But they built a home on Foothill Road, a cabin across the street for their Chinese cook and servants and a stable at the north end of what is now Del Norte Road.

Edward was born in 1854, the son of William L. and Julia (Miller) Libbey of Chelsea, Massachusetts. William Libbey had worked as a confidential clerk for Deming Jarvis, with whom the history of cut glass reportedly began. After just five years with Jarvis and Commeraise, glass importers and manufacturers, Mr. Libbey purchased the small factory, and when he was 19 years-old, Edward joined his father in the business.

William set up a strenuous apprenticeship for his son – one that would fit him for executive responsibilities. And so it was that on his father's death, in 1883, Edward became sole owner of the company.

The discovery of natural gas in northwestern Ohio lured Libbey to Toledo in 1888. He invested all he had in a glass plant there. Five years later, Libbey set up a display at the Columbian Exposition in Chicago to demonstrate the art of making cut glass.

Preparing for this project depleted his limited funds and he asked a local banker for a loan. To his surprise, the banker loaned him the $100,000 he needed. His exhibit was a tremendous success and, when the fair ended, Libbey had collected more than enough to pay the bank back.

Michael J. Owens, a superintendent in Libbey's factory, developed a glass-blowing machine and Libbey financed his project to start the Owens Bottle Machine Company in 1903.

Later, Libbey and his associates perfected a process for making sheet glass, using Irving W. Colburn's basic idea. In 1906, Libbey organized Libbey-

Toledo Museum of Art
Edward Drummond and Florence Libbey.

Owens-Ford Glass Company. Libbey remained involved in each of these companies until shortly before his death.

Despite vast business affiliations, Mr. and Mrs. Libbey traveled extensively in this and others countries. They spent most of their time, however, in Toledo or Nordhoff.

With each passing year as a part-time resident, Libbey became more and more enchanted by the valley's country charm. He felt, however, that the village itself typified most western towns and it lacked distinction. The dusty main street was lined with little shops, hastily built years earlier without much concern for design. He wanted to find a way to preserve the rustic characteristics of Nordhoff while changing those features not in harmony with the lovely landscape.

Libbey discussed his idea with key civic leaders and they thought it was an excellent one. To develop Libbey's concepts, the town chiefs formed the Ojai Valley Men's League with Sherman Thacher as president, Walter Bristol as secretary/treasurer and with Libbey on the executive committee.

On April 24, 1914, eighty-seven men attended a special town improvement meeting at which Libbey introduced his ideas.

Having received overwhelming approval from the community, he hired San Diego architect, Richard S. Requa to look the town over.

Requa prepared sketches of a Spanish arcade which would front Nordhoff's shabby shopping district and contribute uniformity and style to it. Libbey shared the drawings with local merchants and offered to assume financial responsibility for the project if they would each contribute $10 per frontage foot of their store space. With everyone in enthusiastic agreement, Robert Winfield began construction on the north side of Ojai Avenue.

David Mason collection
Ojai Avenue before the arcade was built.

David Mason collection
J.J. Burke of Ojai Realty Company (right) standing with workers during the final stages of arcade construction, 1917

One can only imagine the excitement everyone felt as they watched the transformation taking place. In an article in the September 1, 1916 newspaper, the editor describes there being terra cotta brick and other construction materials piled everywhere in the town as the arches quickly took shape.

The project didn't end with the arcade: the center piece was yet to come. Libbey purchased the land across the street from the arcade and ordered everything removed from the area except the oak trees. Ira Gosnell headed the crew to tear down the dilapidated Ojai Inn and Berry Villa. Also on the south side of Ojai Avenue were the old post office, a plumbing shop, barber shop and Brady's kitchen. The post office was moved across the street just east of Clark's Livery.

They hauled away two truckloads of iron from the former site of Charlie Gibson's blacksmith shop, which was where the post office would go. Requa designed the sixty-five-foot post office tower and had a lovely arbor constructed to the east. Libbey also ordered new tennis courts built in the present-day Libbey Park.

OVM
L-R, Ojai Bank, Pergola, Post Office and Arcade.

When Libbey revealed his desire to finance the project and to donate the post office and adjoining property for a park, town leaders established the Ojai Civic Association for the purpose of accepting the gifts. On March 2, 1917, these people became members: Edward D. Libbey, Sherman D. Thacher, John J. Burke, Harrison Wilson, Harry R. Sinclair, Arthur A. Garland and H.R. Cole.

The following month, the Men's League, in order to express its gratitude and give the community a chance to do likewise, planned a big celebration in the new Civic Center Park. They wanted to call it Libbey Day, but Mr. Libbey asked that they not bestow glory on a man, but instead honor their beautiful town. He called the celebration Ojai Day.

At that first Ojai Day in April, 1917, S.D. Thacher said, during his remarks in accepting the deed for the Ojai Civic Association, "Ojai-Libbey Day is now a fixed anniversary fully as important as Thanksgiving."

In a May 11, 1917 article in *The Ojai,* Richard Requa talked about why he chose this particular design for Nordhoff. He said, "Something had to be devised to take the place of the ugly metal awnings used to protect the buildings and the walk from the heat of summer and the storms of winter. Considering the setting of magnificent trees and semi-tropical verdure, the towering encircling mountains, the desire to maintain the primitive simplicity of the valley and historic architecture of Southern California, nothing seemed so perfectly adapted for the work as a style inspired by the Spaniards in the New World. The simple lines and curves, the early Mission arcades and portales, the wrought grilles and balconies and modest towers, all seemed to take their places among the trees and shrubs as though they had been placed there by nature when in one of her happier moods she fashioned and adorned the valley."

Requa continued, "To complete the architectural scheme and provide a dominant note for the design, a building with a simple yet monumental tower was considered necessary in the corner of the park front." He shares the inspiration for his designs, "The broad elliptical arches of the San Juan Capistrano Mission suggested the treatment in front of the stores. The large and beautiful entranceway on the east of San Louis Rey Mission was modified for use as the entrances to the park. A simple Spanish treatment of the Italian pergola connected these arches and provided the charming framed vistas into the park."

Requa said that the post office is ornamented with simple details of the cathedrals of Mexico, the finials from the convent entrance at Queretaro (a city in Mexico known for its 16th century cathedrals), the portale or combination of column and arch from Calle Principal in Morelia (in southwest Mexico) and the side entrance from a private house in Morelia. The general idea of the tower was suggested by the towers of the Columbus cathedral in Havana (Cuba), although the details were taken from various cathedrals and churches in Spanish America."

Requa brought Robert Winfield in as the builder for this project. The two men had worked together in San Diego. Harry Sinclair supervised the job.

In a 1960 interview in *The Ojai Valley News,* Robert Winfield reminisced about his friend, Libbey. He said, "Libbey was a real pusher and organizer who was continually sparking with ideas. He was full of ideas and he was just as ready to accept anyone else's if he thought they were good."

Who was this man of generosity? How did he come across to the townspeople of the village? In an interview years later, arcade builder, Robert Winfield said that, although Libbey dressed well all the time, he wasn't uppity. In fact, says Winfield, "He loved to sit around and chat with the boys on a warm, dreamy afternoon under the oaks."

The reporter asked why Libbey took such an interest in the Ojai Valley as to drop thousands of dollars here. Winfield said, "Oh that's easy. He told me he'd been all over the world and he'd seen only two places to compare with it – one in Syria and the other on the Bosphorus and Ojai beat them both."

Those living in the valley in the 1950s through the 70s or 80s will remember a ramp along the sidewalk in the arcade. According to Winfield, "Dr. Saeger had a drugstore at what is now the top of the ramp and he didn't want the grade lowered because it would have meant an additional step up to his store. At first there was a step-down and later it was turned into a ramp." My father, Dalton Munger, recalls the steps. His mother had a café in the original drug store building in the early 1930s and he remembers having to maneuver those steps on his clip-on roller skates while entertaining himself by skating along the arcade or while on an errand for his mother.

There's a story in the August. 4, 1916 issue of *The Ojai* about wrecking Clark's stables to make room for a modern garage and auto and horse livery. The reporter said, "The framework of the main part of the old landmark will remain after being shorn of eight or ten feet of frontage." They ended up having to take down the whole barn, though and that's when the rock work on the west side of the building was done. Phillip Scheidecker of Los Angeles was the craftsman on the project. When the arcade was completed, *The Ojai* editor suggested creating a tea garden on the roof. This never came to pass, however.

In 1927, the arcade was extended 100 feet and seven new store spaces created. John Roine was in charge of construction for this project. Already doing business there were W.H. Hays, shoemaker, Alice Misbeek, beauty parlor operator and Dr. Maude Rancia. While the beauty parlor and doctor's office would stay, owner, Eugene Munson planned to replace Hays' building as it was one of the oldest in town. Shortly after starting construction, Munson, said that he had more inquiries for space in the new building than he would have rooms available, but he intended making his selection of tenants carefully, choosing only those who would be most beneficial to the community.

In the late 1980s, the arcade went through a major renovation. The city spent a million dollars to render it seismically safe.

The Post Office

In the early days, a local merchant distributed the mail from his place of business. A new postmaster was appointed on an average of every six years. The reason for this seemingly frequent turnover was the nationwide understanding that all postmasters be of the same party as the current United States president.

In 1893, there was quite a controversy regarding the law. When Grover Cleveland (Democrat) replaced Benjamin Harrison (Republican) as president, Benjamin F. Spencer was expected to turn his postmastership over to a deserving Democrat.

The people of Ojai Valley wanted to keep Spencer, however, and several influential residents signed a letter to the Ojai Club requesting that they arrange a public election for the position of postmaster.

This election aroused widespread interest as, not only was this small town going against United States government policy, but they allowed even the women to vote. Most people agreed that since the women used the post office too, they should have a vote. Ballots issued to women, however, were of a different color for easy identification. There were no nominations. People simply wrote their choice for postmaster on a ballot and Democrat

George Mallory won the four-year term.

In 1897, the town built a small, nondescript structure from which to handle postal duties. Then Libbey built a new post office and it became the most significant structure in town.

The 1,152-square-foot building served the community sufficiently for twenty years, throughout Clara King Craig's term as postmistress. In 1938, after Mattie McCormick became postmistress, Ojai enlarged its post office by 500 square feet and, in 1949, nearly doubled the floor space.

Ten years later, when George Busch was postmaster, the government asked the city to find another location for a new post office building. The city council and the planning commission agreed to consider the move, but members of the Ojai Civic Association were definitely against it. When their limited voice seemed insignificant, they called upon valley residents for support.

One thousand people signed the petition which the Ojai Civic Association drew up, demonstrating that they wanted the post office to remain in its original location. This, one of the largest petitions in the history of Ojai City Hall, was successful. There was just one problem. The government deemed the post office inadequate, so it had to be replaced.

By then, time was limited and there was a cost factor, so the Ojai Civic Association decided to act as contractor for the project. Builders completed the project in 196 days, nine of which were spent razing the old building. They finally had to use dynamite to shake the foundation loose. Postal employees, in the meantime, conducted business in the old Bank of America building which had recently been replaced by a more modern bank structure.

Post office inspectors later were surprised at the quality of workmanship in the job. The fact that the builders finished well within the time limit and under the proposed cost also impressed them.

The spotlight shone brightly on the post office in 1959, as people directed their attention to the activity and progress there. Then, a rumor sprang up that the tower was leaning. People stopped to see this phenomenon for themselves and the more they studied the structure, the more it seemed to tilt. Public concern finally warranted a professional investigation and they asked Major Dron, a local engineer, to conduct an examination. He eventually determined that the tower stood in perfect alignment; it was the Edison power pole next to it that was leaning.

Prior to World War I, female mail carriers were unheard of. The shortage of manpower during the war, however, prompted Helen Robinson to take the job "just to help out." When the war was over, she decided to make this her career. She delivered mail in a horse and buggy initially and then in a black Model T. Since she came into town every day, Helen drove neighboring upper valley children to high school. She retired from the postal department after thirty-four years with the distinction of having only once been unable to deliver the mail and that was because of a landslide on Dennison Grade.

In 1968, the Altrusa Club donated the Westminster chimes to the Ojai Civic Association for the post office bell tower. In 1981, while a repairman was preparing to reinstall the chimes, he turned his back in search of a tool and someone stole them from the sidewalk. Ojai's sense of public spirit prevailed, however, and someone anonymously replaced the chimes for the community.

The Pergola

While the original arcade still stands, the pergola lasted just over fifty years. The park front became a victim of the turbulent 1960s. Piece by piece, vandals chipped away at the pergola and arches. On December 30, 1967, someone made a final protest statement when they bombed the west section of the arbor. While some blame the hippies, others say it was an anti-hippy act.

For the next three years, Ojai Civic Association members and city officials argued about whether to remove the rest of the pergola or to repair it. The community spoke out loud and clear; they wanted it restored. When the board announced its decision to destroy the damaged structure, several hundred people demonstrated against the judgment. Tempers flared and some citizens even threatened violence. The pergola won a temporary stay.

Because of continuing vandalism and other problems over the years, it began to make more sense to Ojai Civic Association members to put the responsibility for the little park in the city's hands. So on March 2, 1971 with permission from the Libbey Foundation, the Ojai Civic Association deeded the park over to the city with all of Libbey's original restrictions.

A group headed by Dr. Charles Butler raised $9,000 to rebuild the pergola. But it was too late. Once in control, the city ordered the unsafe pergola removed. And so it was that early one morning in March of 1971, before most objectors were up

OVM
The pergola and post office covered with snow.

and about, the pergola was secretly demolished. This act angered some and saddened many, but others were glad to see the pretty little park opened up to the street.

In 1999, a committee spearheaded by architect, David Bury, historian, David Mason and Joan Kemper and with the overwhelming support of the community, rebuilt the beloved pergola. They raised the funds for the project and even used Requa's original plans so that it is an exact replica of the original. When workers began the construction, they uncovered the old foundation for the pergola and discovered that they were just one-half inch off by their calculations in replacing it.

Fountains

Evelyn Nordhoff, daughter of Charles and Lida Fallen (Letford) Nordhoff, was a bookbinder. She died in 1898 at the age of 33 of an attack of appendicitis shortly before she was to be married. In 1904, Olivia and Caroline Stokes donated a fountain to the town of Nordhoff in Evelyn's memory.

The Stokes sisters had inherited quite a bit of money. Never married, they spent their time traveling and they gave numerous gifts worldwide. Olivia and Caroline visited Ojai in 1903 and got the idea for the gift at that time.

Built in 1904 and placed in the center of town, an editor for the *Ventura Free Press* said the fountain was "one of the finest in the state."

The fountain was designed by S.M. Jesley, the architect for the Boyd Club and the Foothills Hotel. It was constructed of one large boulder found near the Gridley place. The lion's heads were from tougher stone brought in from Montecito. Hard stone was also used on the coping of the trough to survive the striking of wagon poles as buggy horses drank. This was a unique design as it was convenient for the buggy horse to quench its thirst as well as the saddle horse, dogs and people. The cost for the twelve by nine by two-foot fountain was $1000. A plaque, dedicating the fountain in Evelyn Hunter Nordhoff's memory, was affixed.

During Libbey's town facelift project, the memorial fountain, originally built on the south side of Ojai Avenue across from Barrows store, was moved back four feet and incorporated into the pergola structure.

When the pergola was removed, so was the fountain and its remains were stored in the city yard. Before its removal, however, a member of the Nordhoff family pried off the memorial plaque and took it to the family home in Connecticut for safe keeping. Once they knew that Ojai had a museum where it would be secure and appreciated, they returned it for display.

In the meantime, someone visiting the city yard one day, confiscated the lions heads as they felt they were in danger of being destroyed by weather and negligence. Once word of the pergola and fountain restoration was out, however, these items were returned to the project.

The Tom Clark fountain was built on what was known as the Grand Avenue Trail (Grand Avenue near Gridley) in 1942 as a memorial to the supervisor. This watering trough has been removed and will be rebuilt for use by horses along the Southern Pacific right-of-way walking/biking/riding trail through Ojai.

Sherman Thacher built a Japanese fountain at the northeast corner of Grand Avenue and McNell Road in 1906-07 for students to water their horses on their way home from town. Evidently, there had been some problems with overheated horses arriving at the school after the long ride and he built the fountain to remedy this.

There were several levels of drinking areas in this fountain. The fountain was still in use in 1932.

The fountain inside Libbey Park resulted from a bequest by Mary Gray left in 1953. In 1976, with the pergola gone and the park opened up, the city launched a contest offering $1,000 to the person who could design the best fountain for Libbey Park. A panel of citizens selected Boris Bruenwald's sketch of a nude Indian maiden, but a storm of protests countered this decision. Letters inundated the news editor's desk from people objecting to the ethnic reference and to the fact that the statue was nude. Finally, the city paid Bruenwald for his time and trouble and commissioned a Los Angeles firm to build an ordinary park fountain, which was quietly dedicated in 1977.

A Change of Names

During the town's transformation under Libbey's guidance, an old issue surfaced once again – changing the town name. People had always thought of the valley as Ojai and, over the years, they attempted to give the village that name too. In 1894, residents launched a weak campaign to change the name back to the original Chumash word. Tourism was down then and they felt it was because a place having two names made advertising ineffective.

In 1916, the anti-Nordhoffians assembled and agreed that they resented their town having a German name. The name change came before the Ojai Valley Men's League and the possibilities proposed were Ojai, The Ojai, Ojai Valley and Nordhoff. Hopelessly divided, they placed blanks throughout the town to let the people vote. In October of 1916, ballots were placed in the bank, Mallory and Dennisons store, the drugstore, Burke's office and C.A. Stewart's real estate office. There were 35 votes for Ojai, 5 for Ojai Valley and 107 for Nordhoff, and none for The Ojai.

Mr. Morse, manager of the Foothills Hotel, later appeared with a petition to change the name to Ojai. So mighty is the power of personality and petition that practically everyone signed for Ojai.

206

One argument for the change during that period was that Nordhoff and Norwalk were so similar in spelling it might confuse the postal staff. Ojai, everyone felt, was a name unlike any other. Those against the change were mostly long-time residents with superstitions – thinking bad luck would surely visit their town if they tampered with the name. Coincidentally, it was later that very year that two huge fires burned large sections of the community. (Details of major fires in Chapter Nine).

OVM
The arcade after the 1917 fire.

On March 23, 1917, official notice arrived. The message read, "You may announce change of name from Nordhoff to Ojai. Best wishes, James D. Phelan, U.S. Senator." Mr. Libbey was out of town when this historical telegram arrived and upon his return, he promptly asked Tom Clark, "What town is this?" The answer, "Ojai" pleased him very much.

What with Libbey's drastic village alterations, the dusty, little town was definitely growing up. Soon the question of incorporation came before the community and eighty people signed a petition for incorporation. On August 5, 1921, Ojai became a city with 500 residents.

The first Ojai Board of Trustees meeting was held August 8, 1921. These men were on the board: Earl Soule, Ira Gosnell,

Frank Mead, Glen H. Hickey and Mr. Miller. They appointed Clyde Stewart as City Clerk and Louis C. Drapeau as city attorney. Fred Linder was elected fire chief and H.H. Keil served as Ojai City Marshal, License Collector and Superintendent of Streets and Sewers.

The Marshal's first recorded action was to remove a bootblack stand from the sidewalk and ask the City Garage employees to keep the noise down during Sunday morning services at the nearby Presbyterian Church.

Harry Hunt (not the auto livery owner) was constable in the 1930s and 40s. A one-armed man, Hunt was killed in 1943, when he was shot while trying to apprehend a fugitive in Steckle Park, Santa Paula. The next constable was H.L. Cummings.

Joseph C. Welch, the first city manager, was hired in 1951. John O'Neill was the first building inspector, 1953. Glen H. Hickey was the first mayor.

Other early mayors included Frank Mead, Earl Soule, Alton Drown, George Mallory, Alfred Houk and Fred Linder. Harriet Vonderembs was the first woman council member and the first woman mayor. Robert King Sr., Monroe Hirsch and Robert Lagomarsino all served during the 1950s. The 1960s mayors were Ralph Bennett and A.R. Huckens. William J. Burr, Jr., James Loebl and John Fay held the mayoral position throughout the 1970s and Derald Chisum was elected mayor in 1980.

The first chief of police separate from the superintendent of streets and sewers, was recognized in June, 1950, during Charles W. Robinson's term. James D. Alcorn held that position longer than anyone else – serving for nearly twenty-two years. Vincent France became chief of police in 1975.

Judge Gabbert resigned after thirty-two years as Justice of the Peace in 1954 and Woodruff Deem takes his place.

Ken McDonald was elected Ventura County Supervisor for the Ojai District in 1960.

The Arbolada

It is said that, in the 19-teens, someone was eyeing 360 acres across Foothill Road from Libbey's home for the purpose of establishing a sawmill. Libbey, reportedly, bought the land himself to save the beautiful oak trees from the woodmen's ax.

He built an entrance path across from his home, put up a large, decorative metal gate, and hired F.C. Fassel to landscape the acreage. In the effort, they removed 3,000 tons of rocks and used them to line five miles of winding roads through the tract. In 1917, six train carloads of trees and plants arrived for use in the park. This beautiful property soon became known as Libbey Park.

Libbey originally called the area Encina Vista. In 1922, he hired black Santa Barbara architect, George Washington Smith, to design three Spanish-style houses in his park to demonstrate the type of architecture he felt would compliment the surroundings. To make room for one of the homes, they had to remove an old slaughterhouse. Libbey named the nearest street El Toro to commemorate this historical structure.

Libbey opened the sale of lots to his Eastern friends first. He printed elaborate, multi-paged brochures advertising the Arbolada, claiming that one could build a comfortable home there for $10,000. Unfortunately he didn't live to see this particular dream realized, as it took Detroit real estate man Rawson Harmon until 1958 to sell the last lot.

One early resident in the Arbolada was Bill Lucking who, reportedly, bought Libbey's stable and hired Austin Pierpont to design a home there for him.

Gusta Lundine Linebarger photo
The Arbolada

Edward Drummond Libbey died of pneumonia in 1925 in Toledo at the age of 71. Toledoans flew flags at half mast and many businesses closed for the day. Messages of condolence poured in to his family and friends from all around the world. More than a thousand people gathered at the Toledo Museum of Art in tribute to its principal benefactor. Newspapers everywhere eulogized him as Toledo's foremost citizen, connoisseur of art, glass magnate, multi-millionaire and most generous philanthropist.

Libbey's total estate was reported to be $21,714,087. His will was an interesting one. His cash bequests included almost ten million dollars. He left it not only to family members but also to many institutions, charities and friends, including a $5,000 gift to each of two Ojai friends, C.H. Johnston and Frank Mead and $25,000 to Ojaian Harry Sinclair. He also left his chauffeur and his groundskeeper $10,000 and $5,000 respectively.

Chapter Twelve
Entertainment and the Arts

During those very early years in Ojai Valley, entertainment was pretty much left up to the individual. People weren't used to being formally entertained. They made their own fun, either reading alone or as a family group; by singing or reciting or with friends at a picnic, a taffy pull or a parlor social.

During the 1870s, the scattered settlers threw ghost surprise parties for fun. Thomas Bard had one at his house on Creek Road. The object of these popular parties seemed to be to surprise the guests by revealing who had played the part of the ghost that evening.

In the 1880s, the town staged a few annual community events. The calico ball was a popular affair. Everyone congregated at the Nordhoff schoolhouse – the men wearing their best overalls and the women in colorful calico prints.

Some enterprising person originated the valley's first and only nut social. One could gain admission only by bringing a nut to crack. The Thacher School boys' entries were the most original; they brought coconuts.

In 1882, citizens enjoyed jelly socials where everyone shared their favorite jar of homemade jelly. George Stewart once threw a go-as-you-please party at his home, a forerunner of the come-as-you-are party, no doubt. Young and old alike enjoyed riding atop a wagon load of hay along country roads together or gathering in a neighbor's spacious yard for an ice cream social.

The Jack Bennett family had an enviable reputation for entertaining. In 1894, they threw a party and played musical chairs, had a talent show and enjoyed a sing-along. Someone else invited guests to a cobweb social that year. There they sang, played games and untangled cobwebs for prizes. The Presbyterian Church held a poverty social once, with "hard times" as the theme. Refreshments consisted of bread, water and a toothpick. Anyone who lived through it would surely never forget the April fools dance at the Poplins in 1897. The hosts served a cake filled with cayenne pepper. They made sure that a bucket of water sat nearby, but to everyone's dismay someone had poured salt into it.

David Mason collection
A social at the San Antonio School.

In 1898, some mischievous people staged a watermelon stealing party. They arranged for the farmer to go along with the prank. Later on, Earl Soule became famous for his watermelon patch. Grown men, who are grandfathers and great-grandfathers now, delight in relating stories of their particular expertise at pilfering one of Soule's watermelons.

At the turn of the century, the community held dance parties at the Ojai Inn (the original Blumberg Hotel). Dance instruction was always available for those who needed it.

About twice a year a medicine show came to town. Generally, two or three actors performed attention-getting skits. When the crowd had gathered, a professional hawker described the wonders of his medicinal cure-all. This performance was usually topped off by a movie at the schoolhouse. They couldn't show the motion picture from inside the wooden structure, however, because the celluloid film created an enormous fire hazard. So, the troupe parked their truck close to the building and projected the movie through an open window for the pleasure of the audience seated inside.

Picture Shows and Theater

Two men named F.W. Hawes and Mr. Hayward brought the first real picture show to Nordhoff in 1911. A reported 200 people paid 20 cents each (10 cents for children) to attend this experimental event. The evening was not without problems. The generator ran out of gas halfway through the film showing and when Hawes refilled it, the odor floated heavily throughout the hall frightening the people.

Later, several moviegoers expressed their objections to the behavior of small boys in the theater. Hawes and Hayward were discouraged by the lack of appreciation and the unkind remarks. It cost them $3.00 per hour to run their movie equipment and that expense was another reason why they closed down after just two showings and decided to wait for electricity.

J.J. Burke purchased the southwest corner of Signal Street and Ojai Avenue and moved the print shop, which was headquarters for *The Ojai,* to the rear of the property. Then he built a movie theater, the Isis Theater, which opened in 1914. Lacey Clark operated the theater for a time and then E.A. Runkle took over.

He advertised skilled musicians, clean and interesting amusement, sober drama and hilarious comedy. There were two plays there each week – on Wednesday and Saturday. After Saturday's entertainment, people removed the chairs for social dancing. Runkle charged 5 cents per dance. After each waltz or fox-trot, participants paraded around the room, money in hand, to pay for the previous pleasure. Some say there was more marching going on than dancing.

The first motion picture shown in the theater was Jack London's *Valley of the Moon.* Claude Munger cranked the old projector for Runkle's silent films and Ethel Runkle and Marion Munger (Claude's sister) played the piano. The ladies had no music sheets to follow, so they played while watching the movie, setting their tempo and style accordingly.

Talkies didn't come to Ojai until 1930.

Bands

Ojai seemed always to have its own music-makers. Lowell Otis Reese organized the first Ojai Band in 1894 under the sponsorship of the Ojai Club. They rehearsed at the Nordhoff schoolhouse two evenings per week. The band members originally wore gray uniforms with black trim, but later changed to white duck. The Ojai Band was often commissioned to serenade newly married couples as well as to perform at political functions.

Early band members were Charles Carne, Fred Hudiburg, Eddie Ayers, George Schroff, David Warner, Charles Mathews, Charles Stutsman, Frank Gibson, Schuyler Dennison, Milo Waite, Jack Parker, Arthur Horne, Ezra Taylor, Waldo Dennison and Vernon Gelett. Frank Parrish and William Gray joined the group later. When Reese left the valley, Charles Stutsman, whose home still stands in the upper valley, directed the band.

OVM

Ojai Valley Band, 1908. Front (l-r), unknown, Harry Dennison, Bert Conrey, Levi Bray, Mr. Simmons (band master), Jim Fordyce, Frank Spencer, Jack Bennett, Eddie Schroff, Benny Houk (Mascot). Rear, Tom MacGuire, Boyd Henry, Claude Gallentine, Selwyn Beaman, _____ Wurm, John Fordyce, Charles, Robinson, Charley Stutsman, Ernest Clark, John Thompson, Frank deLine, Charles Baker, Howard Gally.

In 1907, Ojai Valley Band members included Benny Houk, Selwyn Beaman, Boyd Henry, Jim Fordyce, Frank Spencer, Charles Baker, Howard Gally, Claude Gallentine, Bert Conrey, Charlie Robinson, Henry Dennison and Levy Bray. John and Jim Thompson were also part of the band, but John's son, John, Jr. says, "I don't know what they were doing in the band. Neither one of them had any music in them."

The Ojai Band of 1917 included R.O. Robinson, director, Jack Bennett, E.A. Snelling, Dwight Van Fleet, Roy Berry, Grant Stutsman, Abe Downing, Nelson Cota, Charles Stutsman, James Fordyce and E.A. Runkle.

Dick Robinson led a dance orchestra called the Cavaliers in 1924. Members were George Miller, Grant Stutsman, Fred Henderson, George Noble, Charles Stutsman, Melvin Clover, Edwin Joy and Albert Griffin. Their first public appearance was reportedly in what was then called Meiners Ojai Oaks during the big land development promotion there in the 1920s.

OVM

Dick Robinson's Cavalier Orchestra, 1925. Front, Edwin Joy, piano; George Miller, sax; Dick Robinson, conductor. Back row, Charles Stutsman, sousaphone; George Noble, violin; Norton Warden, sax; Grant Stutsman, trumpet; Melvin Clover, banjo and Albert Griffin, Drums.

In the 1930s, a group of musical valleyites gathered under the old name of Ojai Valley Band. Together they scoured county attics and barns in search of idle and forgotten instruments. They found about twenty pieces. The band practiced in the basement of the Boyd Club until the card players upstairs complained about the noise. Then they moved to the Hickey Hardware building.

This assemblage of musicians was diversified, to say the least. The oldest band member was 75 and the youngest was 9. Harry Hunt, the one-armed constable, played bass. The alto horn player was also missing an arm. One man was nearly blind. He played the horn entirely by memory. Lynn Rains and his son, Alan, played trombones, while Roy Hass played clarinet. Bob and Charles Noren, Frank Roller and Ferris McDermitt were also band members.

The Ojai Valley Band performed the opening day concert at the first county fair after World War II and at the cemetery each Memorial Day.

In 1937, Ruth Quimby, the music teacher at Ojai Valley School, organized the Ojai Valley Community Orchestra. Playing violins were Monica Ros, Miss Alice Robertson, Miss Alyce Corbyn, Miss Anna L. Byles, Miss Peggy Smith, Miss Monge and John M. Forbes. Mrs. Howard Gally and Frank Roller played violas. On cello were Dr. Charles T. Butler, John P. Ascot (a teacher at Ojai Valley School) and W. M. Slaughter. Miss Margaret Perkins and Miss Ruth Robertson played the piano.

In 1990, Sara Beeby of Cape Cod, Massachusetts came here and brought the concept of a local band with her, she says, "to offer the community free, wholesome and uplifting musical entertainment." She held auditions for all ages and the first concert was in June, 26, 1991 with an audience of 300 people. Held in the gazebo at Libbey Park every Wednesday evening from July 4th though August at 8, the program always includes charming children's marches which are led by a local celebrity.

By 1993, the band of thirty-five members had outgrown the gazebo, so they built a larger bandstand. In 1999, the community band boasts fifty musicians. Their new director, Joe Boccali, has been with the band from the beginning.

Artists in the Community

Between the wars, Ojai went on a cultural jag. The Ojai Valley Woman's Club started an all-woman community chorus in 1925. After ten years, they invited men to sing with them. By then, some Ojai Valley School teachers had established an English folk dance group. Also notable were the Ojai Community Players, an orchestra started by violinist Roderick White and citizens interested in dramatic performances.

People were engaged in numerous arts and crafts. Creativity was high, but an adequate place to cultivate these talents was lacking. Each group used whatever hotel lobby, schoolhouse, private home or barn that was available when they happened to need it.

During the 1930s, craftspeople gathered in the old library on Friday nights to weave silk, linen and wool and to do raffia work, make wooden toys and decorate with linoleum blocks. The choral group was meeting at the Presbyterian Church and Krotona. The theater branch was rehearsing at city hall and the English Folk Dance Society members were dancing at the women's clubhouse.

In 1936, Dr. Charles T. Butler, being involved with three of these art forms, envisioned a local center where each branch could pursue its interest fully and comfortably. His idea caused great enthusiasm among the artistic community. He just hoped they were also willing to finance it. First, he reportedly went East, contacted those who owned winter homes in Ojai and asked them for donations. He received $6,000 in pledges. With this as incentive, he campaigned locally for an equal amount.

In 1937, the committee was presenting neighborhood teas to acquaint people with the idea of the art center and to get feedback about this project from the residents of the outlying communities.

A thermometer in the post office window kept villagers informed as to how much was being collected. It took a while, but finally donations, ranging in amounts from 5 cents to $499 sent the red line all the way to the top of the gauge. When adding in those who pledged services instead of cash, the list of donors totaled over 500 people.

The committee purchased the former library site on South Montgomery Street. They considered using the old wooden structure as part of their complex, but ended up giving it to the Boy Scouts, instead.

A contest was launched to find an architect who could build the art center for $12,000. Austin Pierpont won. Sam Hudiburg was the builder.

On July 5, 1939, workers broke ground and they completed the project in November. Naturally, Charles Butler opened the dedication ceremonies. He proudly and happily addressed 300 people on the Ojai Community Art Center patio. Mayor Houk laid the cornerstone which contained a lead casket with an American flag, coins, stamps, a picture of Ojai, a list of all of those people having anything to do with the advent of the art center, newspaper accounts publicizing the project, a replica of the thermometer and of Pooh, Austin Pierpont's spaniel, who was always with him on the job.

A variety of artists with assorted styles and mediums have shown some very interesting exhibits in the Ojai Community Art Center over the years. In 1945, for instance, local military men, who were stationed at the Ojai Valley Inn, displayed their artistic talents in the gallery.

The Ojai Center For the Arts, as it is known today, at 113 South Montgomery Street, is a place of fellowship where the community can study and enjoy varied artistic ventures just as Charles Butler visualized it over six decades ago.

High Valley Theater

After the Russian Revolution, Anton Chekov's nephew, Michael Chekov, started an acting group. He gathered performers from all over the world. With Daphne Moore of England, Erica Chambliss of Vienna, Woodrow Chambliss, a graduate of Baylor University in Texas, Iris Tree and others, he held a workshop at Dartington Hall in England. In 1935, the troupe moved to Richfield, Connecticut. They toured the country with a repertoire that included *Twelfth Night* and *Cricket on the Hearth*. At the outbreak of World War II, the Chekov Group disbanded.

In 1940, Iris Tree came to Ojai. The Chamblisses joined her here the following year. Shortly after their arrival they performed at the Ojai Community Art Center. *The Emperor's New Clothes* starred Charles Butler, Constance Wash, Mrs. Gorham, Woody and Erica Chambliss, Daphne Moore and David Heilweil. The group also presented *Macbeth* for the original Ojai Festivals program in 1946. The Chekov Players are said to have brought polished productions to the little community theater. But these artists seemed also to cause some dissension here. Locals wanted to keep the art center for the amateur and began to resent the intrusion of the more professional actors.

As a solution, Mary Frances Clark offered the Chekov Players use of the abandoned upper valley schoolhouse and they dubbed the building the High Valley Theater. Alan Harkness directed most of the performances there. The tiny, country stage attracted some great talent. A most admired Hollywood theater group, the Circle Players, performed there in 1948. The cast included Joe Mantrell, Ford Rainey and Sidney Chaplin, son of Charlie Chaplin. Famous people sat in the audience at the High Valley Theater, too. Bette Davis, for example, attended a performance of *Liliom* there.

Thompson family photo
Children standing on the steps of the Upper Ojai schoolhouse in 1901.

Fry photo
Upper valley school until the 1920s, High Valley Theater in the 1940s, now a private home.

Ann McGarrity remembered Iris Tree. She said that in the mid-1940s, there would be a delightful "twilight procession of man and beast" down McAndrew Road on the east end. She said that Iris Tree would walk with her two white dogs, Jiddu Krishnamurti, the philosopher, often led a cow and a calf on an evening stroll and a sprinkling of Thacher boys on horseback added to what she called "the sunset parade."

After the death of Alan Harkness, the Ojai branch of the Chekov Group was dissolved.

Ojai Arts Commission

Ojai seems to have more artists per capita than many communities. Some attribute this to the valley's aura or energy. Others say it's the natural beauty here that inspires artistic endeavors. Whatever the impetus, many artists claim that their sense of creativity didn't blossom until coming here.

Because we don't take the valley for granted and because we're dedicated to preserving and enhancing it, the Ojai City Arts Commission was formed as an appointed volunteer council that works with city officials in safeguarding the aesthetic qualities of the community. Some of the projects this commission has managed are: an annual art grant designed to benefit children in performing and visual arts and the establishment of a municipal art gallery in Ojai City Hall. The Arts Commission is given the opportunity to review public projects as two percent of funds for these projects are now designated to acquire art or to incorporate an artistic element into it.

Some of this valley's former and present noted artists include, Marty Noble, Sharon and Kent Butler, Gayel Childress, Alice and Richard Matzkin, Bert Collins, Myra Toth, Frank Massarella and Barbara Strohbin.

Beatrice Wood

Not only was Beatrice Wood a world-known ceramist, she was a local icon. She lived in the Ojai Valley for half of her life and died here at the age of 105. Wood studied acting with Marcel Duchamp, learned Russian dancing under Pavlova's master and was taught pantomime by Yvette Gilbert before ever being introduced to ceramics. Glen Luckens of USC was Miss Wood's guide into the world of clay. As with all of her life's endeavors, she excelled.

Beatrice Wood first came to Ojai as an actress in Krishnamurti's Star Camp (see Chapter Eighteen). She performed in *The Light of Asia*. In 1948 she decided to make Ojai her home.

Beato, as she signed her work, set up a studio here and began perfecting her ceramic art. In 1949, she exhibited at the local art center. Six years later the Smithsonian Institution invited her to display her pottery. In 1958, she had a show at the San Francisco Museum of Art and today her works are in permanent collections in famous museums all over the world.

Miss Wood rarely duplicated any of her pieces. She used no molds, but created with a potter's wheel. Some say even her early works showed a sophisticated style that must have been related to her French education. And her glazes are praised worldwide, for she developed her own.

Miss Wood turned the heads of valley newcomers for years. Even those who saw her often couldn't help but stare at her. She was a gracious lady who possessed a special appeal with a foreign flavor. In 1926, Beatrice Wood was the official representative of the U. S. State Department on an educational tour of India. After her second trip to India, she began dressing in saris.

In the 1950s, Miss Wood wore billowy blouses tucked into colorful, gathered skirts and lots of large bangles. Sometimes, during that period, she wore a Western scarf and straw hat. In the 1960s, her everyday dress began to develop a more exotic look and, throughout the remainder of her long life, Beato dressed typically Eastern. Practically until her death at 105 in 1998, Beatrice Wood had audiences every week with people who wanted to meet her. Her business manager set up meetings months in advance. This author spoke with one couple who were eagerly awaiting their opportunity to be with the ceramist. Their appointment was six months away and Ms. Wood was 101 at the time.

When asked about her longevity, Beato always attributed it to chocolate and young men – her two passions in life. She also enjoyed watching Laurel and Hardy. This author had an interview with the famous ceramist one afternoon in the 1970s when she wasn't quite 80 and, having arrived a tad early, had to stand outside the front door for several minutes until Beatrice finished watching the comedians perform on television. Precise in her own scheduling and timing of things, she told me that it was the perfect timing in the comedians' performances that so intrigued her.

Vivika and Otto Heino

Vivika and Otto Heino met in the late 1940s when he visited her New Hampshire ceramic studio. The couple were married in 1950 and spent their lives making beautiful pottery together. Over the years, they were commissioned to do some unusual ceramic work. In 1952, they made a large display of pots for the movie set, *The Egyptian* and another time they designed a ten by forty-foot wall for a swimming pool in Minneapolis.

The Heinos met Beatrice Wood in the 1970s and she is the one who lured them to the Ojai Valley. Like Wood, the Heinos' work has been shown throughout the United States and Internationally.

According to an article by Barbara De Noon appearing in *The Ojai Valley News* just after the Heinos were nominated Living Treasures, Vivika's first introduction to clay ended in disaster. She was just 7. After watching a pottery demonstration, she came home and placed a can of sand on the Victrola and tried to make a pot of her own.

Vivika, a teacher of ceramics for most of her life, carried through with her obligation as a Living Treasure by inviting eight students into their studio to familiarize them with clay.

Vivika has since passed on and Otto is still producing fine ceramics from the couple's studio on McAndrew Road.

OVM
Vivika and Otto Heino.

Chapter Thirteen
Our Neighboring Communities

Ojai Valley was originally made up of two large land grants. Now it's divided into several small communities.

The people who love and live in these unincorporated areas are often disappointed when historians write comparatively little about their towns in books such as this. One must understand, however, that without a daily record of events, such as a newspaper or a town council to document specific occurrences, there are few sources of hard information. *The Ojai* did sometimes include snippets of news about our outlying communities and there are still a few people around who remember life in the early years. We've done our best to capture the essence of these communities and their residents.

Mira Monte

Mira Monte (Spanish for *mountain view*) is the first settlement and shopping area one approaches after leaving Ojai city limits on Highway 33 toward Ventura. Small farm houses and large walnut and apricot groves dotted the Mira Monte terrain for several years, but purposeful development didn't begin until the late 1920s.

In 1927, John Dalton opened a hot dog stand and gas station in Mira Monte across the highway from Mirror Lake. My father, Dalton Munger, recalls stopping at the gas station every Friday when Tony Dalton ran it in the 1940s, and leaving his watch as collateral for a tank of gas to get to work. On his way home from Ventura that day, he'd stop and pay Tony Dalton for the gas and retrieve his watch.

Mirror Lake in Mira Monte.

Man probably effected more physical change in that geographic area in a relatively short span than in any other place in the valley. And most of those alterations were done in modern times. If you had driven through Mira Monte forty-five years ago, you would notice a small airport situated at the southwest corner of Baldwin Road and Highway 33. South of that, was Mirror Lake. You might even see a train loaded with Ojai-grown oranges pass by.

There was a landing field in the valley as early as 1930 – possibly a project of the Ojai Lions Club. Crude maps show it in the vicinity of the Y (roughly near the intersection of Maricopa Highway and Ojai Avenue). Local schools weren't happy about having planes overhead. In one issue of *The Ojai,* Ojai Valley School officials voiced their concern about the planes flying so low over the school as to disrupt classes and potentially endanger students. This landing strip was known as Ojai Valley Airfield.

In the early 1940s, Don Henderson built an airstrip on family property in Mira Monte to facilitate his passion for flying. During World War II, the Army Air Corps commissioned him to run a small flying school there. In January, 1945, the airstrip went public and the following July, 37 year-old Henderson died after crashing his plane near the airfield.

Venturan, Kendall Barr, subsequently took over the operation of Henderson Field. The 2,100 by fifty-foot runway accommodated about twenty small planes per week in those days. In 1949, they built six hangers and a waiting room with restrooms.

During the same year, L.E. Clapp opened a nursery across from Henderson Field and Mirror Lake. Now known as Ojai Valley Nursery, this 50 year-old old business still operates in the same spot today.

Area natives can easily recall visions of Mira Monte in the 1950s and '60s. The attractive lake offered a sense of serenity. Colorful planes landing rather infrequently, caused autoclad passersby to linger along the roadside and watch. And the train chugging past added additional interest. By then, neighborhood horses had become accustomed to the strange whoosh, clatter, clatter of the train and the buzzing of soaring planes as they obediently carried riders through still vast, open fields and along quiet roadways.

It all ended rather abruptly. The trains ceased coming to Ojai, the airstrip closed and the lake was drained to make way for mobile home parks. The horses? Well there are a few, but the vast fields where this author and many others spent long, enjoyable hours riding, are gone forever.

Meiners Oaks

In 1871, George Suhren purchased 800 acres of the western section of Rancho Ojai from John Green. Suhren grew grain there and advertised in the *Ventura Signal* that he had agricultural property and pasture for rent.

Suhren must have run into a bit of financial trouble for, in book three, page 772 of Recorded Agreements, there is a transaction between him and John Meiners for the 800 acres of land. It states that on April 17, 1876, George Suhren relinquished his holdings to John Meiners for the token sum of $1.00. (Some accounts erroneously attribute this transaction to a Mr. Vuerin.)

Since Meiners had not seen the land, he asked a California-bound friend to view it for him. The friend, Mr. Holton, reported upon his return to Wisconsin that Meiners' land was situated in the most beautiful valley he had ever seen. Encouraged by Holton's description, Meiners traveled West to see for himself. He found that all his friend had told him was true and he was also surprised and pleased to discover that the dry valley air gave him relief from his chronic asthma.

OVM
View of Meiners Oaks from above Besant Meadows around 1930.

David Mason collection
View of Meiners Oaks toward Besant Meadows from north of what is now Maricopa Highway.

John Meiners was born in Oldenburg, Germany on November 10, 1827. He received his education in his native land, after which he engaged in the mercantile business. He entered the United States in July, 1848, and immediately settled in

Wisconsin, where he took up farming with Herman Hoyer. Later, Meiners built a starch factory and a sawmill which he ran in connection with the farm.

During the mid-1850s, Mr. Meiners sold out to his partner and moved from the township of Lake to Milwaukee proper, where he became a bookkeeper. Meiners went to work in a distillery during the early 1860s and later he and Ernst Vilter purchased the business, which was then known as Menomonee Valley Distillery. In 1872, Meiners bought Vilter out. Mr. Meiners was also the president and a large stockholder in the Cream City Brewing Company.

John Meiners married Wielyn Thede of Germany in 1853. She died in 1869 leaving six children. In 1871, he married Elisa Meyer.

The Meiners family lived on their ranch intermittently from about 1882 and in 1897, P.K. Miller completed their home, which still stands just east of the present Ranch House Restaurant, at South Lomita Drive. An extraordinary barn stood exactly on the restaurant site. It reportedly held ninety tons of hay, twenty head of horses and farm equipment. The barn and all of its contents were destroyed by fire in 1896.

Some considered Meiners' land a marshy duck pond. It certainly was well-shaded, having probably the largest stand of

OVM
Meiners original ranch house. Mr. and Mrs. Meiners and the Soper family in front. October 19, 1890.

oaks on flat ground in all of California. Meiners was credited with having a superb sense of farm organization. He grew several varieties of fruit in abundance on his ranch, along with wheat, barley and red oats.

The Ojai once carried a strange article about John Meiners. It seems that he planted an apple tree upside down at his distillery. He claimed that the tree grew to be ten feet high and actually bore fruit from its roots, which became so heavy they needed a trellis to support them. Why would someone try to fool Mother Nature in this way? Evidently, it had something to do with an old German legend. According to at least one source, Meiners' apple tree is still on display in Milwaukee where the grounds around his brewery have been preserved as a landmark.

Meiners was successful with his orchards on his California ranch, but the profusion of acorns inspired him to raise hogs as a main product. P.W. Soper was the general manager for John Meiners' Cheery Acres Ranch and he and the ranch hands reportedly walked the fattened hogs to market to Hueneme.

An 1897 map shows Rice as the only road through Meiners' property and the only route to the canyon resorts. Wheeler Blumberg delivered the mail to Matilija and Wheelers in those days. Once, in 1893, as he headed up the canyon with horse, buggy and mail pouch, he found Meiners' gate locked.

Mr. Soper, it seems, had become annoyed with people passing over the property and leaving the gate open behind them and he decided to teach them a lesson. Soper refused to budge in his determination to lock Blumberg out, so Blumberg, it is said, finally unhitched the buggy and rode over the rugged canyon hills that night by horseback. A subsequent discussion a few days later, provided a conclusion satisfactory to both men. Soper agreed to give Blumberg a key if he would always lock the gates behind him.

After John Meiners' death in December, 1898, his only son, Gustav, ran the ranch. Gustav died in 1907 and his son, Carl Meiners took over. Carl asked Otto Busch, an old friend of his grandfathers, to come to Ojai and manage the ranch.

The Busch family lived in part of the old ranch house while part of it was reserved for the heirs' visits. In 1924, the heirs incorporated under the name Ojai Ranch and Development Company. The board members were Carl Meiners, Robert Krull (John Meiners' grandsons), Bernard Goldsmith, Hugo Boorse and C.A. McGee (husbands of Meiners' granddaughters). The property consisted of 1200 acres: 800 level farm land, 200 acres of oaks and 200 of rolling hills. Their plan was to sell off the farm land in ten-acre parcels and larger and the wooded areas would be reserved for cabins.

The corporation hired Tony Sarzotti to clear out many of the oak trees. Then they built a ninety-square-foot dance pavilion, a huge barbecue pit and a few small cabins, in which realtors could close deals comfortably and privately. They marked off several thirty-foot lots to offer for sale.

Their invitation to a free barbecue and dance attracted people from all over this county, Santa Barbara and Los Angeles. Meiners Oaks, first called *Meiners Ojai Oaks* and then *The Oaks,* was open to the public for the first time. To encourage their guests to really get out and look the place over, promoters buried tin cans containing $5 to $20 in gold. On the second day of sales, November 7, 1924, they sold forty-five lots.

The corporation contemplated The Oaks as a recreational resort where a family could own its own cabin. Subsequent improvements included a recreation hall near the northeast corner of Pueblo Street and El Roblar and a swimming pool (actually an old reservoir, according to those few who remember it), on the west side of what is now La Luna. They also put in a baseball diamond and a boxing ring. Behind the recreation hall (later known as the Oaks Community Hall), Sam Booher ran a skating rink for visitors. (The dance pavilion may have doubled as a skating rink.) They also built a barbecue and picnic area in the western portion of Meiners Oaks.

There were just four streets then, thousands of oak trees that were alive with beautiful tree squirrels and a profusion of wildflowers.

Wesley Hickey came from Carpinteria to manage the Ojai Ranch and Development Company in 1927, when just five families lived in The Oaks. Hickey increased the size of the lots to fifty feet and introduced a contract of sale. Lots sold for $270 cash or $285 on the payment plan of $25 down and $15 per month. If the buyer defaulted, Hickey bought the lot back and paid for any improvements on it. The Depression years motivated Hickey's idea, for he felt it gave people a chance for a place of their own. Within just three years, there were reportedly 250 homes in The Oaks.

In 1944, Hickey took over the development company, establishing his office at 312 West El Roblar where the Full Spectrum Landscape Gardening business is today.

Fry photo
Hickey's real estate office in Meiners Oaks during the 1940s.

In the mid-1940s, Mr. and Mrs. Robert Perry bought some property on El Conejo Road between Arnaz and what is now La Luna Avenue (then Tico Road). Mrs. Perry said there were barbecue pits all over the grounds when they moved onto the land and pitched their tent. They promptly built their home and, in 1946, they opened the first mobile home park in the valley. Mrs. Perry still operates Meiners Oaks Trailer Park.

That same year, Charles W. Affeldt built an adobe home on the corner of El Conejo and Padre Juan. His septic tank went into the hole from which he mined clay used to make the bricks for his home. Another Meiners Oaks family constructed their home of ammunition boxes.

The Oaks of the 1940s was mostly a vacation spot. Many Venturans built shanties, set up tents and fashioned crude shelters to use as weekend and summer houses. This soon changed, however, as more and more people became permanent residents. They created activities and entertainment independent of Ojai. They built churches, established a library and organized men's and women's clubs. They encouraged businesses so they needn't rely on larger cities for necessities.

In 1953, the population of Meiners Oaks exceeded that of Ojai proper and the citizens were so enthusiastic over the growth that they wanted to incorporate. Incorporation of Meiners Oaks, however, has not yet occurred.

The mood that the Meiners heirs created seems still to linger in Meiners Oaks. People live in a potpourri of houses on quiet, shaded streets without sidewalks. They shop in small businesses where the merchants know them by name. This could probably be considered one of the last truly typical small California towns.

Early Meiners Oaks Businesses

Dairies were big in the 1920s. In 1928, the El Roblar Dairy operated out of the rock house on East El Roblar Drive. Baron Keen bought it and changed the name to Rose Cream Dairy. In 1929, Mark Markoff brought his family to Meiners Oaks to enroll his children, Mortimer and Sheila (Lodge), former mayor of Santa Barbara, in Ojai Valley School. They bought Keen's dairy and changed the name to Nurse's Dairy because Mrs. Markoff was a nurse. In 1935, the Markoffs bought Le Valley's dairy cows because they were leaving the area.

In 1932, a large dairy opened on Tico Road (now La Luna). This was known as Blue's Dairy. Six years later, Ernest Van Leuven purchased the dairy, which encompassed the area between what is now La Luna and Rice Roads, and changed the name to Royal Oaks Dairy. Absel Klausen bought this business in 1939, ran it for ten years and then sold it to Berl D. Rash.

In September of 1927, Edward Kuhn opened a store and gas station carrying groceries and cigars, presumably on the southwest corner of El Roblar Drive and Lomita Avenue. J.R. Wright and his wife took over the store in 1940 and named it J and G Grocery. In 1943, Pat Patelzik bought the store and the following year he sold it to Royal Danner. Wilbur and Lillian Jackson evidently took it over in 1945 and in 1946, Fred Skill bought it and added a variety store and soda fountain. This is the current site of Jolly Kone.

The Jacksons, in the meantime, opened a grocery store in the building Claude Newton had just completed across the street on the northwest corner of El Roblar and Lomita. "My husband and I were the first to do business in that building," says Lillian Jackson from her Meiners Oaks home. She doesn't recall how long they were there, but there's evidence that they were still there in the mid-fifties. Fred Jue was the next proprietor. Bob and Betty Rhodes bought the building in 1976 and opened Meiners Oaks "Ace" Hardware, which they have operated there since.

A large drive-in market and gas station opened on Martin Green's property on the northeast corner of Lomita and El Roblar in 1929, with Joseph Curren the proprietor. Max Green took over the business in 1935.

In 1929, Harry Cheap built a twenty by forty-foot grocery store of brick with plate glass windows at El Roblar and Pueblo. Cheap leased the business to Guy Little and he called it Little's Cash Store. In 1930, a barber shop opened in the back of the store and two years later, Henry Keller opened a barber shop in a frame building next to Cheap's store. In 1932, it was rumored that there would be a pool room opening in Cheap's building. The pool room didn't materialize, however, and residents expressed relief. Later in 1932, G. R. Davis rented the Cheap building and he sold groceries, notions and hardware from that site. Bert Conrey bought Cheap's building in 1943 and two buildings adjoining it.

In 1946, the Goody Shop opened at 204 West El Roblar – in the vicinity of where the Meiners Oaks Water District offices are now. They served hamburgers and had a full fountain. O.H. Brotherton was the next owner of that property and in 1949, Rice and Turner opened the R & T Market just east of the Goody Shop.

Jack Tulleys ran the Red and White Grocery Store as did G.R. Davis and James Dixon during the 1930s. It is not clear where this store was. In July of 1934, there's a mention that G.R. Davis sold the Red and White to Leo A. Penney and that James Dixon would manage the business.

Often, in those days, people opened grocery stores in their homes and there was one at 150 N. Pueblo. In 1936, G.R. Davis was the grocer there.

Rex Crandall opened Crandall's Market at 520 West El Roblar in 1951 and sold it to George and F.L. Farrell in 1952. The market burned in 1953 and they rebuilt. Joe Cropper and Edwin Justice opened Foodway Market there in 1954. Crandalls Hardware was at 515 El Roblar and Elams auction was at 575 El Roblar, near the southeast corner of Poli Street and El Roblar.

The Oaks Market opened at 339 West El Roblar at the southeast corner of El Roblar and Encinal Avenue in a newly constructed building in 1953. The builder also erected two twenty-foot business spaces east of the grocery store.

The Hut opened in 1946 at the corner of El Conejo Drive and Lomita Avenue. It was originally known as the Barbecue Hut. This business is still operating on the same site.

Bob Wilson started Wilson's Dinosaur Auto Repair at 117 N. Lomita in 1946. George bought it from his brother in 1958. George Wilson still specializes in vintage car repair. There was an even earlier garage in Meiners Oaks. H.A. Rice opened the Oaks Garage on El Roblar, near Encinal Avenue, in the late 1920s and operated this business for some time.

Andy's Liquor opened in 1953 at 138 W. El Roblar, where the vacuum cleaner repair business is now. That business space was built in the early 1950s.

Farming was still going on in Meiners Oaks during the early development days. There were many acres planted to orange trees and at least one unusual crop. In 1934, R.J. Lake planted eight acres of zucca, a vegetable from which they made artificial pineapple and cherries for use in candy and fruit cake. Zucca is described as a zucchini-like vegetable that weighed as much as sixty to seventy pounds each. In 1934, thirty-five tons of zucca was shipped from here.

Meiners Oaks Library

Evidently there was a library here as early as 1929 with Mrs. Tom King as librarian. The following year, the little Meiners Oaks Library, known as the Matilija Branch of Ventura County Libraries was official. Librarian, Miss Topping, of the county library system, traveled here to help make the arrangements. She said, "Find a place and the books will be forthcoming."

Everyone had their own idea about where the library should be. An early variety store offered space for a limited number of books. There was talk of outfitting the community center to house the books. And individuals offered their homes for a library. But no action was taken right away. In January of 1933, the El Roblar Garden Club of Meiners Oaks picked the ball up again. The Markoffs loaned the community a small store building on their property for the library and Mrs. Fred Richardson and Mrs. Davis Adams became the librarians.

In 1934, they moved the library to one of the Richardsons' Cottages on Lomita near Mesa, (now known as the Canary

Cottages). The library had 200 books then, with additional volumes coming from the main library branch each week.

Mrs. Edward Baisselier was librarian in 1935. In 1937, the library was moved from Richardsons' Cottages to Mrs. Henry Koehler's home at 130 South Padre Juan.

The library didn't have a permanent home until September of 1946, when J. H. Penney purchased one of the barracks from Camp Oak, the military camp at Ojai Valley Inn, and moved it to what is now the 100 block of North Encinal Avenue. Long-time residents remember Coral and George Mahr operating the library then while living in the back of the building. Aimee Lett-Haines became the next librarian and she continued in that position through at least the early 1950s.

In the 1960s, the library was at 143 West El Roblar, where the Pregnancy Center is today. In the mid-1970s, the Meiners Oaks Library moved into what was reported to have been an old hardware store at 114 North Padre Juan.

Social Life in The Oaks

In 1924, Meiners Oaks developers advertised a dance pavilion, eating places, an open air plunge and, in the future, tennis and handball courts. By the next year, the pavilion was being enlarged to accommodate more people, a playground had been added and they tried to lure people by offering such activities as wheel barrow races on roller skates.

In 1928, the community established the Meiners Oaks Community Club with the following officers: Mrs. G.H. Stewart, Mrs. G.H. Smith, Mrs. Herbert Smith, John Smith, Harold Rider and Mr. J.U. Tingley. About forty residents met regularly in the Community Center. They discussed community improvement and planned activities such as socials, concerts and plays. They established an athletic club, a garden club, a chorus and activities for the children. The clubhouse became a rest and reading room for visitors to Krishnamurti's Star Camp. On Sundays, it was transformed into a church.

In 1928, for example, Oaks residents enjoyed an evening of music and charades. Guests were also asked to reveal their most embarrassing moments. In the 1930s, the Meiners Oaks Mothers Club was formed. There was also a sewing circle, a dance club, a stamp club, a rifle club and supervised play for preschoolers in Meiners Oaks. In 1934, the Meiners Oaks Woman's Club was started with Miss Nellie Otis as president. The same year, junior high school residents established a social club of their own.

A miniature golf course was also advertised in Meiners Oaks as being at Robles Del Rey at King's Corner.

In 1929, the garden club had a contest with prizes for the prettiest gardens and the best bouquet of zinnias. Two people on North Alvarado won for their creative flower gardens. One particularly beautiful bed of pansies was mentioned. And Mrs. Max Green, on North Lomita, won first place for her zinnias. Residents took pride in their home sites in those days and in 1930, even the children got involved by forming a junior garden club. One charming aspect of this organization was that each child took on the name of a flower.

There was an active Meiners Oaks Theosophical organization then which was considered as much a part of the community as the garden club and traditional church groups. At first, they met in the community hall and later, they built a lodge on Poli Street. With their influence, the community enjoyed astrology classes and, in 1928, residents even attended a reincarnation costume dance.

The swimming pool or plunge was originally opened up to potential property buyers who visited with their families on the weekends. In 1934, it was to become a resident's perk. Fifty cents would buy the resident a key to the pool gate and their family could swim anytime they wanted. Guests could swim for 15 cents per day. The plunge, described as being located on the west side of Meiners Oaks "not far from J.P. Gray's ranch," was a reservoir and was not designed for swimming, however.

Long-time resident, Lillian Jackson tells about a frightening incident she experienced as a child when she visited the valley for a picnic with her family. She and several other children were given permission to go swimming, but when they got into the pool, they couldn't get out because of the slippery, sloping sides. One small boy could not swim and the older children had all they could do to keep themselves and him afloat.

Finally, says Mrs. Jackson, "The adults came along and saw that we were in trouble. They formed a human chain, with the last person holding on to the fence, and were able to pull us out one by one."

The old reservoir was closed to swimmers by county officials shortly after that because it did not meet safety standards.

Services for The Oaks

In 1929, A.W. Helm was the fire chief in Meiners Oaks and he had ten volunteers. They built a small fire station next to the community hall at what was then 112 West El Roblar – just west of where Ace Hardware's main building is today. The building housed a fifty gallon chemical extinguisher. The current fire station, at the corner of West Lomita and La Luna, was built in 1953.

Prior to 1931, the mail carrier would leave Meiners Oaks mail in boxes at the corner of Lomita and El Roblar on the way to Matilija. Door-step mail delivery in this community began in November of 1931 with Hubert Rider as the first mailman.

There are a lot of obstacles to writing the history – imperfect memory being one of them and the other being the familiarity of the times. Everyone writing about events and places then, knew where everything was and didn't feel a need to include addresses in their ads or articles.

Editorials stating that so and so's store was west of the sycamore tree or near Mr. Saunder's camping trailer, are typical, leaving a researcher often scratching his head in puzzlement. In the beginning, there were no house and business numbers because there was no need for them. As time went on and the population grew, numbers became necessary, but they didn't always remain the same throughout the years.

In 1928, in Meiners Oaks, for example, in anticipation of the first local telephone directory, a numbering system was established. Nineteen years later, the numbers were changed. They were rearranged again in 1969.

A regular bus service was established in Meiners Oaks in 1943.

Interesting Characters of The Oaks

Hugo Boorse (John Meiners' grandson-in-law) planted oranges in Meiners Oaks in the late 1920s. By 1931, most of his orange trees were in. His groves, according to one old-timer stretched from La Luna (then known as Tico Road) to Rice and West Lomita to what is now the Maricopa Highway. Boorse built a bungalow on his property and named the place El Rancho Viejo. Orange trees still grace that section of Meiners Oaks and the entrance sign to Boorse's property remains today.

Madeline Baird, a widow from New Foundland; first came to Meiners Oaks to hear Krishnamurti. In 1929, she commissioned John Roine to design a large home for her on the southwest corner of South Lomita Avenue and Mesa Drive. Locals refer to this beautiful structure as the Baird Mansion. Mrs. Baird lived a secluded life here and died in 1939.

Roine is thought to have designed other stucco homes in Meiners Oaks, including one that he built in 1927 and that eventually became an orphanage. Helen Stone first opened the Starling as a home for children. In 1931, Dorothy Rubinfier was running it. In 1938 it was run by Mrs. Greta Parkhust and Mrs. Bessie Maxson.

Wesley Hickey loved Meiners Oaks and he chose to live in the place he promoted. His first home, according to early resident, Mrs. Jackson, was on El Conejo Drive near Pueblo. She says he eventually built a lovely home on the hill overlooking Meiners Oaks, roughly across from the Deer Lodge.

Meiners Oaks residents took much pride in their community and, in 1949, when they heard talk of someone moving in a dilapidated house, the residents were outraged. Before the old building left its foundation in Ventura, the building inspector condemned it and one local resident said, "It's a darn good thing. Our community is slowly building up and improving. As it is, there are a few undesirable shacks like that one here already and we're going to take steps to get rid of them."

Santa Ana Rancho

The Santa Ana land grant includes the Ventura River valley and mesa, sections of Coyote and San Antonio Creeks and what is now Foster Park, Casitas Springs, Lake Casitas, Oak View and Rancho Arnaz. Unlike many California ranchos, much of the Santa Ana acreage still remains in large parcels. There were several early attempts to create subdivisions, however.

In 1875, Santa Ana developers planned a community for which the land agreement carried a temperance clause. No alcohol would be allowed within the boundaries. People showed little interest in this concept and it, along with several other large-scale promotional efforts, failed. When Judge Faucett and Captain Richard Robinson had Santa Ana land holdings, Faucett planned to turn this into a coffee plantation.

Most of Santa Ana Valley was owned very early by the Selbys, Nyes, Wadleighs, Pieranos, Hoffmans and Barnards and it still is.

In 1924, Santa Ana Valley was described as having fine orchards of apples, pears, peaches and apricots and vast grain fields.

In 1953, the Santa Ana Valley Improvement Association was formed to mastermind one of the largest developments predicted to affect the Ojai Valley. Mr. and Mrs. David Alison of El Rancho Cola, planned a resort-type subdivision on their 2,070-acre ranch. They drew up plans for one-acre estates, country club lodging, a shopping center, amusement park and pool. The eventual fate of the old Rancho Cola, however, was not as glamorous as that, for it is among the many acres now forming the bottom of Lake Casitas.

Foster Park

According to legend, the Chumash considered the land we now call Foster Park a sacred place. They believed that the wind started there in a large sycamore. It is told that they left offerings in the hollow of an arched tree which, in more modern times, became known as the Kissing Tree.

The E.P. Foster family gave Foster Park to the county in memory of their son and it was dedicated in 1908. There was one stipulation: that the county would agree to protect the trees and build and maintain the fences.

A tiny community grew up at the park entrance, probably around the 1930s and 40s. People, making the long trip from Ventura to Ojai could stop there (where the Ojai Freeway ends) for gas, groceries and, by 1952, even to mail a letter. All of those services disappeared in 1969, however, to make way for the freeway. Just the park facilities and a few homes remain.

Fry photo
Plaque honoring county pioneers near Foster Bowl at Foster Park.

Roy Wilson designed the Foster Park Bowl in 1928. During the 1930s and 40s, pioneer picnics were held regularly at Foster Park. In 1934, the Ventura County Historical Society honored county pioneers by establishing a large plaque with their family names. Two years later, another plaque was installed including the pioneers with Spanish surnames. One day, long-time resident, Dick Adams was in the vicinity and noticed that the plaques were practically hidden by overgrowth and seemingly forgotten. He launched a project to have the plaques removed to a safer, more prominent place. In July of 1999, the plaques were dedicated to their new home at the Ventura Museum.

Casitas Springs

Late in the eighteenth century, the padres and their charges, walked inland, following the Ventura River, and built a chapel near Canada Larga. They christened it Santa Gertrudis. Historians are not clear as to whether they built the chapel after a fire destroyed the first mission in 1792, or when an earthquake and tidal wave caused extensive damage to the second mission in 1812. Regardless of the twenty-year discrepancy, the mission community used Santa Gertrudis as a place of refuge in time of disaster, in case of pending danger from unfriendly bands of natives or enemy ships and as a rest spot when traveling to the inland valleys.

OVM
Robert Browne excavating at the St. Gertrudis Mission site south of Casitas Springs.

Ed Sheridan, in a speech published in *The Ojai* in 1925, said that the first mission church was abandoned as unsafe and they started a new mission inland. Indian huts sprang up around the chapel, says Sheridan. "It was quite a village of little houses and it was the presence of these little houses (casitas, in Spanish) from which sprang the name *Casitas*."

According to Sheridan, the area was once planted to pears and, in 1925, it was dotted with apricot orchards. There is a marker along the frontage road just south of Foster Park that identifies the location of Santa Gertrudis. Freeway builders unearthed its foundation around 1970.

A post office was established in Casitas Springs in 1928 and the following year, they had a library. The current settlement of Casitas Springs is still appropriately named since the narrow section of land embraces a scattered collection of small homes, most of them built in the 1920s and 30s. It was more widely known then as Stony Flats.

Casitas Springs is the last community before Highway 33 becomes the Ojai Freeway to Ventura. Edison Curve, just south of Casitas Springs, was once known as Adobe Hill. Before it was paved, heavy rains made the mud so sticky that buggy wheels frequently bogged down in it.

Builders began the Live Oaks Acres development, in the river bottom, in the 1940s.

Rancho Arnaz

Rancho Arnaz is located on Highway 33 between Oak View and Casitas Springs. It is not a town but a landmark and an apple ranch where they still make and sell cider. It all began with a Spaniard named Don Jose Arnaz.

Mr. Arnaz was born in 1820. It was part of the educated Spaniard's culture to study medicine and he complied with tradition. Before he could complete his studies, however, his aunt asked him to go to Mexico to collect an inheritance left by her late husband.

Arnaz expected a share of the money for his efforts. They were cheated out of the bequest, however, and Arnaz had to find work. In 1840, he took a job with a German merchant who sent him to Acapulco to exchange merchandise for cotton.

Later that year, the frigate Clarita took Jose Arnaz to the port of San Pedro from which he entered the tiny village of El Pueblo de Nuestra Senora La Reina de Los Angeles de Porciuncula, now known as Los Angeles. He brought to this village, fancy suits embroidered with gold and silver thread and garments of silk, cotton and deerskin collectively valued at $10,000 and sold it all for $64,000. From Los Angeles he ventured to San Buenaventura and established a retail store with a man named Morris.

Arnaz, who once owned the former mission land, acquired a portion of the Santa Ana land grant and, in 1860, he built a large adobe home near the eastern boundary, along the bank of San Antonio Creek. One historian wrote that Arnaz received the property in exchange for assuming guardianship over the unruly children of recently widowed Mrs. Vanegas.

Arnaz married Marie Mercedes de Avila in 1851. When she died, he married one of Juan Camarillo's daughters. Arnaz was a hospitable man, often opening his home to weary travelers. He sometimes entertained up to a hundred guests for a weekend.

On April 7, 1886, Arnaz sold his ranch to John Poplin for the sum of $6,000. He then moved to Los Angeles where he spent the remaining eight years of his life. Poplin reportedly sold half of the 250 acres to his son.

Joseph Goodyear was the next owner. In 1891, he paid $10,500 for 120 acres. W.L. Ferguson married Goodyear's daughter, Fanny, and they took over the ranch. It was Ferguson who planted the apple trees and, in 1922, he opened the cider barn. Thomas Langford bought the ranch in the 1930s and reportedly moved the old barn from across the road to its present location.

The Arnaz adobe still stands southeast of the cider barn. Although it's camouflaged by plaster and boards and isn't recognizable as such, it may be the oldest complete adobe now occupied in the county. The Arnaz adobe is not open to the public.

Motorists often wonder about the large pink house built on a rock at San Antonio Bridge near Rancho Arnaz. This was originally built by Mrs. Ramelli, who, along with Roy Wilson, designed the three-story, eleven-room home for her family.

Oak View

Prior to its development, Oak View was just uninhabited land between Ojai and Ventura. Watermelons grew where Dahl's Market is at 445 Ventura Avenue and apricot orchards covered a great deal of the remaining land. In the late 1930s, people began to build homes there, calling the place *Oak View Gardens.*

Among Oak View's earliest residents was the Hiram Watkins family. Hiram was born in 1866 in Bowling Green, Kentucky. When his parents could not compromise their marital or political differences, Mr. Watkins took his older son, Glyme, to Texas, while his wife, Narcissa, after selling their Missouri home, returned to Kentucky with Hiram.

Hiram married Allie Belle Delp and they set up housekeeping in Summerfield, Kansas, where he grew broom corn and manufactured and sold brooms to support his family which soon included two children, Percy and Florence. Around 1892 they moved to Sterling, Nebraska, opened a rag carpet company and Allie Belle gave birth to four more children, Elva, Ruby (Berry), Clifford and Fern (Munger).

Watkins family photo
Hiram and Allie Belle Watkins.

In 1901, the Watkins family moved to California from Nebraska and rented land in Oak View to raise cattle, hogs and hay. This is where Jane and Irene were born. Around 1903, Hiram purchased seventy-five acres of land on a hill east of Highway 33 in what is now Oak View for $2500 and tended an apricot orchard there. When it seemed that automobiles were here to stay, Hiram opened a service station/grocery at the corner of what is now Watkins Way and Ventura Avenue in Oak View. Allie Belle took over some of the responsibility for the orchard. When the bottom dropped out of the apricot market in 1928, Hiram pulled out most of the trees. He went back to making brooms which he sold to merchants in Ventura, Santa Barbara and Los Angeles. When things were slow, he went door-to-door. He, reportedly, made the brooms in a barn near Mirror Lake.

Percy Watkins married Effie Crose, whom he had met when she worked on the family's apricot ranch in 1917. She was in Oak View helping to care for her brother and signed up for the pitting crew to earn money for college. When the Depression hit, Percy and his Effie moved in with his parents so they could help each other through this period. They remembered eating popcorn from the broom corn for breakfast cereal. They also grew peanuts and often had pan-roasted peanuts for an evening

Watkin family photo
Watkins service station in Oak View, 1920s

meal. They had plenty of fresh milk, though, and they sold it and wood to buy groceries. One year the $7 a month that came from selling their dairy products was the only income they could count on.

Watkins sometimes got something in trade for their milk or the firewood Percy chopped and delivered to neighbors. According to Effie, "Often is was something we didn't want and couldn't use."

Percy and Effie rented the old Kennedy house for a while. Hiram died in 1942 and Allie Belle in 1951, after which Percy and Effie moved back to the ranch land on the hill where the apricot trees once grew. They brought a trailer onto the property and created a lean-to outside it. In the meantime, Percy, who was working in the oil fields by then, was bringing home lumber and scrap wood from the oil derricks and storing it on the property. When the telephone company took out the square telephone poles between Ventura and Ojai, Percy brought some of those home. Effie's brother brought them truckloads of rock from a quarry in Northern California where he worked – all of this for their future home.

Effie drew pictures of her dream house and Percy started building it in 1961 using the materials he'd been hoarding – the square telephone poles as beams, the stone as flooring and to build the massive fireplace. The house didn't go up overnight. In fact, it would be another ten years before Effie realized her dream as the Watkins didn't move into their home until 1971.

Percy died at the age of 93 in 1983. Effie was also in her 90s when she died in 1997.

Mrs. Jessie R. Caldwell opened a gas station and grocery in Oak View Gardens in 1927 where the Shell Station is on Highway 33 and Santa Ana Road. Reverend Craig established a Holiness Church in Oak View in 1928. By 1929, it was necessary to start a school and it opened with sixty-eight pupils. There was no heat in the building, so school started at 10 a.m. to give the building time to warm up before the children arrived.

There is mention of a library in Oak View as early as 1930. At one point it was housed in a garage.

In 1945, the community created a memorial park at Apricot Street and Mahoney Avenue. It was named, Glenn Memorial Park in memory of Captain Glenn A. Loban and others who had lost their lives in the war. Local families of servicemen planted shrubs and roses and labeled them with the names of their sons.

Upper Ojai

The first mention of the restaurant in Upper Ojai was in 1928 when the newspaper ran an article about Arthur and Carolyn Lee and Lee Kimbro operating the Triangle Inn and service station, halfway between Ojai and Santa Paula. At that time, they served homemade food and boasted a fireplace, barbecue pit, dance floor and dining room.

Chapter Fourteen
Development of Ojai Industry

What is the heart-capturing quality that still entices folks here? The lack of people? Uncrowded streets? The unrushed atmosphere? The weather? Actually the answer is: all of the above. The absence of noisy, repugnant industry also contributes greatly to Ojai's appeal. That is not to insinuate that this is a dependent community – very much to the contrary. Ojai attracts clean, non-offensive and often visually agreeable industry. But it wasn't always that way.

Oil, Gold and Other Minerals

Oil was the first marketable product derived from this valley. Ever since the initial discovery of black gold here, oil people have shown an interest in both the upper and lower valleys. They come and make their geological determinations, dump big money into exploration and, when their efforts are not amply rewarded, they leave, only to return again and again.

Almost every decade, someone has launched a major oil operation here. Historically, residents fought as hard for their right to peace, quiet and the preservation of their land as the crude seekers battled for their prerogative to drill. These conflicts still occur regularly in Upper Ojai.

During the early 1950s, those living in the lower valley became irate over an oil well situated just west of where the Y shopping center is now on Maricopa Highway. Not only did the populace object to the sanity-threatening noise of machinery, which operated twenty-four hours a day, but the visible aspects of this well were also a constant irritant. As with many valley oil exploration attempts, this well, Carty No. l, produced only salt water.

Had our history been different – had the petroleum experts found the oil that they expected in Ojai – our valley might be dotted profusely with oil machinery instead of agricultural enterprises. And the Ventura Avenue oil fields, once a lovely little valley, might now be a charming community where people from all over the world come to play and rest.

The Chumash discovered and utilized asphaltum here long before settlers began repairing their roofs with it. In 1892, *The Ojai* reported that the Ojai Asphalt Company hauled twenty tons of asphalt from its mines to be used in paving and sidewalks. A short time later, however, the company closed the mine due to a financial tangle. Interest in mining this substance here seemed to diminish from then on.

Gypsum is usually found in volcanic areas. Someone discovered gypsum on the Leach/Rynerson property (near modern-day Reeves Road) around 1880. A company was formed and the owners planned to hire a hundred men to mine hydrated calcium sulfate for use in fertilizer, plaster of Paris and the manufacture of porcelain, glass and alabaster. In 1890, gypsum was discovered on the Dennison ranch and by the turn of the century, gypsum was a minor but promising industry here.

Another mineral rumored to have been found locally is gold. In historical reports, someone claimed to have found traces of gold near Matilija Hot Springs in 1890. The major gold excitement in town, however, occurred seven years later when a prospector showed around some ore he had found on Mr. Wilsie's ranch, which was most likely in the vicinity of what is now Wilsie Canyon in Upper Ojai.

Word spread fast. By the next day, Randolph Freeman, editor of *The Ojai,* had printed and sold 380 claim blanks. Almost the entire male population scrambled to the foothills and spent days raking the chaparral, dislodging stones and putting the terrain in a general state of disarray. Their objective – immediate wealth.

Rumors of a gold strike traveled fast and people came from all over Ventura and Santa Barbara counties to find their share of the riches, only to return home in the same economic state as when they arrived. If there was gold in them thar hills, it is still up there.

In the early 1900s, Seymour Munger and his brother-in-law, Marlon Robison, manufactured cement irrigation and drainage pipes and poured sidewalks. Their specialty was cement floors. In 1915, they added decorative artificial stone to their line.

Munger and Robison poured the 4,850-square-foot cement floor in the packing house on Bryant Street. They built the first sidewalk in front of the Catholic Church on Ojai Avenue. They replaced many outdated irrigation systems, including Edward Thacher's wooden flume – the one Buckman had built nearly fifty years before. Some say that a good portion of the pipe under Ojai was laid by the old firm of Munger and Robison, whose business was on Fox Street near Munger's boarding house.

Agriculture

Ventura is one of the principal agricultural counties in the United States, ranking seventeenth out of 3,175 counties and tenth among the fifty-eight counties in California, in 1981. Ventura is also ranked fifth in dollar value of fruits and nuts produced nationwide. The valley contributes greatly to that status. Agriculture has always been an important industry here. As an example, according to the *Ventura Signal,* in 1883, Ojai was known as the place where crops never fail.

One of the first farm products to be harvested in the valley was grain. Although Jose Arnaz grew wheat around his adobe in the 1860s, Jacob Wilson, who lived in the Tico adobe in 1870, is reported to be the original sower of wheat in Ojai proper. As people moved in they followed Wilson's lead. In 1872, valley farmers reaped 16,200 bushels of wheat, providing grain for much of Southern California, according to the *Ventura Signal.* The Bartch brothers produced 1,200 sacks; Riggins, Proctor and Dennison harvested 600 each; while Pinkerton, Todd, McKee, Hueston and Wilson each harvested 500 sacks that year. Tom Clark produced 1,000 sacks; A.J. Bryant ended the year with 300 and Robert Ayers, just 200.

Ojai's principal products in 1875 were wheat, barley and potatoes. In 1880, wheat grew profusely under the oaks in Ojai, according to Sol Sheridan, *The Signal* editor, and reached the remarkable average height of four and a half feet.

The Original Ojai Orange

F.S.S. Buckman came to Ojai about 1872 and was appointed county school superintendent. Education was a prime concern of his, but mainly he dreamed of turning his 1,500-acre east end ranch into a lush orange orchard. His neighbors scoffed at this idea. They ridiculed Buckman as he laboriously cleared his land of rocks and burned the brush. They jeered while he built a wooden flume designed to convey water from what is now known as Horn Canyon to his orchard. People stopped laughing, however, when in 1880, Mr. Buckman marketed what was reported to have been the first citrus in Ojai. His 8 year-old trees produced 4,000 oranges and 3,000 lemons.

Robert Lyon brought back memories of fragrant orange groves from South America. And in 1874, he planted oranges on his Matilija Canyon property. Other agriculturalists in the canyon and both valleys observed Lyon's and Buckman's success with citrus and began including orange and lemon trees in their orchards.

Topa Topa Ranch

Edward Thacher, after studying to become an architect, discovered that he disliked working indoors. In fact he suffered the symptoms of a nervous breakdown, for which agricultural work was the therapy in those days. He left his comfortable New Haven home for therapeutic ranch work in Kansas.

OVM
Edward Thacher, 1886.

Edward's boss, Mr. Krutz, sent him to California in search of good orange property. It didn't take Edward long to develop a foolproof method of evaluating the myriad types of oranges he encountered all over the state – he tasted them.

No one will ever know Mr. Thacher's mental posture when he arrived in Nordhoff. Was he sick of eating oranges? Could he have been tired of traveling around? Was he simply enchanted by the Ojai Valley? Or did he, indeed, prefer Mr. Buckman's crop of citrus over any other, as he proclaimed? In 1887, Mr. Krutz and his partner, Mr. Leighton, bought the Buckman place on what is now East Reeves Road and hired Edward to manage it.

In 1890, Thacher married Lucy Smith and fourteen years later he bought his employers out and formed the Topa Topa Ranch Company. He ran the ranch until his death in 1923. When Thacher's heirs sold the ranch to George A. McKenna in 1936, it was considered one of the largest real estate transactions in the history of the valley.

The Ojai Orange Association

In 1894, local ranchers formed the Ojai Citrus Growers Association. They elected W.E. Wilsie as president and George Taylor as secretary. Each ranch had a packing facility where growers washed, graded and packed their own fruit. The primary responsibility of the association was to arrange for the citrus to be transported.

OVM
Jack Bennett delivering oranges to the SP Depot, circa 1910. Howard Bald on saddle horse.

In 1908, the Ojai Orange Association replaced the former citrus organization. Those most active in its formation were Edward Thacher, Sam Brown, W.C. Hendrickson, H.E. Stetson and Fred Sheldon. The local coalition served as purchasing agent for fertilizer, farm machinery and supplies. Its managers employed a picking boss and gang who moved from ranch to ranch and they directed fumigation and hauling work. Perhaps the main function of the O.O.A. was to pack and ship the fruit in response to the buyers near and far. Growers were assessed $20 per acre to join the association – the money would go toward building a packing house.

A packing house was built west of Bryant Street near the railroad turntable. In 1917, William C. Raddick became the manager of the packing house – a position he held for nineteen years. James Van Antwerp took his place. He resigned in 1952 and Alfred Reimer took the position the following year.

The little packing house grew by 7000 square feet in 1935.

Originally there were no conveyors and no way to cool the fruit. Employees wrapped and boxed the citrus individually, by hand. Eventually they upgraded the plant.

In the 1940s, probably due to the war, labor problems hampered the future of the orange industry. But in January of 1945, the O.O.A. imported thirty-four Mexican nationals to help with the crops. The association set up a bracero camp behind the packing house and hired a contractor to feed and manage these willing workers.

In June of 1945, it was discovered that more help was needed and twenty German prisoners were brought in from the war camp in Saticoy. A German-speaking instructor came in to teach these men how to pick and they made from 80 cents to $1.20 per day. The men worked until their quota was met. The war prisoners soon left for their homeland and the Mexican pickers stayed on.

As time went on, more pickers were needed until the association was hiring sixty to seventy-five men during the peak of the season. This came to an abrupt halt, though, when, in 1965, the bracero program ended by federal law. This decision damaged Ojai's citrus industry. The Mexicans were such good workers that costs rose as much as twenty-five percent when unaccustomed pickers took over.

People often wonder why, with such an abundance of good oranges growing in the valley, we are seldom served fresh squeezed orange juice in our restaurants, we often find only small inferior citrus in local markets and all over California they advertise "orange juice from Florida." It's because local orchards do not grow oranges for their own community.

In 1964, for instance, 32% of Ojai oranges went to the Midwest, 17% to the East, 15% to Canada, 5% to the Pacific Northwest, 11% were exported, a mere 3% stayed in California and the rest were sold at auction.

Orientals once bought a great many Ojai oranges. All of a

sudden, however, sales to the Orient dropped and no one knew why. An investigation uncovered the fact that the buyers were actually spooked by the orange label. It seems that the Ojai Orange Association had replaced an old crate label with one picturing a distant orchard. To the Oriental buyers, this scene resembled a cemetery. They were superstitious about such things and refused to handle boxes sporting those labels.

When the train ceased coming to Ojai, other arrangements were made for transporting local crops. With no train and with larger and more modern packing facilities elsewhere, orange growers had no use for the old packing shed. In 1970, they razed the building, also destroying the colorful labels that were left inside. Packing crate labels have since become collectibles.

The orange was destined to have a beautiful future here. Imagine, the first orange trees were carefully planted amid much skepticism in 1872 and by 1903 over 100 railroad cars left Ojai carrying oranges. Eight years later, Ojai orchards produced enough oranges for every man, woman and child in the United States. In 1925, the county produced 529,281 boxes of citrus. Ojai contributed 90,000 to that figure at a revenue of $450,000. In 1950, marketable Ojai oranges filled 500 railroad cars.

Elmer Friend

Elmer Friend was born in Ojai in 1897 to William and Annie (Beers) Friend. They lived on the east end near the San Antonio School. William planted almonds on his land in 1887, later replacing them with lemons and then with oranges. The orange trees were planted in 1891 and some of them still bore fruit in 1983.

In 1962, Elmer purchased the old Sheldon place in Matilija Canyon and, up until 1998, the family offered excellent, locally-grown fruit, nuts and honey for sale from a roadside barn on Highway 33, north of Ojai.

Stone Walls of the East End

People who travel through the orange groves in Ojai's east end usually wonder about the origin of the beautiful stone walls that surround certain orchards. In the early days, in order to ready the groves for planting, ranchers hired Orientals to remove the rocks and paid them 50 cents per day. They were told to pile the rocks at the outer perimeters of the land and they did so, in some cases, forming walls.

Fry photo
Rock wall in the east end of Ojai.

The asymmetrical stacks of stones which form crude walls are theirs. The beautiful, artistic rock walls that catch the eye of passersby today were built in the 1920s by craftsmen, not by the original Oriental farm workers.

One will notice that the early rock walls were built without mortar – they're dry walls. Later, craftsmen began to create walls using mortar. The rocks in the early walls in the east end are sand stone. Now, craftsmen are more apt to use river rock in constructing the many, fine decorative walls going up all around the valley.

The 1000 foot rock wall running in front of St. Joseph's Hospital was built in 1928. Ed Wiest owned the property then.

Olives

In the 1880s, Seymour Dalton Munger planted the valley's first olive orchard on the east end property he purchased from his father, Dexter. On February 14, 1889, 46 year-old Hugh MacMillan bought that ranch, known as Los Olivas, for $3,500 in gold coin. MacMillan was a native of Scotland who had earned prominence in his profession as an agent for the Webster Transportation Company of Chicago.

MacMillan and his wife, Annie (McKay), lived in Ojai on a part-time basis. While in Illinois, their lives were hectic. On their olive ranch, they could relax free from the pressures of a demanding business and social world. MacMillan took quite an interest in his olives, even to the point of making his own olive oil.

He built a crude olive crusher on his property. First, he located an oak tree with a cavity. He placed a large, flat rock with a groove notched for a drain next to the hollow. He inserted one end of a large beam into the tree opening and crushed the fruit on the rock with the other. The juice followed the groove into a pail.

In February, 1897, Hugh MacMillan drowned in the Santa Paula Creek. Later, someone concocted a story about his death saying that he drowned while returning from a fair. When he was found, according to the anonymous fabricator, his lifeless hand clutched a bottle of his olive oil on which there had been placed a blue ribbon. The actual obituary simply stated that Mr. MacMillan was on his way to the East on business when he drowned in an attempt to cross the swollen creek. According to Yda Storke, Susie (MacMillan) Gibson, Hugh MacMillan's daughter, took over the property after his death.

There was a great deal of interest in olives by 1892. Local ranchers experimented and proved that olive trees would grow on rocky land and with a minimum of cultivation and fertilizer. By then, besides MacMillan's forty acres of olives (which were later determined to be planted too close together), Earl Soule had twenty, Captain Richard Robinson had three acres, Edward Thacher had forty of his own and another twenty planted for Easterners and H.L. Hall had three acres. These people must have believed in the old Italian adage, "An olive orchard is a gold mine on the face of the earth."

In 1901, Edward Thacher, Thomas Corwin, H. Waldo Forster, J.J. Burke, Earl Soule, Walter Hall, Charles Bigelow and Edwin Fowler formed the Ojai Olive Association and they built a mill. During its operative years, through 1903, they marketed 11,000 gallons of oil from 100 acres of locally grown olives.

The mill was a two-story structure with a basement. Growers brought their olives to the east side of the mill where the fruit was transferred by elevator to the upper floor and spread on trays to dry. Ten to twelve days later, the operator dumped the olives into a large hopper and then down a shoot to the crusher on the lower floor. The crushed olives resembled raspberry jam. They filtered and bottled the oil on the premises, saving the pulp to use as fuel and hog feed.

George Bald was the only man ever to operate the olive mill. He refused to shut it down during the season and even slept there on a small cot. His son, Howard, brought him meals. Howard said that his father loved to drink the olive oil straight from the bottle, even though he was allergic to it and would always break out in hives.

George Bald

George Bald had come to Ojai in 1886, when he was 22 years old. He worked for local ranchers earning 50 cents per day and later, he went to work setting out trees for Edward Thacher on the Topa Topa Ranch. George married Catherine Clark (County Supervisor Tom Clark's sister), and they moved to Washington, where they lived for ten years. Howard was born there.

Howard was a sickly boy and in 1900, when he was about eight years old, the doctor recommended that Howard's family take him to a dryer climate where he might gain strength by roughing it. So back to Ojai they came. His father never like it here, according to Howard, but he stayed.

The olive mill closed down in 1903, because local oil couldn't compete with the Italian variety, and George became a forest ranger. He kept that job for nineteen years. He once said that when a fire broke out or he spotted smoke, he would grab a sack of barley for his horse, lunch for himself and his firefighting tools (rake, shovel and ax) and he'd head for the hills not knowing how long he would be gone. He earned $60 per month (four times that of twenty years earlier) from which he purchased all of his provisions.

In 1921, George was offered a job as superintendent of the Topa Topa Ranch. He held that position until the ranch was sold in 1936, then he retired.

Howard Bald married Nordhoff High School teacher Alice Mabryn Chapman, in 1917.

The old mill, having been extensively remodeled several times, is now a private residence. It stands at the south end of the street named for its dedicated operator, George Bald.

Valley Wineries

In the 1870s, Tom Clark (the supervisor's uncle), hired an Italian from the Santa Clara Valley for his threshing crew. His name, Nicolo Noce, translated to English is Nick Walnut, and that is how he wanted to be known in America. Nick homesteaded several acres northeast of Clark's on what is now Reeves Road. He began making wine in 1883 and dug a cave into the side of a hill in which to store it.

Nick had come to America during the gold rush. His wife and sons traveled from Italy to be with him but soon returned, never to see Nick again. He was a short man with a thick, strongly built body and a bushy, brown beard. He was good-natured, had a pleasant voice and radiated a friendly face, which was probably what attracted children to him.

OVM
Nick Walnut (center) in front of his home on Reeves Road.

John Thompson remembered him as a kind man. John was a child when he knew Nick Walnut. Once when he was returning home from delivering butter for his mother, he met Nick walking with a large sack slung over his shoulder. The boy asked Nick where he was headed. Nick said he had heard that the Horne place was on fire and if they were burned out they would need something to eat.

Nick died at the age of 73, in 1898, and shocked everyone by leaving his entire ranch to Willie Thompson, a 5 year-old boy. Nick wanted to be buried on his ranch under an olive tree he had planted and had rested under many times. His friends respected his wishes and his grave is still marked by native rock and shaded by the old olive tree.

Tony Sarzotti owned the old Walnut ranch for quite a while and, in 1921, Fred Carfi and Andrew Fontana bought the property. Mr. Carfi left his portion to his wife, Mary, who married another Italian named Simoni. In 1935, Mary became the sole owner and ran the winery until at least 1949. Her facility was designed to crush eight tons of grapes at once, producing over 1,000 gallons of wine at a time.

Apricots and Avocados

In 1927, Ojai orchardists tended 925 acres of apricots. The total agricultural area in Ojai then was reported as only 2,500 acres.

Most of the valley apricots were planted in Oak View and Upper Ojai, with but a few orchards on the valley floor. The Watkins in Oak View provided cabins with dirt floors and straw bedding for their imported pickers each season. The 1940s brought labor problems and growers relied on housewives and storekeepers to pick and pit the crops.

My recollections of a pitting crew were established through a child's sensibilities. We children could play together on the ranch while our mothers earned a little extra money pitting apricots. The sweet, ripe fruit drew swarms of bees and we got stung regularly. I remember running around about half the time with a little glob of mud where a bee had put his stinger into me. Today there are just a handful of apricot growers in Ojai and they are concentrated in the upper valley.

Edward Thacher is reported to have brought the first avocado trees to the valley from Mexico around 1886. Hobert R. Cole, who developed the Cole avocado of the Fuerte strain, was one of the first serious avocado growers in Southern California. Cole moved to Ojai around 1912 and lived here for forty years. He died in 1952. Cole brought the Cole Fuerte from the Hawaiian Islands about 1925.

By 1927, there were ten acres of avocados in the entire valley. Today it seems that more new orchards are being planted to avocados than to any other fruit. The Bacon variety grows best here because it can survive more cold than Haas or Fuerte. Bacon avocados are thin-skinned and green in color.

It would be interesting to know just how many Ojai acres are planted to avocados now. Although the agricultural commission and the farm advisor receive many such requests, no one has felt impelled to divide county statistics into communities. The official 'guesstimate,' however, is 1,500 acres.

One thinks of beans growing in Oxnard, not Ojai. Earl Soule, however, planted eighty acres of his ranch to beans in 1927, making this the largest planting of this vegetable ever here.

The Orchid Industry

In 1939, Louis M. Boyle bought Loring Farnum's Rancho El Rinconada on Fairview Road from C.V. White and developed Orchid Town. After several major setbacks, due to his ignorance of the flower business, Boyle became the largest and most successful producer of cymbidium orchids in the world. The seventy-seven-acre ranch was a remarkable showplace of blooms and animals and featured a most charming little town.

According to David Mason's research, Boyle built the Western village in order to make the orchid greenhouses more interesting. He salvaged building materials from local junk yards to create the front pieces for his lath houses. There were replicas of a hotel, schoolhouse, bank, Chinese laundry, saloon, church and so forth. The grounds were also decorated with hundreds of rose and camellia bushes.

Mason says that Boyle's Orchid Ranch suffered great damage in the devastating 1948 fire and that they had to bring in smudge pots to protect the orchids the following year when it snowed on the valley floor. Boyle died in the mid 1950s. Camp Ramah now uses the land.

Silk, Bees and Lumber

In the 1950s, a Mira Monte woman was reportedly growing silk stockings at home. Mrs. Eugene Charles had 15,000 cocoons on mulberry leaves which were capable of producing nearly seventy pounds of silk.

In 1879, there were twelve apiaries here, but none of the early beekeepers made history the way George Biggers did. In

1950, he shipped the largest transport of bees ever in this county. He hauled 75,000,000 bees in over 1,000 hives to Colorado by truck. He made the trip at night to allow the bees to leave their hives during the day. In 1952, *Ripley's Believe It or Not* featured Biggers when he wore a beard of live bees. In 1964, this county produced 1,800,000 pounds of honey which was worth $225,000 and $35,000 worth of beeswax.

Early settlers removed thousands of oak trees to make room for themselves and people yet to come. There were so many trees that no one could imagine their total existence being threatened. Quite a wood-cutting operation took place at W.B. Hunt's ranch on Creek Road in 1890. It was rumored that they got thirty-four cords of wood and the largest butcher-block ever built from one especially large oak tree.

By 1891, the community began to express concern for all the trees being downed on Creek Road. The possibility of man rendering Ojai Valley oakless became frightening. Later, a newcomer suggested that this was a prime place to manufacture wagons because of the dry air and ample wood. Luckily he and others interested in removing our oaks, met with discouragement, or else today we would have no leafed canopies of shade and beauty.

The Old, the Young and the Visitors

Retirement is also a big business in Ojai. We have several residential care homes, a retired teachers' home, senior housing facilities and many mobile home parks where mostly seniors reside.

Some people claim that our most important product is an abundance of happy, healthy children.

Tourism is the number one industry in Ojai Valley. The constant flow of visitors can find diverse recreational activities available, some of which serve both to entertain people here and also to attract out-of-towners. People come to play tennis or softball in the yearly tournaments, ride horseback, hike, fish, view art, play golf, pursue photography, attend our famous annual events or to simply relax in the resort-like atmosphere.

Chapter Fifteen
Bringing Water to Ojai

An important factor in raising good crops is, of course, water. People found water here, but it wasn't always easily obtainable. Farmers had to devise methods of getting the water to where they needed it. This chapter tells of the struggle for that crucial commodity.

Fresh, clear water is as convenient as the nearest spigot. It wasn't always this simple to procure, however, and it is not by accident that we now enjoy this luxury. Those who came before us labored relentlessly so that we might have a reliable source of good water.

Ventura was the first place in the county to be settled by non-native Americans. The padres and their advisors saw a permanent Chumash community living near the mouth of a wide channel, later to be known as the Ventura River. One reason they chose this location for the mission was because of the abundance of water.

In the 1790s, the padres recruited hundreds of natives to dam the Ventura River several miles north of the mission and build a stone aqueduct through Canada Larga to the mission. The diverted water gravitated through

Fry photo
Old mission aqueduct near Canada Larga.

260

a filtration system before draining into adobe reservoirs above the mission grounds.

The storm of 1861-62 heavily damaged the aqueduct and it no longer functioned. Subsequent rains over the years have washed away most of the stones. Its meager remains are still visible, however, to one who gazes east from the Ojai Freeway near the Canada Larga offramp.

In 1873, Thomas Bard and Walter Chaffee organized Ventura's second water system, the Santa Ana Water Company. Using the same idea as the padres did, they channeled Ventura River water along a ditch from the Foster Park area to the old mission reservoir above Poli Street and laid pipe through the city to carry water to key residents and businesses.

Early Ojai settlers were pleased to discover artesian wells abundant here. These naturally flowing wells served households, stock and crops sufficiently at first. Some landowners utilized water directly from the creeks.

Because of the influx of people, the water supply from 115 small artesian wells soon became inadequate for homes, street sprinkling and garden irrigation, let alone putting out fires.

In 1887, a group of progressive farmers excavated a reservoir on Gridley Road. They built the stone and cement basin fifteen feet deep and ten feet in diameter with a 350-barrel capacity. They siphoned water from the San Antonio Creek 300 yards away with six-inch pipe and carried it to town in four-inch pipe at 200 feet of pressure. They completed this project for $3,000. Research indicated that this was done by the Ojai Valley Water Company.

The San Antonio Water Company was established before 1892. San Antonio creek supplied this association through deep ditches.

In 1892, George Stewart headed a study to propose a tunnel through the mountain to obtain more water. Stewart organized the Nordhoff Water Company. He built a 2,500-barrel capacity reservoir one-half mile north of Nordhoff and laid four-inch pipe into town, offering water to a limited number of families. Pure mountain water helped eliminate disease in the valley. This fresh supply decreased the number of typhoid cases from about fifty per year to the same number over a fifteen-year period.

Capable men located and utilized more and more water sources, but still, too much water went to waste. It was frustrating to watch winter's rain water rushing down streams with no way to stop it.

Water Companies are Established

J.J. Burke stated once that an abundance of water would be the greatest blessing ever to be bestowed upon Ojai. And, in 1910, the Water Development Improvement Company, which he headed, drilled a well at the mouth of the canyon near the Foothills Hotel.

In 1912, O.W. Robertson, C.M. Pratt, E.D. Libbey, William Ladd, F.H. Osgood, H.R. Sinclair and J.J. Burke bought the Gridley Ranch solely to secure the water rights. They provided gravity water for domestic purposes.

In 1913, J.B. Berry, manager of Nordhoff Water and Power Company, claimed that Nordhoff could have all the water it needed. The equivalent of 190 barrels per hour was rushing into the reservoir north of town through George Stewart's 20 year-old water tunnel. However, by 1919 water was again scarce. That year the wells reportedly pumped the San Antonio Creek dry.

Water was a highly valued element. It was a farmer's livelihood and a family's lifeblood. History teaches us that when something is in demand, but in short supply, greed abounds – and so it was in Nordhoff.

Doc Stuart and Mr. Gibson owned a diesel engine. Each night they used it to fill the Gridley reservoir so that they could irrigate their respective crops on alternate days. A couple of times, when they arrived at the reservoir to release the water, they found it empty; water thieves had struck. Thereafter, Stuart and Gibson actually stood shotgun over their water at night.

In the mid-1920s, a concerned group engaged J.P. Lippincott, an engineer from Los Angeles, to help with local water problems. Among his early suggestions was to dam up the Sespe River at Cold Springs and pipe the overflow through the mountains to the valley. At that time, he also surveyed Matilija Canyon as a possible dam site. Apparently the public wasn't ready to commit themselves to such an expense, however, and they dropped the whole idea.

In 1924, a group organized under Ojai Valley Water Committee, was formed to study water issues and Guy Stetson was appointed chairman. In 1929, under the title, Ojai Domestic Water Co., they met to evaluate irrigation styles of local ranches. Experts visited ranches and determined that water was being wasted. Ranchers were using too much water and instructions were given to help them use water more efficiently.

In 1931, a 2,600-foot water tunnel was opened at the mouth of Senior Canyon to allow the water that accumulated in a natural reservoir there to rush, instead of trickle, into the valley. But that was not the answer to Ojai's water dilemma, either.

Matilija and Casitas Dams

The rising population increased the demand for water. That demand was also evident in Ventura and in 1944, an act of the legislature formed the Ventura County Flood Control District. They employed Donald R. Warren as consulting engineer to evaluate the local water situation and he recommended a $3 million bond issue to construct a dam in the Matilija Canyon and another on Coyote Creek.

The Matilija Dam project met with major problems. Unexpected delays, rising costs and heavy criticism plagued the job. Clay began oozing from under the dam foundation in Matilija Canyon, and the carpenters walked out. The dam was eventually deemed unsafe and a lawsuit against the engineering firm ensued. This proved to be a very costly decision.

Finally, despite all of these adversities, the site was judged safe and the workers completed the Matilija Dam in 1948. But the beautiful new dam stood embarrassingly empty for three

David Mason collection
Matilija Dam

years, as a severe drought was in progress. There wasn't enough rain during that time to make more than a mud hole of the huge reservoir and that is what water customers were getting – mud. Finally, during the winter of 1951, a storm produced enough rain to fill the reservoir to capacity and the first spill occurred the following January. Conduit pipe carried water to the spreading grounds near the mouth of Senior Canyon at a rate of 1,350 gallons per minute. This water percolated into the ground and helped replenish the wells below.

By March, 1952, 44,960 acre-feet of water had been lost over the Matilija dam spillway to the ocean. It was evident that a larger facility was necessary, especially when considering the long-range water picture. In the meantime, geologists tested a dam site at Coyote Creek. A possible fault caused the project to be canceled, but after further investigation, this decision was reversed. Consultants for the flood control district recommended a 90,000 acre-foot reservoir on Coyote Creek to stop the Matilija overflow, and the project was approved.

The Federal Bureau of Reclamation completed Casitas Dam in 1959. When Lake Casitas was filled, the water covered part of the original Casitas Pass and part or all of the following ranches: Hoffman's, Dunshee's, Chismahoo and Rancho Cola. The first spill-over at Casitas Dam was in April, 1978. Casitas Municipal Water District presently operates Matilija Dam, which is owned by the Ventura County Flood Control District. No water is served to customers from this source. Lake Matilija is used primarily to store water during flood periods for later transfer to Lake Casitas.

Watkins family photo
One of several Santa Ana Valley Ranches now under Lake Casitas

Chapter Sixteen
Ojai Flashbacks: Fifty Years

In writing this book, my primary concern was with the very early, less easily obtainable history of the valley. The period between the 1930s and 1980s, however, marked a time of considerable change. I feel it is pertinent to our understanding of the past to include some of the happenings occurring within that time span. Here is a chronological listing of various newspaper accounts denoting important or interesting Ojai events.

1920: Sunday motorists were swarming to Ojai. With the introduction of the auto, tourism was on the rise.

State speed cops from the Automobile Club of California visited the valley regularly to explain and enforce traffic laws.

1921: The City Garage was built on the southwest corner of Montgomery Street and Ojai Avenue. The building is currently occupied by the Ojai Valley Cleaners.

1924: Ojai experienced a building boom.

1925: The Ojai-Santa Paula Road to Santa Paula was completed and paved.

1927: There were two doctors practicing here: Dr. Saeger and Dr. King.

1928: The city placed signs to identify streets.

H.R. Roberts bought a tract of land from George Hall east of the Soule property, named it Seite Robles (seven oaks) and opened the sale of lots there.

1930: The Ojai Theater, on the southwest corner of Ojai Avenue and Signal Street, installed 'talkies'.

1932: The Deer Lodge opened on Maricopa Highway. It is still operating nearly seventy years later.

Mr. Slater purchased the pool hall and smoke house from George Macleod and was refused a license because officials suspected him of allowing gambling there.

Mr. Swanson bought the Ojai Theater.

1933: Workers finished the Maricopa Road to Cuyama, after which there was a big celebration held in Cuyama.

1935: The first five and dime store opened here.

1936: George A. McKenna bought the Topa Topa Ranch from Thacher heirs.

1938: Harold Clausen opened Ojai's first funeral home on Matilija Street in the rooming house that was once John Montgomery's residence.

1939: The county established the honor farm on Rice and Baldwin Roads as a rehabilitation center. Inmates were brought from Ventura daily to farm the county ranch. Clarence Barrows was in charge there.

1941: Ojai prepared for the war: Women learned to shoot at the target range that was erected on the Soule property.

1942: The army turned the Boyd Club into a recreation hall.

Sugar was being rationed.

1943: Los Angeles experienced a "daylight dim-out." This was the first smog reported in that city.

1944: Mr. and Mrs. Glen Wills and Mr. and Mrs. Melville Danner bought the movie theater from Swanson.

1945: Firefighters protested Captain Bill Bowie's resignation by refusing to work.

Bert P. Hanson built the Ojai Frozen Food Locker on Ojai Avenue and Fulton Street.

1946: George Schroff bought the bowling lanes.

1947: Some reported spotting a flying saucer hovering over Ojai.

Kenneth Ayers was the fire captain.

The city established a building code. Fred Pfiffer, former City Marshal and Superintendent of Streets and Sanitation, was the inspector.

Sixteen homes were established in Siete Robles.

There were 1,411 phones in the Ojai exchange.

Bunce Lumber Company opened east of the Y intersection off Highways 33 and 150.

Walter Bristol's *Story of the Ojai Valley* was being circulated at $2.00 per copy.

1948: There was a dog pound at the Ferguson Ranch on Creek Road.

A total of 3,661 deer hunters registered that year.

Ojai experienced a gas shortage.

1949: Pyramid clubs were the rage.

Fireman Frank Keyes rescued a cat from the post office tower.

The city issued $315,862 in building permits for the year.

Retail sales in Ojai were at the two million dollar mark for the year.

1950: Building permits valued at $50,000 were issued during the months of January and February.

Twenty merchants gave green stamps.

Local merchants established the Welcome Wagon.

The city approved the proposal to build a Shell gasoline station at the triangle (Ojai Avenue, El Paseo Road and Canada Street).

Ojai enforced rent control.

C.R. Craft opened a health food store in Ojai.

1951: Builders planned an extension to the Shady Lane tract.

The Skyline tract, north of Oak View, was subdivided.

Officials hired Joseph Welch as the first city manager. His salary was $400 per month.

There was a restaurant in Ojai called The Nest.

Midway acres, on Rice Road, was subdivided.

The Hub, now a cocktail lounge in the Arcade, served food and catered to families.

Crandall's grocery market opened in Meiners Oaks.

Planning was underway for an expansion of the Drown tract.

Building permits exceeded a million dollars for the year.

1952: The Mercer tract was subdivided.

The Arbolada and West Hills area (west of the Arbolada) were rezoned from agriculture to residential use.

This year marked the first organized issuance of house numbers in Ojai proper.

Talk in town centered around trying to control growth in Ojai.

Slim Bayless built a new market at 131 West Ojai Avenue, across the street from his Santa Cruz Market. He later changed the name to Bayless Market.

There were two newspapers and one bank in the Ojai Valley.

In June, the city issued $52,000 in building permits.

A police chief and two officers handled law enforcement.

Ojai's assessed valuation for the year was $2,142,380.

The population was 3,000.

1953: Ojai's entrance sign was dedicated on Highway 33.

John O'Neill was the building inspector.

1954: The Grandview tract was started.

In June, there were $91,000 in building permits issued.

The 24-hour restaurant called End of the Trail, also known as Anderson's, closed only once in twelve years of business.

There were 219 homes proposed in July including the Ojai Terrace tract – this was the greatest number ever approved at one time.

Developers planned to build 158 homes on the Ayers

Ranch (where Ayers Street is now).

The twelve-unit Ojai Rancho Motel was completed at 615 West Ojai Avenue.

1955:   A 52-acre tract near Foothill Road was started.

Strong and serious campaigns were launched to ban uncontrolled growth.

Experts expect smog here within five years.

1956:   Retail sales in Ojai amounted to four million dollars for the year.

Someone slashed the seats at the theater.

In a six-week period, three motorists collided with the train.

During 1955-56, there were 41 accidents at the Y intersection. Finally a larger stop sign and a sign warning motorists of the approaching stop sign were erected.

The Ojai editorial pages reflected the community's concern over accelerated growth.

1957:   There were parking problems in the city and numerous accidents reported.

Charles Marrone proposed a race track, ball park, dance pavilion and shopping center on Gridley Road.

The city hired its first recreation director: Michael McKissick.

1958:   Ojai received mention as an All-American City from the National Municipal League.

Butman Road, which in the 1930s was known as San Antonio Road, was changed to Country Club Drive. People named Butman had once owned property in that area.

1959:   Retail sales in Ojai totaled eight million dollars for the year.

Two million dollars in building permits were issued. This was over six times the figure from ten years ago.

St. Joseph's Hospital, near Gorham on East Ojai Avenue, was dedicated.

Ken Hasse and Bill Akins opened the Firebird Restaurant

in the old Ojai American Legion building at 960 East Ojai Avenue.

There was an open house at the new Ojai Valley Community Hospital on Maricopa Highway. This project took eight years from its conception to completion.

1960: Postal workers served 16,000 patrons per day over a thirty-square mile area of Ojai Valley. Joe Potts was the postmaster. It cost five cents to mail a letter.

The city manager was James F. Sullivan.

Using dynamite, John Dron demolished the fifty-year-old Bank of American building on Ojai Avenue just west of the present bank.

Sixty-five percent of all local parents earned their livelihood outside the valley.

The Y shopping center opened on Maricopa Highway.

The Red Cross taught 99 valley children how to swim during the summer.

One could dine at the Oaks Hotel for $2.95.

There were seventy-five new homes approved in December.

The city issued $1,650,000 in building permits during the year.

Ojai assessed valuation was $6,270,000.

1963: The El Roblar Movie Theater was built on Maricopa Highway where the Ojai Valley State Bank is now.

1968: Citrus was the number one product in Ojai – tourism was second.

1970: There was a severe shortage of homes priced under $20,000.

1976: A research team from New York listed Nordhoff, Lyon Springs, Matilija, Ozena and Stauffer as being ghost towns.

1980s: The world's only roller skating elephant, Tarra, lived and skated in the Ojai Valley.

Chapter Seventeen
Ojai Today

In 1917, Libbey transformed Ojai from a common, little, dusty town to a distinctive and attractive village. As the preceding outline indicates, the next significant change occurred in the 1950s. This is when people started the metamorphosis of Ojai from a rural, horsy, country town.

A rural community suggests such things as farms, barnyard animals and quiet, tree-lined streets without sidewalks. It implies a slower pace, friendliness, trust and knowing just about everyone in town. These are some of the qualities people relocate here for, while others remain because of them. And still others, convinced that this aspect is gone, leave Ojai in search of a place that still

Fry photo
Pergola, rebuilt in 1999

represents their idea of "small-town America." Even those living here for as few as six years have observed changes resulting from growth. Inevitably, with growth comes change and, if growth is to happen, the community must adapt. As these changes take place, the way is cleared for even more new residents.

When the population increases, the community must provide more services and conveniences to accommodate the influx. We build new schools for children yet to come. We make better roads so people can travel into Ojai effortlessly. We erect new tracts on what were once open fields or producing orchards. Then we need more shopping centers. New laws are written because more people drastically complicate the social system. Consequently, the more people we invite here to stay, the less solitude and privacy we enjoy and the less rural Ojai will be.

Growth and Change

Despite the fact that Ojai Valley is growing and changing, compared to other cities we have managed to maintain a relatively small-town atmosphere. How, with all of Southern California bursting at the seams, is this possible? We reject freeways, large discount houses and all of the other things that denote big city. People must understand that, to enjoy a rural atmosphere, one must sacrifice a few conveniences.

If the city allowed buildings higher than two stories, if we cut down the trees, brought in the freeway and allowed industry indiscriminately, much of what the valley has to commend it would be lost. Ojai would become an ordinary place full of smog, noise and people, with concrete and cars stretching from foothill to foothill.

Ojai still possesses the ability to fascinate, attract and delight. Some people claim that this place has bewitched them. Ojai is quaint (pleasingly old-fashioned, attractively unusual), unique (rare, choice, matchless) and all of these qualities add up to one thing. We cannot buy it, but we can preserve it; above all else, we must not destroy it.

Ojai's Charm

Ojai is charming and here are some reasons why. Ojai is where only the tourists turn their heads to stare at famous personalities, because the residents are accustomed to seeing them.

On the outskirts of Ojai Valley, south of Foster Park, stands a very special People's Christmas Tree. It is an ordinary tree, probably of the fir variety. One December, road crews cut back some shrubbery and trees along that stretch of the freeway. Someone spotted the then tiny tree and, in an effort to save it from the ax, hung a couple of Christmas ornaments and some tinsel on its branches. Others stopped and added their meager adornments. Soon the little tree was so beautiful that it was allowed to live.

The People's Christmas Tree is much larger now. And still each year, as if by magic, it is decorated more and more elaborately. Harried Christmas shoppers, grumpy commuters, and hundreds of visitors experience a calming sense of Christmas spirit and brotherly love when they drive past and notice the tree the community has decorated together.

The world famous Police Blotter originated in Ojai. Fred Volz began this feature in the *Ojai Valley News* some years ago. The purpose was to inform the public of their police department's routine. The Police Blotter included such things as: A deer was eating on the library lawn. A Blanche Street dog was barking. A woman reported her purse missing. Someone found the purse on a bus bench and brought it to the police station intact.

Police were always chasing someone's pony, sheep, goats or geese up or down city streets. And then there were our local characters, some of whom had extremely vivid imaginations.

Johnny Carson discovered the Police Blotter and used to close his show with excerpts from it. Larger newspapers used the Ojai Police Blotter to entertain their readers. In Ojai, crime was refreshingly humorous. As Ojai grows, however, so does the seriousness of the crime. Consequently, the crime report continues to become less and less humorous.

We no longer have a police department. In January 1980, the Ojai Police Department became a unit of the Ventura County Sheriff under a police-sheriff contract for law enforcement services.

Ojai The Beautiful

Despite wild building spurts and great waves of growth, Ojai remains appealing to the eye. There are three major reasons for this. One is the constant battle waged by the Ojai Valley Garden Club to protect the life and limbs of our native trees. We have an architectural board that carefully monitors our building designs and we have a strict sign ordinance. We also have volunteer commissions which operate through the city. The Historic Preservation Commission assists in preserving Ojai's history and the Arts Commission helps to enhance the aesthetic quality of this place.

This notice appeared in *The Ojai* around the turn of the century: "Those who distribute advertising literature or post signs should exercise better judgment. The average citizen does not like to see our grass lots covered with glaring paper or the tree trunks of the valley disfigured with flashy pasteboard. Every breeze now, across our green community, lifts a flight of red, yellow or white circulars." The continuity of this attitude through the decades led to the eventual development of our sign ordinance.

During the 1950s, with such a flurry of real estate activity going on, officials began looking for ways to prevent the proliferation of signs that grossly marred the appearance of the city. In 1953, they formed a committee and appointed Edward Callender as chairman. He was to gather information regarding the feasibility of establishing some type of regulation.

On May 17, 1956, based on the committee findings, the Planning Commission recommended a sign ordinance. And on June 11 of the same year, the Architectural Board of Review was established. The mayor, with the approval of the council, appointed five people to this board. At least one of them, it was decided, must be schooled in architecture, while one has to hold a license from the California State Contractor's License Board.

Their purpose is to promote orderly and harmonious development within the city, ensure enhancement of this city's unique character and, at the same time, sustain property values. Their concerns include style, size of the proposed building and its color.

This committee also reviews sign proposals. Their attitude is that signs should identify and not advertise. They allow no flashing signs. There can be no more than four colors in a sign and those colors must be compatible with the surroundings. Size and placement of the signs are also important criteria.

Ojai is the browser's delight and the serious shopper's paradise. From Ojai's hundreds of businesses I've isolated a few which are unique, historical, famous or all of these things.

Rains Department Store

Glen, Wesley and Floyd Hickey opened a general merchandise store in Carpinteria in 1904. Twelve years later, they heard of a business for sale in Nordhoff and Wesley came to check it out. He rode the train to Ventura and, after a long wait, he boarded the Ojai special which brought him only as far as La Cross because the bridge was washed out. Tom Clark met the merchant on the other side of the creek and brought him into Nordhoff.

Glen Hickey bought Barrows' old store, known as Ojai Hardware and Implement Company from the most recent owner, Mr. Soliss. Just before the disastrous 1917 fire, Hickey purchased Mallory and Dennison's dry goods store.

In a 1948 newspaper interview, the Hickey brothers recalled the honesty of people in the early days. When they received a shipment of valuables such as guns, shotgun shells and expensive hardware items, it often sat in the back alley for three days before their small workforce could put it away. The Hickeys were sure that no one ever took any of it.

Lynn Rains joined the firm, known as Hickey Hardware, as a warehouseman and general helper when he was still in high school. He worked his way up and, in 1934, became merchandise manager for all four stores: Ventura, Carpinteria, Fillmore and Ojai. The Hickeys took him in as a co-partner in 1938 and made him general manager of the Ojai store.

In 1944, Lynn Rains opened Rains Realty Company. He bought the Hickeys out in 1960, formed a partnership with his son, Alan, and they changed the store name to Rains Department Store. Alan purchased Lynn Rains' interest in the store in 1969. His son, Jeff, joined the business in 1988 and now he is running it.

In tracing the history of Rains store, the trail leads back to the tiny store first run by the newlywed Herberts so long ago. This confirms Rains as the oldest continually-run business in the Ojai Valley. Rains Department Store is located in the center of the arcade.

Bill Baker's Bakery

During World War I, the government offered $500 to the person who could develop a recipe for the best wheatless bread.

Wilhelm Koch, a chef at the Huntington Hotel in Pasadena, entered the contest and vowed that if he won, he would use the money to have his name changed. That is how Mr. Koch became William Cook Baker.

Bill Baker settled in Ventura in 1917 and ran the American Bakery for six years.

In the meantime, E.F. Carle had sold his Ojai Bakery to Emile K. Gerstenmeyer in 1919. Gerstenmeyer ran the bakery, known as The Cookie Shop, as a retail store – baking bread for local grocery stores. Bill Baker bought the Cookie Shop, at 457 East Ojai Avenue, from Emile Gerstenmeyer in 1923.

Gusta Lundine Linebarger photo
Ojai Bakery, presumably the building Bill Baker first occupied in Ojai.

In 1926, Baker tore down the old barn-like building and built a new one. This modern building had a retail store and a sales and equipment room with a covered driveway between. Roy Wilson designed the building, George Noble was the contractor and Frank Harrow did the concrete work.

Mr. Baker had a soft heart for those less fortunate and a flair for the dramatic. After the Santa Barbara quake, he baked bread for the hungry. He often created huge cakes for monumental occasions, such as the U.S. Presidents' birthdays. In 1934, Baker made the world's biggest cake. This nearly one-ton fruit pound cake was reportedly twenty-one feet in circumference and seven feet in diameter. It was decorated with 2000 frosting roses and 1000 birds. Just getting the cake to its destination in Los Angeles to celebrate the 75th birthday of the school system there, was quite a production. It took ten men and a ten ton truck to move it and they, reportedly, had to take the sides off the bakery to get it out. In 1939, Baker baked a 1000-pound cake for the World's Fair in San Francisco. Bill Baker is also credited with originating lima bean and gluten bread in the 1930s. And he's among the first to bake a soybean loaf.

As a youngster, Bill Baker showed talent as a sculptor. In fact, he planned to be an artist.

Bill Baker died in 1942 after contracting poison oak, according to historian David Mason. After Baker's death, Harmon and Helen Vaughn, who had been working for Baker since around 1936, stayed on to run the bakery. They bought the business from Baker's widow in 1946 and operated it until 1974.

Bill Baker's Bakery continues to serve the community in the original building at 457 East Ojai Avenue.

Bart's Corner

Richard Bartindale of Santa Monica originated Bart's Corner at 302 West Matilija Street in 1964. He combined his love for books with the dream of opening a farmers market and created a unique atmosphere. This may be the only outdoor bookstore in the United States. People come from all over the world to browse among books sheltered by giant oaks. The open-air patio is a perfect place to sit quietly and read or to attend an occasional autograph party for a local author. Gary Schlichter owns Bart's Corner now.

Bart's Corner is the only business in Ojai where one can make a purchase after hours. A customer chooses a book from those shelved outside along the sidewalk and places the designated amount into a slot in the gate. Schlichter doesn't know of anyone ever lifting one of their outside books.

Ranch House Restaurant

The well-known philosopher, Krishnamurti, drew Alan and Helen Hooker to Ojai in 1949. They moved into the old Meiners' ranch house in Meiners Oaks, refurbished the large, place and opened it to overnight guests. Alan did the cooking, offering a primarily vegetarian menu at first. They charged $14 a week to board and that included meals.

In 1950, the Hookers got serious about their business. Alan obtained a license to operate a restaurant and Helen named it Ranch House Restaurant. They stayed in the Meiners home until 1954, when the property sold.

Alan then took a job in the kitchen at Happy Valley School to support himself and Helen. Two years later, their friend, Frank Noyes, suggested Alan buy half acre of land below the old ranch house and build a restaurant there. Alan liked the idea, but lacked the funds, so Noyes put up the money. Thanksgiving Day, 1956, the Ranch House opened on South Lomita Avenue.

Alan hired a baker, but he did the cooking himself. Helen was the hostess and the waitress. At first, they could seat sixteen people for dinner, which cost around $3.50 a plate in those days. The following spring, they expanded. Alan bought wrought iron furniture from the Oaks Hotel and fifty chairs for $1 each from a local Mexican restaurant (possibly the popular Angie's Restaurant then on Maricopa Highway at Fairview Road). Beatrice Wood offered to paint the chairs. Now they could seat forty.

In 1958, the Hookers started serving meat to draw a larger

OVM

John Meiners' ranch home as it looked when Alan and Helen Hooker operated the Ranch House Restaurant there during the 1950s.

crowd. That's the same year they built a studio on the site where they lived until 1969.

In the beginning, they allowed customers to bring their own wine for 25 cent a bottle which they chilled in the brook in the garden. In 1964, they were issued a license to serve beer and wine. Knowing relatively nothing about wines, Alan bought it from the corner liquor store at first. Now the Ranch House offers over 600 fine imported and domestic wines.

According to Ralph Edsell in his story of the Ranch House, Alan Hooker had a lifelong love affair with food. At the age of 3 he would stand outside his home in Carpentersville, Illinois and invite passersby in for dinner. In the Roaring '20s, he played piano in a jazz band and, while on the road, he'd prepare dinner for the other members of the band. He was constantly experimenting and kept track of his creations in a food diary. Alan, who became noted for his baking, is reported to have made his first loaf of wheat bread in an old washing machine. Hooker ran a pie company before coming to Ojai.

Alan died in 1993 at the age of 90. Helen, now in her 90s, is still living.

The Ranch House Restaurant, named for the old Meiners' home, still attracts diners with discriminating taste from all over the world. It's a favorite restaurant of movie stars. An evening at the Ranch House features patio dining and guests are encouraged to stroll along the bubbling stream among the lovely gardens where herbs, used in the food preparation, grow amongst roses and other flowers.

Ojai Seniors

Many people have discovered that Ojai is a perfect place to retire. The mild climate that historically lured the ailing to Ojai may also be one inducement that attracts the elderly. Couple this with the lush scenery, relaxed lifestyle and congenial environment and it's practically the ideal retirement spot.

Mrs. H. LeBel Winnette, a nurse and Swedish masseuse, opened Ojai's first rest home at the corner of Aliso and Ventura Streets in the 1920s. She may have been responsible for starting a trend, for now there are approximately ten rest homes and nursing facilities expressly for the elderly. There are half a dozen large mobile home parks, which are usually dominated by those 60 years of age and over and a 100-unit senior housing facility on East Ojai Avenue.

In 1969, valley churches combined their work forces and established HELP of Ojai. Together they provided the community with needed services like aiding shut-ins and tutoring failing students.

They found that the community's most fervent requests were for transportation, however, and most of those came from the seniors. In 1975, HELP sponsored a group called Retired Senior Volunteer Program (RSVP) expressly to provide transportation for handicapped people and seniors. A federal grant bought their first multi-seated vehicle and the city purchased their second. They added a third bus to their collection in 1980.

RSVP has branched out; using the services of able seniors to help those who need assistance in a variety of ways. Hospice is part of the RSVP program. Crime prevention is another area where seniors are actively helping and guiding other seniors through Ojai Valley Volunteer Security Patrol.

This posse of seniors, under the direction of RSVP and the Sheriff's Department, aid local law enforcement agencies. They write citations on abandoned cars, run errands for the department, do home security checks and maintain surveillance over local businesses. This program, the brainchild of Undersheriff John Gillespie and his wife, Carol, was the first of its kind in the state. Senior volunteers also promote and help launch Neighborhood Watch programs throughout the valley.

The small building on city hall grounds, at 401 South Ventura Street, called Little House, is a recreation center for Ojai seniors. Not only are the RSVP and HELP offices located there, but that is also where seniors receive their specially prepared hot meals daily. They can participate in a variety of programs at the Little House. They exercise, play games, learn new crafts, receive blood pressure checks, obtain legal aid, have their pets licensed and much more.

Day care services are also provided for the elderly.

Grey Gables

In 1954, Dr. Ethel Percy Andrus, founder of the National Retired Teachers Association, viewed the property at the northwest corner of Grand Avenue and Montgomery Street. What she saw there was a high stone wall around a building and overgrown grounds. Barbed wire had been strung across the top of the wall and the gate was heavily barred. She saw a future there, however, purchased the eyesore and established Grey Gables as a home for retired teachers.

Living Treasures

Sanford Drucker started Living Treasures in Ojai in 1993. Living Treasures is a local mentor program designed to honor those who excel in their field and requiring them, in turn, to share their expertise with others. Drucker's vision for the Living Treasures program is to provide role models and mentors who focus on the positive by igniting the dreams and talents in each of us. And his vision is being played out as some of the community's greatest resources – the Living Treasures – are working with individuals and groups in the arts, communication, community service, education, environment, finance, business, government, health, human relations, physical fitness and technology.

Contact Living Treasures by writing, POB 1777, Ojai, CA 93024 or email: info@livingtreasures.org. Their web site is: http://www.livingtreasures.org

Ojai Valley Youth Foundation

Caryn Bosson is the executive director for Ojai Valley Youth Foundation (OVYF), an organization cosponsored by the Ventura County Sheriffs Department, Ojai Unified School District and the City of Ojai. A major goal of OVYF, according to Bosson, is to have "every valley teenager feel included, connected and respected." The Foundation helps existing efforts and sponsors new programs to make Ojai a better place for young people and their families. Their mission statement is: "To create a youth master plan to ensure that our community is a safe and nurturing one for our young people to grow up in and reach their full potential."

According to Bosson, "Our mission is to support families and promote responsible parenting; increase educational, recreational and employment opportunities and promote the positive participation and interactions of young people and adults in community life."

A unique aspect of Ojai Valley Youth Foundation is that there are as many young people involved in decision-making and the necessary work as there are adults. The board of directors, for example, is composed of youth and adults paired as co-chairs of each committee.

Ojai Valley Youth Foundation just received $1,000,000 grant from the California Wellness Foundation and, included in their future plans are a youth fitness center, a bicycle repair business and a community organic garden all to be planned and implemented by diverse youth-adult committees. The OVYF also operates as an employment agency for valley youth.

Contact Ojai Valley Youth Foundation at 805-640-9555 or visit their office at 201 Church Street in Ojai.

Ojai Historic Preservation Commission

The City of Ojai has created commissions dedicated to various crucial aspects of the valley such as recreation, art and historical. Volunteers are selected from the community to serve on these commissions. The Historic Preservation Commission studies issues around our historic structures and designates buildings for historic landmark status.

The city now has seven historic landmarks: Nazarene Church (the original Presbyterian Church), Woolsey House, Ojai Arcade, Ojai Post Office, Nordhoff Cemetery, St. Thomas Aquinas Chapel (now the Chamber of Commerce office and home to Ojai Valley Museum) and the Ojai Valley Woman's Clubhouse. Structures currently in line for historical designation include, Libbey Park Jail, Bill Baker's Bakery, the original building at Ojai Valley Inn, Gateway to the Arbolada and the Ladd and Libbey homes on Foothill Road.

With the advent of this commission, interest in historic buildings and local history in general has accelerated. In 1999, the Ojai Unified School District was one county district to

Fry Photo
Historic Preservation Landmark plaque for the Theodore Woolsey house.

282

receive a grant from the Annenberg Rural Challenge Foundation to fund an oral history program. As part of this project, local grammar school students contacted local historians and old-timers and interviewed, recorded and filmed them and various historical sites throughout the valley. The results will be exhibited in the Ojai Valley Museum.

Fry photo
Topa Topa School fifth grade students and their teacher preparing to film a local historian for an oral history project.

Chapter Eighteen
The Essence of Ojai

The last quarter of the twentieth century is widely referred to as the Aquarian Age. Spirituality is the predominate motivation. Ojai seems to lure students of the New Age. They settle here, bringing with them organizations that flourish in this environment. Ojai is considered one of the first New Age centers in California.

It is believed that, over many years, certain forces, through a concentration of positive thoughts, have accumulated here. Some people, upon entering the valley, feel a magnetic pull. Those with spiritual awareness claim to see a luminous canopy – Ojai's aura. Others can feel powerful vibrations here – vibrations created, perhaps, through collective mental efforts of the varied spiritual groups.

It has been going on for a long time and it continues. An 1878 issue of the *Los Angeles Times* carried an article about Ojai from which this observation was taken: "The magnetic center for the earth is here. Spirit-minded people come to reach the God centers in themselves."

People come, bring their ideas and either start a spiritual group or become a participant in an established organization. Their combined goals are to preserve and improve upon humanity. By expanding one's own individual awareness, by transforming one's attitude to the positive, by learning to live in harmony with oneself, a person contributes to the harmony of the world; thus helping to create a more positive and peaceful atmosphere. And all of mankind benefits.

Some New Age and spiritual groups that have filtered into the valley are the Church of Tzaddi, Life Divine Center, Sufi Order,

Unitarian Fellowship, Vortex Institute, Science of the Mind, Siddha Yoga Dham, Huna, ECKANKAR, Church Universal and Triumphant, Ananta Foundation and Sathya Sai Baba.

Following are sketches of some of the valley's most prominent spiritual organizations.

Meditation Mount

At the end of Reeves Road, atop a knoll, perches the Western headquarters of MGNA, or Meditation Group for the New Age. Forty years ago, a group of individuals from the United States and Europe gathered in England at the express request of Dr. Robert Assagioli. At this meeting, Assagioli. a psychologist, explained his concepts regarding a new, more effective method of meditation. And MGNA was born.

This group is composed of people from all over the world who meditate to further the evolution of humanity. MGNA offers a study course which is mailed from Meditation Mount to individuals everywhere and is translated into eight languages.

The buildings on Meditation Mount, all nestled among the sage brush and wild flowers, are Oriental in design. The facilities are open to the public daily from 10 a.m. until sunset. Anyone may attend the monthly meetings which take place at the full moon. Members of MGNA believe that when the moon is full, the doors to heaven are open wider, allowing them to make more effective contact with the higher spirits. Visit the Meditation Mount web site: www.meditation.com.

Fry photo
Meditation Mount

Krotona

In 1906, Albert Powell Warrington, a 40 year-old lawyer from Norfolk, Virginia, and theosophist, first envisioned Krotona. He planned to build a center on the James River where cultured people and overworked city folk could rest in beautiful surroundings. Theosophy was to be the inspiring feature. When Annie Besant, world president of the Theosophical Society, asked Warrington to head an esoteric school in California, he agreed and decided to bring his concept to fruition here.

In 1912, he purchased fifteen acres in the Los Angeles foothills. There he established Krotona, "the place of promise." Warrington got the name from a colony in Italy where the great philosopher, Pythagoras, once had a school of life. Crotona, of the third century, was the center of spiritual enlightenment, just as Warrington's new Krotona was to become.

When the movie industry began their mass infiltration of Southern California, giving birth to Hollywood, Warrington decided to move. In 1924, he led the faithful to Ojai, a section of Southern California he thought to be "impregnated with occult and psychic influences."

The Krotona Institute of Theosophy is composed of members of the Theosophical Society which was founded in New York City in 1875 by Madame Elena Petrovna Blavatsky, a Russian religious leader. She wrote *The Secret Doctrine,* a textbook for theosophists.

Annie Besant of England joined the Theosophical Society as a student of Madame Blavatsky, who was an important political figure in India. Besant founded the Central Hindu College at Benares in 1898 and the Indian Home Rule League in 1916. In 1917, she

Courtesy of Krotona Library
Annie Besant

served as president of the Indian National Congress.

The Order of the Star of the East was started in 1911 by members of the Theosophical Society. In 1928, the organization bought land adjoining Krotona, in the area of what is now Besant Road and including the Meiners homestead, on which to hold their annual camp congress.

This project caused quite a stir in the valley and put a lot of locals to work. With Sam Hudiburg overseeing the project, they built three large bath houses with twenty showers and twenty toilets each, dressing rooms to accommodate 400 and a large kitchen. Fred Linder was hired to install the modern kitchen equipment such as dishwasher, ice cream freezer, electric potato peeler and salad chopper at Starland.

Jiddu Krishnamurti was recognized as the leader of the Order of the Star of the East then and people came from near and far to hear him speak – a reported 1,500 people in 1928.

In 1929, Krishnamurti decided against affiliation with any organization and he dissolved the Order. But many who came to Star Camp stayed on. Madeline Baird, as an example, built the mansion at 205 South Lomita Avenue in Meiners Oaks in 1929, just to be close to Krishnamurti, who maintained a home in the east end called Arya Vihara.

Many visitors enjoy the scenic drive through the wooded grounds of Krotona and a walk around the lotus pond and rose gardens. People come from all over to browse through the bookstore or to use the library, as it is one of the largest occult libraries in the world.

The Memorial Gateway to Krotona was designed by Austin Pierpont and built by Ben Noren in 1952. It was dedicated to Albert P. Warrington and Miss Marie Poutz.

Krotona is at 46 Krotona Hill, which is across from Hermosa Road on Highway 33. Contact them through krotona@jetlink.net. Their web site is: www.theosophical.org

Jiddu Krishnamurti

It was Charles W. Leadbeater, a Theosophical leader, who first saw the wonderful aura of 13 year-old, Jiddu Krishnamurti, in 1909. Annie Besant was so impressed with the young man that she virtually adopted him. She had great expectations for him and demonstrated her willingness to help him reach the heights she knew him capable of. He was thought to be the new Messiah.

Courtesy of Krotona Library
Nityananda Krishnamurti, Albert P. Warrington and Jiddu Krishnamurti

Krishnamurti first came to Ojai in 1922 with his ailing brother, Nityananda, in hopes that the climate would save him. His brother died here three years later.

The expectations of others must have overwhelmed young Krishnamurti. He became uncomfortable with the image people bestowed upon him. Throughout his life, he continually claimed that he was not a world teacher, that he had simply found a way of living "intelligently, happily and without sorrow." He hoped that others could also find truth and wisdom within themselves.

Kristnamurti did not encourage followers. He felt it was wrong to follow another through the "difficult process of life." Individuals should explore their own minds and ultimately draw their own conclusions independent of the spoken or written thoughts of others, he said. Through his talks, Krishnamurti led self-explorations, hoping that he would awaken a latent thought in an individual mind in his audience and that he would encourage its development.

Krishnamurti was born in Madras, India in 1895. His father was a theosophist who worked in the headquarters in Adyar.

Ojai Foundation

In 1927, Annie Besant bought upper valley land on which she planned to build a religious center with Krishnamurti at the head. Lack of water in Upper Ojai prompted a shift of venues, but Besant held onto her property in the name of Happy Valley Foundation. Happy Valley School is now on part of that land and The Ojai Foundation uses 40-acres of it.

According to their brochure, the purpose of The Ojai Foundation is to create and nurture an educational sanctuary for youth and adults. The Foundation provides a learning community and a place for retreat, reflection and healing. The Foundation's focus on education has been coupled with a firm commitment to land stewardship and environmental awareness. Most of the structures on the property are wood and canvas powered by solar energy and their land development includes an organic fruit orchard and herb garden.

For more information about the programs and facilities in this beautiful semi-wilderness, contact The Ojai Foundation at 805-646-8343 or visit their web site at www.ojaifoundation.org.

Meher Mount

Atop Sulphur Mountain on 170 acres, perches Meher Mount. Meher Mount was founded in the 1940s, in response to Avatar Meher Baba's (1894-1969) request for a place of pilgrimage for those who revered him.

Agnes Baron was the long-time caretaker of Meher Mount. According to Kendra Crossen Burroughs, current caretaker, Baron was highly involved with community service. She established the Head Start programs in the county, conceived and developed the Ventura County funded Drug Abuse Reorientation Training (D.A.R.T.) and helped found the Ventura County Suicide Prevention program. Baron died in 1994.

Meher Mount still exists, although several original buildings were destroyed by the 1985 fire. Currently, the Burroughs host weddings at Meher Mount, concerts, meditation groups and individual and group retreats. Contact them by phone: 805-640-0000 or Internet: www.bigfoot.com/~mehermount

Chapter Nineteen
Events and Sights

In 1933, James Hilton wrote about a hidden paradise called Shangri-la in his novel *Lost Horizons*. When Ronald Colman made the movie based on this book in 1937, it is thought by some that Ojai played the leading role. Other people, however, doubt that any part of the movie was filmed in this valley. Those who believe that Ojai was Colman's Shangri-la, don't all agree about what view was used in that brief scene.

With or without Colman's enticement, Ojai lures people here. But once here, they will find that this place offers more than beauty, charm and a good ambiance. There is more to do than gaze at the beautiful oaks. Following are our major annual events and most interesting sights, along with the history of each.

Ojai Day

We're so proud of our town that we honor it annually with a celebration reminiscent of Ojai Day, 1917. Music, hay rides, historical trolley tours and an array of entertainment for all ages are just some of the events featured on Ojai Day. Ojai Avenue is roped off to traffic and the street is lined with booths where browsers can buy food, merchandise and learn about various local organizations and agencies. This popular affair is typically held in the fall.

Tennis Tournament

William Larned Thacher joined his brothers, Sherman and Edward, in Nordhoff for a three-week stay in 1890. He had studied for the ministry in a theological seminary and planned to serve as pastor for a Presbyterian Church in Bradford, Pennyslvania.

William's main sports interest was tennis. He was a member of Yale's tennis team where he earned the honor of intercollegiate doubles championship and runner-up in the men's singles division. When he arrived at Thacher School, Sherman said, "William, if you have brought white tennis trousers, tennis shoes and a racket and white hat in your trunk, please, please keep them there. We, here, do not play tennis at all. We work and play with horses." That statement, according to a letter written by William Thacher in 1938 to Miss Smith, was the first mention of tennis in the valley.

The second mention was in 1893 when the Thacher boys used their newspaper column in *The Ojai* to invite "all-comers" to a tennis tournament at Thacher School. The only "comers" were S.D. Thacher, O.H. Bronson (Thacher School's first hired teacher) and six of the students.

In 1895, William Thacher organized The Ojai Athletic Club mainly to promote the sport of baseball. Soon there were eighty members who also promoted a bicycle club and a rifle club. They turned a portion of the Chrisman home into a clubhouse. This also provided a place for the men's social clubs to meet, play billiards, read or write letters. A.D. Williams operated a barber shop in one room of the building and he also served as caretaker. J.J. Burke was treasurer and Sherman Thacher was president. Several months passed before they announced the inclusion of quoits (a game like horseshoes) and tennis, however. The club

OVM
Tennis party at the Dennison Ranch, May, 1897. Zaidee Soule is on the far right in the black dress.

was designed with the men in mind, but later that year they opened the dirt tennis courts to women who were willing to pay the dues of 10 cents per month.

By the end of the year, W.L. Thacher had formed the Ojai Valley Tennis Club with himself at the head, Miss Alice Baker as vice president, J.C. Brown, secretary and J.J. Burke, treasurer. They held their first tournament in 1896, between the Ojai champs and the Ventura champs. Ojai won. In 1897, the Ojai and Ventura champs challenged the best from Santa Barbara and won. Then Ojai, Ventura and Santa Barbara beat Los Angeles and Pasadena. In 1898, Southern California played against Northern California and the prize went to the north.

The true foundation for the Ojai Valley Tennis Tournament was laid in 1899, when the club staged a contest with three divisions: men's singles and boys' interscholastic singles and doubles. In a plea for funds to finance the tournament, this editorial appeared in *The Ojai*. "Dear people, go down in your jeans, socks, stockings, moneybags and tills and bring forth cartwheels, spondulix, bills, eagles and other lucre – let us not invite the guests to a feast and then make them catch the fowl and wait until it is made into tamales before partaking."

That first tennis tournament attracted 500 players. And that is when the tournament leaders began restricting the number of events one could enter. Some participants had collapsed from overexertion. Until 1925, when they covered the courts with asphalt, contestants played on dirt. Before each tournament, several men laboriously sifted pebbles from the surface and tamped sand into the area – a long and tedious process.

Hospitality was always a hallmark to the tournament. People still open their homes and private tennis courts to players. Since 1899, hosts and hostesses have managed refreshments for participants and spectators. The tea tent came into being around 1904 and the popular orange juice stand was a byproduct of the Depression.

In the 1930s, oranges were so cheap that local packing houses donated several dozen crates of them to the tournament. And until the 1920s, when they became scarce, ladies picked fresh poppies, brodaea, lupin and mustard from the countryside to decorate the refreshment booth.

The Men's All-Comers Championship cup for singles is inscribed with such names as Tom Bundy, Bill Johnston, Maurice

McLoughlin, Harvey Snodgrass, Bill Tilden, Keith Gledhill, Ellsworth Vines, Lester Stoefen, Jack Tidball, Francis Shields, Jack Kramer and Bob Falkenburg.

Quite a collection of names has accumulated on the women's singles trophy also: May Sutton Bundy, Florence Sutton, Mary K. Brown, Caroline Babcock, Alice Marble, Dorothy Bundy and Louise Brough, to name a few of them. Ruby Garland won the first ladies singles around 1900.

The boys' interscholastic cup also has some impressive names engraved on it. They include: Hal Gorham, Cliften Herd, Harvey Snodgrass, John Doeg, Keith Gledhill, Ellsworth Vines, Jack Tidball, Gene Mako and Bobby Riggs. Nearly all American tennis champions have played on the Ojai courts at some time during their careers.

The tennis tournament has always represented an important event in the lives of Ojaians. In earlier years they even closed the schools for the tournament. The tournament was canceled only twice: in 1924 when a hoof and mouth epidemic threatened parts of California and officials decided to discourage movement between counties and during WWII

William Thacher, who had introduced the popular game of tennis to this small community, making it a famous place for athletes of the courts, played tennis practically until the day he died at the age of 87.

The tennis tournament is held yearly in late April.

Festivals

In 1926, an Easterner, Elizabeth Sprague Coolidge, and Frank Jefferson Frost of Ojai, sponsored the first important musical happening ever held on the West Coast. They assembled 500 seats in the Foothills Hotel lobby which were filled at every performance. Incredibly, an estimated one-third of the audience came from outside the valley.

Mrs. Coolidge offered a prize of $1,000 to the composer of the best string quartet. The judges, a panel of famous musicians, presented the generous award to Albert Huybrechts of Brussels, Belgium.

Twenty years later, the dream of many – to make Ojai synonymous with good music, culture and art, without the element of commercialism – came true when the Ojai Music Festivals began.

Nordhoff High School housed the annual event until 1953, when they presented it outdoors for the first time. The musicians performed on a wooden stage under a canvas shelter in Libbey Park. Everyone liked the idea of listening to great music in the open air, so the Festivals Committee established a thrift shop and raised funds for a permanent bowl, which they built at Libbey Park in 1954. Roy Wilson and Austin Pierpont designed the Ojai Festivals Bowl. Frames for seating came from a brick schoolhouse torn down on Main Street in Ventura. They expanded the seating in 1967 and the Rotary Club built dressing rooms in 1980.

Fry photo
Festivals Bowl at Libbey Park

The bowl is used for many purposes today, including graduation exercises, dramatic productions and other musicales

The Ojai Festivals Thrift Shop closed its doors after forty years. The internationally acclaimed Music Festival, however, still attracts music lovers each year during the last weekend of May.

Folk Dancing

It was in 1946 that the California Folk Dance Federation roped off the main street of Ojai and introduced the first statewide Folk Dance Festival in California. It has been held biennially, in even years, ever since.

Historically, the festival draws representation from many

countries. The dancers exhibit their talents, offer lessons and encourage participation. Their authentic costumes turn Ojai ablaze with color. As long as the folk dances took place in the streets, the fire department faithfully hosed the pavement down before and after each event. Today's folk dance demonstrations are held at the Ojai Art Center during late March.

Independence Day Parade

When Ruth Melhorn came to Ojai, in 1962, and discovered that the town had no plans for Independence Day, she invited everyone to her parade. Through the years, the Fourth of July celebration maintains emphasis on family togetherness and clean entertainment. Along with the Independence Day Committee, which works all year round, most local service clubs become involved to insure a day of fun for all.

A popular pancake breakfast, hosted by the Ojai Lions Club, gets everyone off to a good start. This is followed by Ruth's old-fashioned, small-town parade, after which everyone gathers at Sarzotti Park on Park Road with their picnic baskets. Various organizations set up refreshment booths and games for the children. The festivities include live entertainment and sports events. At dusk, a pyrotechnician delights young and old with a huge fireworks display at Nordhoff High School.

Mexican Fiesta

A group of Mexican Americans started the Mexican Fiesta in 1967 to commemorate their Independence Day, September 16. They had some money left over that first year and decided to use it for scholarships for local students of Mexican descent. This tradition continues.

The Fiesta Committee prepares authentic Mexican food wrapped in handmade tortillas. Entertainment representative of their native land is featured and many interesting items are available for purchase. It is not difficult to find one's way to the Fiesta when it is in progress. People just follow the huge, colorful paper flowers that brilliantly decorate the Libbey Park entrance.

Softball Tournaments

Softball has become a leading sports activity for much of

Ojai's population. The fields aren't being monopolized only by youngsters either. Men and women combine athletic abilities each spring representing their churches in a slow pitch league. The Ojai Valley Men's and Women's softball leagues take turns using local diamonds throughout the summer months. Over Labor Day Weekend, this community hosts the Ojai Valley Softball Tournament enticing sixty teams, including thirteen local ones, with 900 players and hundreds of spectators. This event, which began in 1973 and draws participants from all over California, is considered one of the largest tournaments in the West.

Crafts Festival/Peddler's Fair

The Crafts Festival is a relatively recent addition to Ojai's list of annual events. California artists present this show and sale in December at the Ojai Center for the Arts on South Montgomery Street. Along with a magnificent array of crafts, they also offer entertainment and food.

Craftspeople, artists and antique dealers have been selling their wares through the monthly Peddlers Fair for fifteen years in Ojai. Now benefiting the Ojai Valley Youth Foundation, the Peddlers Fair operates from the Chaparral School auditorium at 414 East Ojai Avenue every third weekend of the month.

Ojai Valley Museum

The Ojai Valley Museum was established in 1966 primarily

Mullican photo
Ojai Valley Museum, formerly the Catholic Church.

296

by Robert O. Browne and Effie Skelton with the support of the Ojai Board of Realtors. Browne was the curator from its inception until his death in 1993 at the age of 91. The museum opened in April of 1967 at 841 East Ojai Avenue. In January of 1970, they moved to the old Ojai City Hall building at 338 East Ojai Avenue and nine years later, the museum moved to the abandoned fire station building at 109 South Montgomery Street.

The museum is currently housed in the historic St. Thomas Aquinas Catholic Church building at 130 West Ojai Avenue.

The museum houses many exhibits depicting early life in the valley, displays many authentic artifacts and presents numerous programs for adults and children. The museum is open Wednesday through Sunday from 1 to 4 p.m. Trained docents are available to answer questions and conduct tours. Although there is no entrance fee, a donation for the museum's upkeep is appreciated.

Historic City Hall

Our city hall, like so many things about Ojai, is unique. The government offices are housed in an elegant home set in lush, well-kept grounds. The Hobsons built the estate as their home in 1907 and the family of Grace Hobson Smith generously donated the property, at 401 South Ventura Street, to the city in the 1970s. Architect, Zelma Wilson, designed the remodel which transformed the site into a municipal facility. The Hobson estate began as a single, rather simple home structure. The family, reportedly, added on over time, eventually building a separate house next to the main home. Wilson, found a way to connect the two structures so the place was functional and the integrity of the original design was preserved. A Fellow of the American Institute of Architects, Wilson was one of the first Living Treasures nominated.

Biblical Gardens

When Mary Lapham Hunt realized the similarity between our climate and that of the Holy Land during Biblical times, she decided to collect the plants that grew there. During the early 1950s, she was president of the Ojai Valley Garden Club and she often exhibited her hobby at membership meetings. Her program created such an interest that the Reverend Gearhart asked if she would plant a Biblical garden at the Presbyterian Church at 304 North Foothill Road.

Today Mary's garden is home to many plants, trees and shrubs – all of them referred to in the Bible. Mary had spent years researching Biblical botany and locating the plants that are not native to Southern California in various parts of the world.

She said that those who translated the Bible were not botanists, consequently, many of the plants mentioned therein were mislabeled. The rose, in some instances, was actually an oleander. Mary has identified each plant in her garden with a tasteful redwood sign that gives the Biblical passage in which the plant is mentioned.

Mullican photo
Biblical Gardens at the Presbyterian Church.

Even though some local people are not yet aware of the Biblical Gardens, countless out-of-towners certainly are, as it has received publicity in the *Los Angeles Times, Westways Magazine, Santa Barbara Magazine, Midnight* and on NBC television. The garden is open daily for self-guided tours.

George Stuart Figures

George S. Stuart, a lifelong student of history, has combined his curiosity about the past with his impressive artistic talent to create incredible figures depicting personalities of yore. He began this unusual art form as a hobby in the 1950s. Now he has hundreds of beautiful quarter-life-size figures from American, European and Asian history.

Although his studio is in Ojai, his figures can be seen at the Ventura County Historical Museum at 100 East Main Street, where they are on permanent display.

Whale Rock Ranch

On the east end, amongst sage brush, slitherers and skitterers, is a giant boulder that nature shaped to resemble a whale. In 1916, Mr. and Mrs. Harry M. Gorham built a weekend retreat near there. They constructed a house of stone and aptly named their place Whale Rock Ranch.

Florence Halliday Rogers, a widow with two young children to raise, had moved to France to insure that her son, Emery, would have a proper education. Well-meaning people convinced her that he would become a womanizer if influenced by French scholars, so she frantically wrote to her lawyers asking them to locate a school somewhere in the United States. They suggested Thacher School, but warned Mrs. Rogers that this area of Southern California was still wild. The reputation of the school, however, was great enough for her to risk a few inconveniences and so the Rogers came to Ojai Valley in 1907 and stayed in the Pierpont Cottages. Later they built a home on McAndrew Road.

Harry Gorham, nephew of the Jones boys who found the Comstock mine in Virginia City, Nevada, accompanied his son, Hal, to a tennis tournament in Nordhoff in 1905. He liked it here and visited occasionally. He met the widow Rogers here and they were married under a tree in Yosemite. Deciding to live at least part-time in Nordhoff, they purchased 323 acres from Walter Hall and built the Whale Rock Ranch.

While Emery attended Thacher, his sister, Constance, had her early schooling at home. The family spent every winter here and toured either abroad or in the East during the summer months.

People remembered Mr. Gorham as a good dresser who was always well-groomed and never without his hat and gloves. He died in 1951 at the age of 92.

Other Sights

In the Siete Robles tract at the east end of the valley, amid orange groves and a cluster of typical Southern California dwellings, stands a splendid replica of India's Taj Mahal. Edward Martin, a priest in the Liberal Catholic Church, and his wife, having traveled extensively throughout the world, asked John Roine to design this house in honor of Krishnamurti.

The Taj has changed owners several times over the years, but has never ceased attracting and fascinating sightseers. It is a privately owned home which is not open to the public. The curious do enjoy driving by for a glimpse of this unusual Eastern beauty, however, in its unlikely surroundings.

Chapter Twenty
Fun in the Sun

Man cannot live by work alone, so he invented recreational sports. The earliest mention of physical amusement in the county, other than the old Spanish pursuits of horse racing, cock fights and lassoing bears and pitting them against bulls, appeared in the *Ventura Signal* in 1871. The editor stated that every town of any size had a roller skating rink. "Occurring everywhere," he wrote, "is the rise and fall of many individuals."

When bicycle-mania struck, people were convinced that the wheel would replace the horse. There were fifteen bicycles in Ojai in 1892. The Sheldons had one, as did John Suess, Ed Zimmerman, J.J. Morris, Charles Morse, Fred Hudiburg, Albert Van Curen, Charles Walker, Jennie Blumberg, Alice Howe, Belle Wisecrans, Edith Baker and L.H. Mesick. Otan Montgomery made local news when he rode his bicycle twenty miles to Ventura from his home in Upper Ojai in less than two hours.

In 1895, mountain climbing was the rage, particularly for women. Women, they say, succeeded in "planting many flags in high points locally."

Horseback Riding

Horseback riding purely for pleasure became popular here around the turn of the century. In fact, for many years riding was the principal recreation of winter guests in Ojai. With Margaret Clark Hunt as their guide, hundreds of riders kept the trails behind Nordhoff open.

In 1911, Tom Clark led a group which included Mabel Gage and his daughter Dortha (Roberts) to Yosemite by horseback. Dortha told me that it was a rugged trip, but she wouldn't have missed the experience. She and her horse returned home by train.

In 1927, the Ojai Valley Trails Association was formed to maintain and enhance the trails in Ojai backcountry. The original officers were, Forest Cooke, Elizabeth Mosle, Helen Robertson, George Bald, Margaret Hunt and W.A. Kimball.

In 1930, a riding group calling themselves the El Camino Trails Association was formed in the valley. In 1931, local riders organized the Ojai Trails Association (OTA) to establish and maintain local trails. They, reportedly, connected the Pratt, Foothill and Gridley trails with the state trail that leads from Mexico to Oregon.

The Caballeros riding club made it's debut in 1944.

Members of OTA, the Ventura Saddle Club (formed in 1946) and Equestrian Trails, Inc. later became active in showing their horses. Every weekend during the 1970s both the Foster Park arena (which has since been removed) and the one at Soule Park were alive with horses and those who loved them. There was also an active arena across from the entrance to Lake Casitas for a while.

Jay Cortner family photo
Riders in the Wheelers area.

Southern Pacific Right-of-Way Trail

There's an overwhelming inclination here toward environmental awareness and the preservation of health and safety. Forward thinking leaders considered all of the above when they visualized creating a walking, biking, riding trail on the old Southern Pacific Railroad right-of-way. Today, people of all ages and capabilities ride, walk/run, skate and bicycle along that trail that runs from Bryant Street, in Ojai, to Ventura.

Fry photo
Old Southern Pacific right-of-way trail.

302

Baseball

Valley schools were poorly supplied for recreational endeavors in the early days, so the children learned to make their own sports equipment. A boy would wind yarn from old stockings around and around a bit of bark until the wad was the size of a baseball. After scrounging for an old, flat board to use as a bat, the only remaining challenge was to locate a space among the oaks large enough to play a game of baseball.

Softball became the favorite sport in the early 1880s. An amateur team, the Santa Ana Ball Club, won the county championship in 1886 by beating Ventura 15-13. The team had these ten players: John and Jim Fox, Tom and A.J. Dickerson, Otan Montgomery, J. and L. Medibles, A. Dubois and Richard and Charles Robinson.

By the 1892 season, they wore uniforms consisting of white shirts with letters across the front boldly spelling OJAI. Their navy blue pants had narrow red side-stripes and they wore black socks, tennis shoes and caps. They had a favorite bat which they affectionately called "old toothpick."

By 1945, five Ojai teams competed three nights a week. As enthusiasm for softball grew, local storekeepers often closed early so they could attend these games. Local Ojai women formed a softball team in 1948.

Golf Courses

There are two golf courses in the valley. Soule Park, at 1033 East Ojai Avenue, has an eighteen-hole championship course built around its one-thousand trees. It's a par seventy-two course with a 69.0 rating. The Ojai Valley Inn, on Country Club Drive, is a semi-private course. It is an eighteen-hole championship course with a par seventy and a 70.4 rating. Reservations are required at both courses.

Parks and Recreational Facilities

Our climate entices us out-of-doors often and we are fortunate to have many lovely places to go with our families and guests. Each of Ojai's major parks has a unique history interwoven with lives of early families.

Camp Comfort

The lovely, shaded spot on Creek Road known as Camp Comfort, was thus named by Sarah McFarland, Reverend Townsend Taylor's daughter, around 1873.

In 1904, the Ventura Board of Supervisors met in Camp Comfort and agreed to purchase thirty-seven and a half acres for $2,500 in gold and turn the land into a park. The people of Ojai, concerned about the large tree-cutting operation on Creek Road, were grateful to have this pretty, shaded spot saved from the woodman's ax.

In 1924, the large barbecue pit, tables and benches were installed under the direction of Tom S. Clark. Charles Linnville was the builder. The meeting hall was built in June of 1938.

Camp Comfort is two miles south of Ojai on Creek Road. There are shaded picnic areas, horseshoe pits, playground equipment and a large meeting hall and barbecue area which accommodates up to 3,000 people on a reservations only basis. There is an entrance fee.

Libbey Park

Edward Drummond Libbey gave seven and a half acres to the city for a park in 1917. Situated in the center of town across from the arcade, Libbey Park offers easy access to a restful and lovely setting. There is a large play area for small children and plenty of picnic space as well as tennis courts. No entrance fee is charged for everyday use.

This park also has an outdoor bowl where concerts, plays and other activities are held throughout the year.

The original name for the park is Ojai Civic Park. In 1971, however, the year we celebrated the city's 50th birthday, officials changed the name to Libbey Park.

Dennison Park

The Dennison family donated over thirty-two acres of their ranch for a park in 1924. The pine and oak covered land at the crest of Dennison Grade, six miles southeast of Ojai, offers seclusion, camping, hiking, barbecue facilities and a magnificent view.

Sarzotti Park

Anthony Sarzotti deeded his ten acre Park Road land to the city in 1933. Ojai was unable to maintain it, however, and Ventura County took it over in 1939. In 1957, the Boyd Clubhouse was moved from its original Ojai Avenue location to the park grounds, where it remains today as headquarters for the Ojai Recreation Department.

Ojai's recreational program is an active one, offering organized soccer, softball, football, basketball, tennis, volleyball and exercise classes for people of all ages. A supervised children's program, including educational outings, pet parades and games, makes summertime in Ojai fun for the youngsters. There are numerous other activities and several of them are specifically to attract senior citizens.

The baseball field and bleachers were built at Sarzotti in 1939 and summer night baseball began there in the 1940s. A Quonset hut was set up in the park, reportedly, so the players would have a place to shower and dress. Today, hundreds of valleyites participate in coeducational church league slow-pitch and men's and women's softball on the park's diamonds throughout the summer months. This sport draws nearly as many spectators as there are players.

Sarzotti Park has a barbecue facility to rent for large parties. This was added in 1941. In 1953, the Ojai Valley Garden Club planted torrey pines in Sarzotti Park – some of which, no doubt, shade picnickers today.

Soule Park

In 1957, Zaidee, the only remaining member of the pioneer Soule family, gave some land to the county for a park. Excited by this generous gift, county leaders began talking of building a pool, trout ponds, bridle trails, an archery and pistol range and riding stables – none of which were feasible at the time. In 1961, despite public protest, they tore down the Soule home where Zaidee had been born eighty-three years earlier. The original home was reportedly on the spot where the golf clubhouse now stands.

Presently the beautiful, grassy park on Boardman Road includes a softball diamond, horse arena, tennis courts, playground equipment, barbecue pits and lots of open space where children can fly their kites or just run and tumble.

Mullican photo
Entrance to Lake Casitas.

Lake Casitas

Lake Casitas is one of the largest lakes in Southern California and among the most popular recreational facilities. There are about 400 pleasant camp sites – fourteen with hookups, twelve large picnic areas and a water park for small children. There's a bait shop, boat rentals and a place to eat. Many special events are held each year at the lake, such as the Renaissance Faire, the Indian Pow Wow and the Ojai Wine Festival. In 1984, the Olympic rowing and canoeing events were held at Lake Casitas.

The lake's main attraction is the marvelous fishing which draws both the skilled and the novice angler. In April, 1980, Randy Easley caught the big mouth bass that held the state record until 1996. It weighed just over twenty-one pounds and was almost twenty-eight inches long. This bass is still a lake record. The world record bass caught by a woman came from Lake Casitas. Jan Detzel's fish weighed in at almost fifteen and a half pounds.

In 1991, Wayne Chappel caught the lake record catfish. It weighed 42 pounds. The biggest rainbow trout caught there weighed almost nine and a half pounds. This angler has held the record for almost fifteen years.

Lake Casitas is operated by the Casitas Municipal Water

Mullican photo
Lake Casitas. Dam in background.

District. It has a 254,000 acre foot capacity and it is a domestic water supply. Swimming is not allowed.

Jerry Clausen is credited with being the first to take a boat on Lake Casitas in February of 1959. He claims the same distinction for Matilija Lake.

Oak Dell Park

The entrance to Oak Dell Park is just north of Oak View on Highway 33. Oak Dell boasts a ball field, motorcycle course and picnic areas.

Wheelers Gorge

The United States Forest Service maintains Wheelers Gorge campground for public use. It's eight miles north of Ojai on Highway 33 and offers wilderness campsites, easy access to all forest activities and miles of hiking trails.

Chapter Twenty-One
Flora and Fauna

Among Ojai's scenic attractions is the most beautiful of backyards – Los Padres National Forest. This wilderness, once known as Santa Barbara National Forest, was renamed in 1936 in honor of the San Franciscan padres who founded the California missions. The part of the forest that is in Ventura County contains 516,000 acres of mountainous and wooded areas, valleys and 140 miles of well-stocked streams. The entire forest, however, the second largest in California, covers 1,948,983 acres (U.S. Department of Agriculture Forest Service figures).

Hunting, hiking, camping, fishing, off-road sports, target shooting, swimming, sightseeing and photography are some of the activities available to those entering our immense forest wonderland. During the winter, cars stretch for miles bumper-to-bumper along the winding Highway 33 while hundreds of families enjoy the mountain snow.

Nordhoff Peak is the tall pinnacle directly north of Ojai at the 4,477-foot elevation where Nordhoff Lookout stands. The lookout was built in the 1940s but thirty years later, when it no longer met regional criteria for lookouts in national forests, its use was discontinued. When the fire of 1979 destroyed the old lookout, volunteers from a four-wheel-drive club repaired the structure and the public now uses it as an observation tower.

Chief Peak is the high mountain slightly northeast of Ojai. A huge likeness of an Indian in full feather headdress lies peacefully there. Gaze in that direction and see if you can spot the resting chief. He can be viewed from many points in the valley. To locate the chief, I recommend glancing ahead at the mountains while driving northeast on Ojai Avenue just after

Fry photo
Chief Peak

passing the Bristol Street intersection.

The sheer, craggy face of the Topa Topa Bluffs, part of the huge Topa Topa Mountain Range, looks down on Ojai from the northeast. The bluffs are actually situated in the Sespe Condor Sanctuary behind the upper valley.

Black Mountain is southeast of Ojai and just north of the larger Sulphur Mountain range that runs from Upper Ojai west toward Oak View.

Fishing and Wildlife

Several people who are still living today relate stories of local boyhood fishing trips when they caught their limit of fifty trout in an hour. And, according to tales, the fish were big. Elmer Friend recalled once that there were "millions of fish in the Sespe River."

Arthur Waite remembered catching his limit any time he fished the Matilija River or the San Antonio Creek. My dad, Dalton Munger, recalls catching large steelhead in the creek running through the east end of the arcade. There was one newspaper account in 1909 stating that someone had seen a trout swim by in the creek near the Jack Boyd Clubhouse that measured over two feet long.

Fish are no longer that abundant and the limit is no longer that generous, but many fishermen still gain pleasure from fishing our beautiful mountain streams and they even catch a few.

The subject of wildlife in the Ojai Valley belongs within the pages of this history, for the animals were the first to make this land their home. Because of the many acres left in their natural state and the vast national forest at our doorstep, most original species still flourish here.

Early issues of the *Ventura Signal* reported two grizzly bear attacks per month in the county, most occurring in the Ojai and Santa Clara Valleys. It is said that Thomas Bard was once confronted by a bear in his bedroom.

Prior to 1870, John T. Stow reportedly killed a dozen grizzlies during one summer in Ojai and he observed more than a hundred. Emigdeo Ortega hired natives to watch for bears while he gathered timber for his adobe home.

Instead of shaking in his boots with fear of Ursus horribilis, Julio Peralto hunted them. He killed one per week and sold the carcasses to Detoy's Meat Market in Ventura, where residents could buy the meat for domestic use.

Due to many methods of extermination, including traps and poison, there are no more grizzly bears in the county. Our forests are home now to the smaller, gentler and much shyer black bear. Most experts do not believe that the grizzly shared his territory with the black bear, but that black bear were brought here as late as the 1930s.

People rarely see this timid species, even deep in the backcountry. When they do, they are surprised that the coat of the black bear is usually a shade of brown. A few years ago, Ventura County established a short hunting season for black bears, whose meat is rich and very much like pork.

A black bear's diet consists of wild berries and other fruits, beetles, grasses, the inner bark of evergreen trees, bulbs, acorns, honey, eggs, fish and meat. Black bears usually live to be about 15 years-old.

The California mule deer is so called because of its mule-like ears. Chumash remains contain evidence that this species was extremely numerous here at one time. The mule deer is still California's most important big game animal.

During the 1937 season, 1,005 hunters bagged 105 deer. Hunters numbering 3,661 registered in 1948. In 1960, 12,500 hunters killed 100 deer the opening weekend and 1,180 bucks during the season. The 1980 season saw forty-five bucks dropped during the first hunting weekend in the county, which is usually during late summer. These animals are hunted for their meat, for sport and for trophy antlers.

Of course hunting isn't the only activity involving the mule deer; probably the biggest sport is observing them in the wilds. Deer still roam occasionally into residential areas along Creek Road, Upper Ojai and in the Santa Ana Valley. People spot them less and less frequently, however, grazing at Lake Casitas, on Sulphur Mountain Road, along the valley foothills and in the pasture along the freeway in Canada Larga.

The mule deer, a vegetarian browser, feeds mainly in early mornings and late afternoon. Typically deer will live to be 14 to 16 years of age.

Fry photo
California mule deer

The mountain lion is also referred to as a cougar, puma or panther. Hunters stalked this large, sleek cat extensively until 1972, when the Department of Fish and Game, fearing its extinction, called a moratorium on the destruction of the lion. Mountain lions are seldom seen any more, although alert hikers sometimes spot their paw prints on mountain trails. Theirs are easily distinguished from those of a dog or coyote, as the cat's retractable claws rarely show in their prints. A mountain lion diet consists of deer, which they stalk and kill, and small mammals. The life expectancy of a large cat is 12 to 14 years.

People were concerned about the destruction of the condor as early as 1920, but it wasn't until 1950 that a county refuge was contemplated. Although it may be considered just an unattractive vulture, its saviors do not want to see any more wildlife become extinct. People used to shoot these large birds on sight, because some of them believe the story that a condor once swooped down and flew off with a human baby. Others kill for sport.

The California condor is the largest flying bird in North America. It has a wing span measuring approximately nine feet. In 1983, there were twenty to thirty-five birds living safely in the 53,000-acre Sespe sanctuary located twenty miles northeast of Ojai. Since then, there have been some successful hatchings and there have been some losses. All in all, the future looks a little brighter for this nearly extinct bird.

Our forest is home to many other wild animals, some of them commonly seen in residential neighborhoods. There are tree and ground squirrels, bobcats, coyotes, cottontails, brush rabbits, jackrabbits, quail, dove, raccoons, ringtailed cats, skunks (spotted and striped), badgers, chipmunks, weasels, foxes, opposums and porcupines. Rattlesnakes, gopher snakes, king snakes and tarantulas live on our valley floor as well

Plant Life

Much of Ojai's appeal is in its scenery, including many varieties of lovely plant life. The observant backcountry hiker, armed with a little botanical knowledge, might spot and identify some of these area flowers and plants: lupin (lavender stalk), snowberry (shrub with white berries), pink owl clover, monkey flower (spotted flower that resembles a face), blue-eyed grass (grass having blue flowers), mariposa lily (tulip-like flower), Indian paint brush (red flower), golden yarrow, California aster, goldenrod, yellow daisy, bleeding heart (heart-shaped flower), clarika, baby blue eyes, currants, gooseberries, bush poppies, morning glory, chocolate lily and death camas, to name but a few.

Following are descriptions of the most common and popular plants and trees found growing here.

Probably the most entrancing aspect of Ojai is the abundance of trees. Incredibly, native oaks still tower over most buildings. Here, we drive around trees and we build so as not to disturb them. We take care that the natural beauty remains unspoiled. In Ojai, the trees have rights.

There are two main types of oak tree found in Ojai – the live oak and the white oak. Live oak leaves are edged with tiny, spiny barbs. This tree maintains year-round foliage. The live oak drops leaves, usually in spring and fall, but never goes completely bare in the process.

The white oak drops all of its deeply lobed leaves in the fall.

The shape and size distinction between these two oaks is difficult to define, since it depends more on location and care than species. In other words, both can grow to be wide and full-leafed or tall and sparse.

The scrub oak is a close cousin to the live oak and is found mostly in the backcountry. It grows in a low bush and has leaves like those of the live oak, only smaller.

The Chumash used the yucca plant for a multitude of life-sustaining purposes. In 1924, the large desert plant was in danger of extinction. Anyone caught destroying a yucca was fined $50 and jailed for thirty days. Today the yucca grows profusely in the backcountry, as well as in the foothills and in parts of the valley floor. It is recognizable by a clump of large pointed leaves from which three to six-foot spikes grow, opening into huge clusters of cream colored flowers during spring and summer.

The Matilija poppy, also known as the California tree poppy, was first discovered by the Chumash and used as a medicine. There is a local legend that the poppy first bloomed over the grave of Princess Matilija and her lover on a hill above Matilija resort.

In 1845, a man named Coulter classified and named the plant. He called it Romneya Pappaveracoe or Romneya Coulteri, after an astronomer friend, T. Romney Robinson. The Matilija poppy grows in Southern California, parts of Mexico and most profusely in our backcountry. The large, delicate, white flower has a golden center and grows on long stems on bushes anywhere from one to seven feet tall. No trace of this poppy plant can be found here throughout the winter months, but from May to mid-August their beautiful flowers decorate our neighborhoods and mountainsides.

Fry photo
Yucca

Fry photo
Matilija poppies.

Although the Matilija poppy plant develops a strong root systems that insures its return every spring, it is very difficult to transplant with any success. In 1908, nevertheless, people dug up the poppy plants by the thousands and sold them in Los Angeles. There was fear of its extinction here, but the poppy did survive and in 1964, the city of Ojai adopted the Matilija poppy as its official flower.

An Outline of Disasters,
Unusual Weather Conditions
and Certain Other Statistics

1808   A violent earthquake shook this coast badly.

1812   An earthquake caused a tidal wave in Ventura.

1857   A great earthquake caused internal disturbances near the base of Mount Pinos.

1860   Santa Barbara County, of which Ventura and Ojai were a part, had a population totaling 3,543.

1861-62 Heavy rains altered the face of the county. The Ventura Avenue bluffs were completely reshaped by this storm and it washed away sixty buildings from the mission settlement.

1863-64 A serious drought killed hundreds of cattle.

1867-68 A total of 25.19 inches of rain caused much flooding.

1870   Santa Barbara County population reached 7,784.

1871   An extreme heat spell inspired this tip: Put ice on the stomach to keep cool and comfortable.

1873   There were fifty people living in Ojai Valley.

1874-75 Ojai received ten inches of rain in a twenty-four hour period.

1876-77 There was a severe drought.

1876   The *Ventura Signal* reported fog in Ojai Valley.

1878   Flooding resulted from a devastating storm.

1880   There was an earthquake.

1881   Goleta experienced a tornado.

1882   Five inches of snow was reported on Santa Rosa Island.

1883-84 Ojai received sixty inches of rain in an eleven-day storm.

1887	This valley was considered by its enthusiasts to be exempt from fog.
1891	There were 300 people in the town of Nordhoff.
1894	An earthquake caused no damage but widespread nausea was reported.
1898	Many people were overcome by a heat spell in July and the local paper suggested that citizens tag themselves so officials would know who they were and where to take them if they swooned from the heat.
1909	The most disastrous fire in the valley occurred. It started from a gasoline engine and threatened to burn Thacher School and several homes before racing up Twin Peaks, across and up Horn Canyon and over the Topa Topa Ridge.
1911	Twelve days of rain washed out the railroad tracks.
1914	The railroad was washed out again, after the worst storm in thirty years. Ojaians tolerated fifty-four straight hours of rain.
1916	It snowed in Ojai.
1917	Two disastrous fires occurred this year, one in June and the other in September.
1920	Eleven hundred people lived in the valley.
1921	The city population was 500.
1923	The railroad was washed out.
1925	An earthquake occurred.
1927	There were 2,100 people living in Ojai Valley.
1932	There was an eleven-day brush fire.
1932	It snowed in Ojai.
1933	An earthquake shook the valley.
1938	The worst flood since 1914 hit the county and washed out the railroad tracks.

1940	A storm dropped 36.71 inches of rain.
1943	The railroad tracks were washed away again.
1943	Greta Garbo visited friends in Ojai.
1946	A drought caused a severe water shortage.
1947	The drought continued.
1948	The drought continued and 1,500 firefighters fought a major fire that burned 30,000 acres including thirteen homes.
1949	Smudge pots caused smog in the valley.
1949	The heaviest covering of snow ever to fall in the valley did so during this year. By noon, every store in the valley had sold out of film.
1950	There were 2,519 people living in Ojai city.
1952	There were 12,000 people living in the valley.
1960	The post office claimed 16,000 postal patrons in the valley.
1963	There were 18,000 people living in the valley.
1969	Rain totaling forty-seven inches caused much flooding and the railroad tracks washed out for the last time. Matilija Dam totals hit an all-time record of 70.04 inches.
1970	Storms dumped fifty-two inches of rain in the valley and great flooding occurred.
1980	Ojai again experienced serious flooding.
1980	Ojai Valley's population reached 25,000, and the city's population topped 7,000.
1985	One of the most threatening fires in the valley occurred in July of this year.
1997	Ojai Valley experienced an extremely wet winter due to a condition called, El Niño. Almost all areas of the county and the valley, except Matilija Dam, broke rainfall records this year.

Pink Moment

We began this book with the dawning of recorded time. We will now end with dusk, when a special phenomenon occurs in this peaceful valley. When day is done, we face east and behold the sunset palette that gloriously paints the Topa Topa Bluffs. The last rays of sunshine, magnified by thicker layers of atmosphere, bathe the bare ridge in brilliant pink, creating for us the incredible *pink moment*.

Additional Books By Patricia Fry

Nordhoff Cemetery – Book One.
Matilija Press: 1992

A Thread to Hold, The Story of Ojai Valley School.
Fithian Press, 1996

Quest For Truth, a Journey of the Soul.
Matilija Press: 1996

The Mainland Luau,
How to Capture the Flavor of Hawaii In Your Own Backyard.
Matilija Press, 1996

Creative Grandparenting Across the Miles,
Ideas for Sharing Love, Faith and Family Traditions.
Liguori Publications, 1997

Matilija Press
PMB 123
323 E. Matilija Street
Ojai, CA 93023

email: matilijapr@aol.com

Bibliography

California History

BANCROFT, HUBERT HOWE. *History of California.* Volume XX. Wallace Hebberd: Santa Barbara

BANCROFT, HUBERT HOWE. *History of California.* Volumes XV111, X1X, XX1V. A.S. Bancroft and Company: San Francisco, 1884.

BOYLE, LOUIS M. *Out West.* Mirror Press: Los Angeles, 1952.

BREWER, WILLIAM H. Francis P. Farquhar, editor. *Up and Down California.* University of California Press: Berkeley, 1949.

California Historical Society Quarterlies.

CAUGHEY, JOHN WALTON. *California.* Prentice-Hall: New Jersey, 1954.

GUINN, J.M. *History of California.* Volumes 1 & 2. Historic Record Company: Los Angeles, 1907.

HANNA, PHILL TOWNSEND, compiled by. *The Dictionary of California Land Names.* Los Angeles, 1951.

HUTCHINSON, W.H. *Oil, Land and Politics.* Volumes 1 & 2. *The California Career of Thomas Robert Bard.* University of Oklahoma Press.

McGROATY, JOHN STEVENS. *California of the South.* Volumes 1-5. S.J. Clarke, Inc., 1933.

McNARY, LAURA KELLY. *California Spanish and Indian Place Names.* Wetzel Publishing Company, Inc.: Los Angeles, 1931.

McWILLIAMS, CAREY. Erskine Caldwell, editor. *Southern California Country: An Island on the Land.* American Book; Stratford Press: New York, 1946.

NORDHOFF, CHARLES. *California for Health, Pleasure and Residence: A Book for Travelers and Settlers.* Harper and Brothers Publishers: New York, 1872 and 1882.

PAULSON. *Handbook and Dictionary of San Luis Obispo, Santa Barbara, Ventura, Kern, Los Angeles and San Diego Counties.* Francis and Valentine/Commercial Steam Presses, 1875.

PITT, LEONARD. *California Controversies.* Scott Foresman and Company: San Francisco State College, 1968.

RENSCHI, HERO EUGENE & ETHEL GRACE. *Historic Spots in California: The Southern Counties.* Stanford Press, 1932.

ROBINSON, ALFRED. *Life in California.* Thomas C. Russel, 1925.

SALITORE, EDWARD V. *California Information Almanac.* Published for Bank of America, 1968.

SHARP, ROBERT P. *Down Coastal Southern California.* Kendall-Hunt Publishing Company, 1978.

SPEER, ALLINE MERCER. *History of California* #16. Typewritten manuscript, 1933.

TAYLOR, FRANK J & EARL M. WELTY. *Black Bonanza.* McGraw Hill Book Co., Inc.: New York, 1950.

WOOD, RICHARD COKE & GEORGE LEON BUSH. *The California Story.* San Francisco, 1957.

WOOD, RUTH KEDZIE. *The Tourist's California.* Dodd, Mead and Company: New York, 1914.

California Land Grants

AVINA, ROSE H. *Spanish and Mexican Land Grants in California.* University of California, 1932.

Magazine Articles

GULLIVER, HAROLD G. *Arbolada.* Country Life Magazine, 1924.

HARPER'S WEEKLY. New York, 1871-72.

KOUWENHOVEN, JOHN A., compiled by. *Adventures of America From 1857-1900.* Harper and Brothers: New York and London, 1938.

SANCHEZ, NELLIE VAD GRIFT, editor and translator of *Memoirs of a Merchant... Jose Arnaz Story.* Touring Topics. Automobile Club of Southern California, 1928.

Miscellaneous History

ANDERSON, WINSLOW, M.D. *Mineral Springs and Health Resorts of California*. Bancroft Company: San Francisco, 1890.

CALLAN. A. *A Brief History of St. Joseph's Convalescent Hospital*. Valley of the Moon: Apple Valley, 1974.

CLARK, ARTHUR MILLER. *From Grove to Cove to Grove: A Brief History of Carpinteria Valley, California*. 1962.

CONRAD, HOWARD L. *History of Milwaukee County From its First Settlement to the Year 1895*. Chicago, 1896.

FLOWER, FRANK A., editor. *History of Milwaukee, Wisconsin*. Chicago, 1881.

ILSLEY, SAMUEL. *Walter Nordhoff pamphlet*.

Krotona Scrap book.

LYON, MISS BELLE G. *Early Development of Matilija Canyon at Lyon's Springs*. Essay.

MONTGOMERY, JOHN, his diary.

MOTT, D.W. (Mrs.), compiled by. *Legends and Lore of the Long Ago*. Wetzell Publishing Company: Los Angeles, 1924.

O'NEILL, OWEN H., editor. *History of Santa Barbara County*. Harold McLean Meier: Santa Barbara, 1949.

Ventura County Labor News.

World Book Encyclopedias.

Miscellaneous Material

BUREAU OF RECLAMATION, UNITED STATES DEPARTMENT OF INTERIOR. *Ventura River Project*. Pamphlet, 1960

FAUNTLEROY, S.H. *Wildflowers of the Ojai*. 1936

Foothills Hotel advertising pamphlet.

GARNSEY, MARY VESTA (Mrs.). *Ojai, The Valley of Homes*, advertising pamphlet distributed by Hickey Bros., A.F. Knudsen, 1943.

HOTCHENER, MARIE RUSSACK, editor. *The Star*. volume 11 #5. Star Publishing: Hollywood, 1929.

Ojai Festivals Limited program, 6th season, 1952.

OJAI VALLEY CHAMBER OF COMMERCE brochure, *Ojai Valley California.* 1957-58.

Ojai Valley California sketch report on growth. 1969-70.

Pierpont Cottages, advertising pamphlet.

Presbyterian Centennial Program Booklet.

Presbyterian record book.

SANDERS, F.C.S., M.D. *California as a Health Resort.* Bolte and Braden Company: San Francisco, 1916.

SENATE, RICHARD. *Historical Adobes of Ventura County* and *Haunted Ojai.*

THACHER, WILLIAM. Letter to Miss Smith, 1938.

Ventura Abstract Company records.

VENTURA CHAMBER OF COMMERCE. *Ventura County, Your Opportunity in California.* Ventura, 1924.

WAITE, HELEN HARDIN, compiled notes of Miss Clara Smith.

Wheelers Hot Springs advertising pamphlet.

Mission Period

BAUER HELEN. *California Mission Days.* Doubleday and Co. Inc.: New York, 1951.

COMSTOCK, ADELAID. *San Buenaventura Mission.* Ventura, 1902.

ENGLEHARDT, FR. ZEPHYRIN O.F.M. *The Missions and Missionaries of California.* Volumes 1 & 2. The James H. Barry Company: San Francisco and Santa Barbara, 1912 & 1929.

GEIGER, MAYARD J. *Life and Times of Fray Junipero Serra.* O.F.M. Volumes 1 & 2.

SIMPSON, LESLEY BYRD, editor. *The Letters of Jose Senan* O.F.M. 1796-1823. John Howell Books.

Native Americans

ANDERSON, EUGENE N. JR. *The Chumash Indians of Southern California.* Malki Museum Press: Banning.

BAUER, HELEN. *California Indian Days.* Doubleday: New York, 1963.

BLACKBURN, THOMAS C., editor. *December's Child*. University of California Press, 1975.

BOARDMAN, MATT. *Badger Claw of Ojai*. Ventura County Superintendent of Schools: Ventura, 1971.

BROWN, ALAN K. *The Aboriginal Population of the Santa Barbara Channel*. Reports of the University of California Archaeological Survey #69. University of California Archaeological Research Facility: Berkeley, 1967.

BROWNE, ROBERT O. *Indian Cultures of The Ojai*.

CAMPBELL, GRANT. *The Rock Paintings of the Chumash*. University of California Press: Los Angeles, 1966.

GREENWOOD, ROBERT S. & R.O BROWNE. *A Coastal Chumash Village*. Anderson Ritchie, Simon: Los Angeles, 1969.

HARRINGTON, J.P. *Notes on a Ventureno Chumash Shrine*.

HEIZER, R.F.& M.A. WHIPPLE. *The California Indians*. University of California Press: Berkeley, 1971.

HEIZER, ROBERT F., editor. *Handbook of Northern American Indians*. Volume 8, Smithsonian Institution: Washington, 1978.

HUDSON, TRAVIS & ERNEST UNDERHAY. *Crystals in the Sky*, Ballena Press: Santa Barbara, 1978.

JOY, CHARLES, R. *The Heritage of the Ojai and Chumash* (part two). Essays, 1976.

KROEBER, ALFRED LOUIS. *Handbook of the Indians of California*. California Book Company, Ltd.: Berkeley, 1967.

LANDBERG, LEIF C.W. *The Chumash Indians of Southern California*. Southwest Museum Papers: Los Angeles, 1965.

SAN LUIS OBISPO COUNTY ARCHAEOLOGICAL SOCIETY. Papers on the Chumash, #9, 1975.

ZIEBOLD, EDNA B. *Indians of Early Southern California*. Perc B. Sapsis, 1969.

Newspapers

LOS ANGELES TIMES, several articles.

NEW YORK HERALD, early issues.

OJAI VALLEY NEWS, most issues.

THE OJAI, all issues.

THE OJAI PICTORIAL EDITION, 1922 & 1925.

VENTURA SIGNAL, early issues.

VENTURA FREE PRESS, early issues.

Ojai History

BEE, POLLY, editor. *The Golden Book Honoring Ojai's 50th Anniversary*. Fred Volz, Ojai Valley News: Ojai, 1971.

BRESSLER, R.W. *Round the Clock*. Ojai, 1950.

BRISTOL, WALTER, W. *The Story of the Ojai Valley*. Ojai Publishing Company: Ojai, 1946.

CHASE, ELIZABETH. *The History of the Ojai Valley*. Thesis, 1933.

EDSELL, RALPH. *The Ranch House Story, Forty Years of It*. A booklet, 1991

FRY, PATRICIA L. *Nordhoff Cemetery: Book One*. Matilija Press: Ojai, 1992

GERARD, FRANK R.J. & FRANKLIN H. PERKINS. *Ojai the Beautiful*. Ojai Publishing Company: Ojai, 1927.

HUBLER, RICHARD G. *The Ojai Story*. Ojai Valley Chamber of Commerce: Ojai, 1956.

JOHNSON, AUDREY HOYT. *Away in Ojai*. Volume 1, Number 1. Ojai, 1965.

REYNOLDS, HELEN BAKER. *Family Album*. Self published.

TRUSTEES OF THE OJAI PRESBYTERIAN CHURCH. *The Presbyterian Church of Ojai, 1874 - 1926*.

WILLIAMS, MERRILL. *Tid Bits – a Brief Look at the Historic Ojai Valley Inn and Country Club*.

WOOLMAN, ARTHUR ERWIN. *The Ojai Valley, Gateway to Health and Happiness*. Kheil Press: Upper Ojai, 1956.

Schools

FERRIER, WILLIAM WARREN. *90 Years of Education in California*. 1846-1936. West Coast Printing Company: Oakland, 1937.

FRY, PATRICIA L. *A Thread To Hold: The Story of Ojai Valley School*. Fithian Press: Santa Barbara, 1996.

HOOBLER, VIVA UTTERBACK. *A History of the Nordhoff School District.* Unpublished thesis, 1964.

MAKEPEACE, LEROY. *Sherman Thacher and his School.* Yale: 1941

Ventura County History

CAMARILLO CHAMBER OF COMMERCE. *Greater Camarillo- Then and Now*, 1978.

GIDNEY, C.M. *Gidney's History of Santa Barbara, San Luis Obispo and Ventura Counties, California.* Volumes 1 & 2. Benjamin Brooks of San Luis Obispo, Edwin Sheridan of Ventura. Lewis Publishing Company: Chicago, 1907.

HALL, THRONE, editor and publisher. *Odyssey of the Santa Barbara Kingdom and 138 Miles North.* 1963.

HENDRICKS, YETIVE. *The Camarillo Family.* Typewritten manuscript.

HOBSON, EDITH M. *The Romantic History of San Buenaventura.*

KAGAN, PAUL. *New World Utopias – a Photographic History of the Search for Community.* Penguin Books: 1975.

M & N PRINTING. *A Comprehensive Story of Ventura County, California.* 1979.

MASON, JESSE D. *History of Santa Barbara and Ventura County.* Thompson and West: Oakland, 1883.

Ojai Historic Preservation Commission Reports. 1990 - 99

SALINAS, THOMAS A. Typewritten manuscript.

SHERIDAN, EDWIN M. *History of Ventura County, State of California. Its People and Its Resources*, edited by Harold McLean Meier, 1940.

SHERIDAN, SOL N. *Ventura County California.* S.T. Clark Publishing Company: Chicago, 1926.

STORKE, MRS. YDA ADDIS. *A Memorial and Biographical History of the Counties of Santa Barbara, San Luis Obispo and Ventura.* The Lewis Publishing Company: Chicago, 1891.

The Ventura Story. Centennial Publications: 1966.

Ventura County Historical Society Quarterlies.

Index

Arundell, Mr., 96

Ascot, John P. (teacher at OVS), 216

Ash, William, 145, 151

Ashcraft, Roscoe (early school principal), 68

Asphaltum, Chumash uses for, 7, 8, 9, 11; the industry, 141, 247

Assagioli, Dr. Robert (Meditation Mount), 285

Automobiles, 178-186

Avatar, Meher Baba (Meher Mount), 289

Avocados, 257-258

Ayala, Chrisogono, 16

Ayala, R.G., 185-186

Ayers, Agnes (Robert and Christiana's daughter), 50

Ayers, Christiana (Conner) — Robert's first wife, 50

Ayers, Edwin (Robert and Christiana's son), 50, 151, 192, 214

Ayers, Elizabeth (Conner) — Robert's second wife, 50

Ayers, Fannie (Smith) — Frank's wife, 50-51,

Ayers, Frank (Robert and Christiana's son), 50-51

Ayers, Henry (Robert and Christiana's son), 50

Ayers, Ida (Robert and Christiana's daughter), 50

Ayers, Jennie (Robert and Christiana's daughter), 50

Ayers, John (Robert and Christiana's son), 50

Ayers, Kenneth (Robert and Christiana's grandson), 266

Ayers, Montgomery (Robert and Christiana's son), 50

Ayers, Robert, attended Nordhoff Hotel opening, 27; Nordhoff Road to Ojai, 44; profile, 49-50, 157, 248

Ayers tract, 268-269

Ayers, William (Robert and Christiana's son), 50

Babcock, Caroline (tennis player), 293

Bailey, Gertrude, 188

Baird, Madeline (Meiners Oaks resident, 1930s), 238, 287

Baird Mansion, 238

Baisselier, Mrs. Edward (Meiners Oaks librarian, 1935), 235

Baker, Alice (Edwin and Sarah's daughter), 292

Baker, Bill, established Bill Baker's Bakery, 275-277; bakery: historical landmark, 282

Baker, Charles (Edwin and Sarah's son), 215

Baker, Edith (Edwin and Sarah's daughter), 158, 300

Baker, Ednah (Edwin and Sarah's daughter), 158

Baker, Edwin, cemetery trustee, 39; profile, 124-126, 137, 149, 180

Baker, Helen, *see* Reynolds, Helen

Baker, Sarah (Miller) — Edwin's wife, profile, 125-126, 158

Bald, Catherine (Clark) — George's wife, 152, 255

Bald, George (operated olive mill), 89; horse/car mishaps, 179, 180; profile, 255, 301

Bald, Howard (George and Catherine's son), 142-143, 179, 180, 255

Bald, Mabryn (Chapman) — Howard's wife, 73, 255

Ball, Katherine (early teacher), 75

Bands in Ojai, 214-216

Bank of America, established, 170-171; as post office, 202;

building demolished, 270

Bank of Italy, 170

Bank robbery, 171

Baptist Church, *see* First Baptist Church

Bard, Cephas, 22, 38

Bard, Elizabeth Memorial Hospital, 22

Bard, Thomas R., early oil days, 19-22, 24, 26, 27, 28, 31, 41, 70; donated to Presbyterian manse, 87, 122; lead Judge Wolfe's funeral procession, 157; social event at his home, 211; organized Santa Ana Water Company, 261; bear in bedroom, 310

Bard, Mrs. Thomas, 138

Barnard, Irwin, 54

Barnes, Mrs. Morgan, 166

Baron, Agnes, 289

Barr, Kendall (Henderson Field), 225-226

Barrington, Frank (El Roblar Hotel, 1920s), 105, 163

Barrington, Mrs., 105

Barrows, Albert (Frank and Julia's son), 84, 192

Barrows, Charlotte (Thomas' daughter), 192

Barrows, Clarence (honor farm), 266

Barrows, David (Thomas' son), 192

Barrows, Edward (Frank and Julia's son), 192

Barrows, Ella (Cole) — Thomas' second wife, 192

Barrows, Frank Peleg, Nordhoff High School Board member, 73; church affiliation, 82, 84, 96; started early library, 135, 136; Nordhoff Board of Trade, 149; started first YMCA, 166;

early merchant, 184, 185, 186, 187; profile, 191-192; Rains Department Store, 275

Barrows, Julia (Smith) — Frank's wife, library board member, 137; Ojai Club, 148, 192

Barrows, Sarah (Coffin) — Thomas' first wife, 192

Barrows, Stephen S. (Frank and Julia's son), 84, 174, 185, 192

Barrows, Thomas, 52, 84, 124, 127; profile, 191-192

Barry, Richard (*The Ojai* publisher, 1903), 133

Bartindale, Richard (Bart's Corner), 277

Bartlett, John, 17

Bart's Corner, 277

Baseball in Ojai (also *see* Softball), 303

Bayless Market, 268

Bayless, Thomas (Slim), 191, 268

Beal, Miss (early teacher), 65

Beaman, Frank S., 97; fire chief, 1904, 174

Beaman, Mrs. Frank, 159-160

Beaman, Selwyn S., 188, 215

Beardsley, J.A., 20

Bee business, Bronson, 53; Hund, 56; Sheldon, 122; Sayre, 127; Leslie, 144; Maddox, 194; Biggers, 93, 258-259

Beeby, Sara (Ojai Band, 1993), 216

Beecher, Reverend Thomas K. (first preacher in Ojai), 81

Beekman, Alice and Nellie, 72

Bell, William F. (built Ojai Valley Inn Golf Course), 106

Bella, Frances (early teacher), 71

Bennett, Anita (Jack and Hattie's daughter), 129

Bennett, David (Jack and Hattie's son), 129

Boyd Clubhouse, as a classroom, 68; USO, 109; honor roll, 150-151; building of, 161-162; Teen Town, 165; bank robbery, 171; building moved, 170-171; fire station nearby, 176; meeting place for band, 216; at Sarzotti Park, 305

Boyd, Jack, 161

Boyle, Louis M. (Orchid Town), 258

Bracken, Mr., 62, 89

Bradley, John H. (established *Ventura Signal,* 1871), 131

Bragg, Kitty (teacher at OVS), 76

Brakey, J.R. (house mover), 86

Bray, Levy, 215

Bray, Mrs. L.A., 188

Brick Schoolhouse, 63-67

Bristol, Esther (Walter and Olive's daughter), 75

Bristol, Olive (Lamb) — Walter's wife, 75

Bristol School, 75, 76; fire, 177

Bristol, Walter, 29; principal Nordhoff High School, 73; Bristol School, 75, 95; donated to library fund, 138, 149; first president Ojai Valley Chamber of Commerce, 150; member Ojai Valley Men's League, 196; published book, 267

Bronson, A., 53, 148

Bronson, O.H., 291

Brotherton, O.H. (Meiners Oaks merchant), 233

Brough, Louise (tennis player), 293

Brown, Agnes (Duncan), profile, 86

Brown, Benjamin F., 33

Brown, J.C., 292

Brown, James D., 82

Brown, Mary K. (tennis player), 293

Brown, R.M. (San Buenaventura Springs), 113

Brown, Ray (boxer), 113

Brown, Robert G., 82

Brown, Sam, 250

Brown, Thomas Steele, 82, 86

Browne, Robert O. (founder Ojai Valley Museum), 3, 296-297

Bruenwald, Boris (designed Libbey Park fountain, 1976), 206

Bryant, A.J., 47, 248

Buckman, F.S.S. (first county school superintendent and first orange grower), 55, 63, 64 248-249

Builders in Ojai, 144 - 146

Bunce Lumber Company, 267

Bundy, C.E. (published *The Ojai,* 1901), 133

Bundy, Dorothy (tennis player), 293

Bundy, May (Sutton) — tennis player, 293

Bundy, Tom (tennis player), 292

Burger, Don (manager Ojai Valley Inn, 1947), 109

Burke, John J., managed Blumberg Hotel, 96; Ojai Improvement Company, 97; movie theater, 134, 213; train committee, 140; Nordhoff Board of Trade, 149; founding of Ojai State Bank, 170; profile, 170-171; Nordhoff Water and Power Company, 173 Volunteer Fire Department, 174; Ojai Realty, 186, 187; Ojai Civic Association, 199; 206; Ojai Olive Association, 254; water issues, 262; Ojai Athletic Club, 291

Burket, Harold (Cottages Among the Flowers), 111

Burr, Dorothy, 13

Burr, Wallace (headmaster at OVS, 1940s), 13, 76

Burr, William J., 208

Burroughs, Kendra Crossen (Meher Mount), 289

Craig, Reverend W.J., 87, 245

Crandall, Rex, 233

Crandall's Market, 233, 268

Crawford, Reverend J.M., 83, 147

Creasinger, S.P., 114

Creek Road, description, 42; old Creek Road, 44, 46, 157

Crespi, Juan, 4

Cromer, Hiram Imboden (Bodees), 112

Cromwell, Alexander (El Roblar Hotel, 1950), 106

Cropper, Joe, 233

Crowder's Market (1940s), 190

Cummings, Harry, night watchman, 189; constable, 208

Curren, Joseph, 233

Curren, R.E. and R.G. (newspaper publishers, 1890), 131

Curtis, Nell (OVS teacher), 76

Cutting, Bayard W., Jr., 133

D.A.R.T., 209

Dahls Market, 182, 242

Dalton, John and Tony (early Mira Monte merchants), 224

Daly, J.C., 124, 140

Daniels, Reverend Allen Gatch, 43, 127

Danner, Melville (bought movie theater, 1944), 266

Danner, Royal (early Meiners Oaks merchant, 1944), 232

Davenport, Clara (Robison), 88

Davis, Bette (actress), 219

Davis, G.R., 233

Davison, Margarette, 129

Dean, William, E., 123

Deem, Woodruff (Justice of the Peace, 1954), 208

Deer Lodge, 238, 265

Del Pozzo, Julie (Adopt-a-Grave), 40

Deline, Lotta (Greenleif), 124

Dempsey, Jack (boxer), 112-113

DeNoon, Barbara, 222

Dennison, Cora Edna (H.J. and Margaret's daughter), 57

Dennison, Elias (Henry Jackson's father), 57

Dennison Grade (also see Ojai-Santa Paula Road), 44

Dennison, Henry (H.J. and Margaret's son), 57, 215

Dennison, Henry Jackson, profile, 56-58; first teacher, 63; church member, 81; train committee, 141; charter grange member, 157, 248

Dennison, Ida Belle (Lamb) — Robert's wife, 75

Dennison, John Franklin (H.J. and Margaret's son), 57, 173, 174 184, 192

Dennison, Junius Waldo (H.J. and Margaret's son), 57, 214

Dennison, Margaret (Rapp) — H.J.'s wife, 56-58, 81

Dennison Park, 304

Dennison, Robert S. (H.J. and Margaret's son), 57, 75

Dennison, Rudolph Rapp (H.J. and Margaret's son), 57

Dennison, Schuyler (H.J. and Margaret's son), 57, 214

Detzel, Jan (caught record fish), 306

Dickerson, A.J. and Tom (Santa Ana Ball Club), 303

Dickinson, Fr. Edwin, 90

Dickson, Reverend Robert, 83

Dixon, James (Meiners Oaks merchant, 1930s), 233

Dobbins, Reverend H.H. (early preacher), 81

Doeg, John (tennis player), 293

Fleegle, George, 117

Foothills Hotel, building of, 102-103, 144, 146, 173; fire, 177, 195; music festival, 293

Font, Fr. Pedro, 5

Fontana, Andrew, 257

Forbes, John M., 216

Fordyce, Harry (early rancher), 53, 127-128

Fordyce, Jim, 215

Fordyce, Stubby, 86

Forster, H. Waldo, 97, 148, 149, 254

Fortnightly Club, 157

Foster, E.P., 239

Foster, Mrs. E.P., 138

Foster Park, history of, 239-240

Fountains, 146, 204-206

Fowler, Edwin, 254

Fox, James B., 45, 47, 124, 186

Fox, Jim and John, 303

Fox, Rebecca (Roberts), 47

France, Vincent (Chief of Police, 1975), 208

Frances, Myrtle Shepherd, 28

Fraser, Mrs., 154, 189

Freeman, A.E. (early grocer, 1900s), 66, 187

Freeman, Ethel (librarian, 1910), 137-138

Freeman, Randolph (*The Ojai* publisher, 1896), 133, 141, 247

Fremont, John, 23

French, Mary (first woman voter in Nordhoff), 125-126

French, Dr. W.H., 37

Friend, Annie (Beers), 252

Friend, Elmer (William and Annie's son), 122, 191; profile 252, 309

Friend, William , 71, 128; profile, 252

Friends of the Library, 139

Frost, Frank Jefferson, founding of OVS, 75-76, 145; founding of music festival, 293-294

Frost, Mrs. Frank, 163

Gabbert, Judge Boyd (Justice of the Peace, 1922-1954), 155, 186, 208

Gabbert, Walker, 189

Gage, Mabel, 138, 300

Gallentine, Claude, 215

Gally, Agnes (Lord) — Howard's wife, 216

Gally, Benjamin, profile, 99-100, 137

Gally Cottages, Nordhoff visits, 33; establishment of, 97-101, 126; phone line, 172

Gally, Howard (Benjamin and Mary's son), 215

Gally, Mary, 39; profile, 99-101, 114, 129, 147

Gambling in Ojai, 168-169

Gardner, Erle Stanley, 138

Gardner, Captain (Matilija Hot Springs), 113

Gardner, Mr., 96

Garfield, Lucretia (guest at Pierpont Cottages), 105

Garland, A.A., 33, 97, 148, 174, 186, 199

Garland, Ruby (tennis player), 293

Garner, Sam (early newsman), 131

Gateway to the Arbolada, 282

Gearhart, Reverend William, W., 87, 297

Gearhart, Mrs. William W., 87

Gelett, Charles Wetherby, 84; profile, 123

Gelett, Jane (Russel), 123

Gelett, Vernon, 148, 214

346

White, Roderick (musician), 217

Whitmore, E.W., 157

Wickenhaeuser, Otis (teacher at OVS), 76

Wiest, Edward L (banker), school built on his property, 71; his ranch, 127; banking career, 1910-1928, 170, 171; Nordhoff Water and Power Company, 173; treasurer for fire department, 175

Wiggins, Colonel C.P., 29, 95

Wilcox Cottages, 117

Wilcox, Etta (Blumberg), 114, 117

Wilcox, J.W. (discovered hot springs, 1872), 113

Wilcox, Webb, 116-117

Wilcoxen, Mrs. 113

Wilde, Judge W.H., 140

Wilder, John J., 81

Wildlife in Ojai, 309-312

Wilkie, Wendell (guest at Pierpont Cottages), 105

Wilsie, W.E., 84, 140, 145, 247, 250

Wilson, Bob and George, 234

Wilson, Frances (librarian, 1911), 138

Wilson, Harrison, 155, 199

Wilson, Jackie (boxer), 113

Wilson, Jacob, 248

Wilson, Roy (architect), designed Ojai Elementary School, 68; designed San Antonio School, 71; designed high school gym, 74; profile, 146; designed Foster Park Bowl, 240; designed Ramelli house, 242; designed Bill Baker's Bakery, 276; designed Ojai Festivals Bowl, 294

Wilson, Zelma (architect), profile, 146; designed Ojai City Hall, 297

Wilson's Dinosaur Auto Repair, 234

Winchester, Henry K., 123

Wineries, 256-257

Winfield, Robert (early builder), built El Roblar Hotel, 105; profile, 145; built arcade and post office, 197, 200

Winnette, Mrs. H. LeBel, 279

Winslow, Carleton (architect), designed Presbyterian Church, 1930, 85; designed library, 138; profile, 146

Wisecrans, Belle, 300

Wolfe, Charlie (Irvin and Philena's son), 65, 156

Wolfe, Frank (Irvin and Philena's son), 157

Wolfe, Jessie (Irvin and Philena's daughter), 156

Wolfe, Judge Irvin W., son dies, 65; property holdings, 124; train committee, 141, 155; profile, 156-157; fire marshal, 174

Wolfe, Nellie, *see* Pelter, Nellie

Wolfe, Philena (Eddy) — Irvin's wife, 156-157

Women's Christian Temperance Union, 168

Wood, Beatrice (ceramist), 221-222, 278

Woolsey, Heathcote, 85

Woolsey, Theodore S., 103, 127, 135, 155; home as historic landmark, 282

World University, 77, 92

Wright, John C., 109-110, 128

Wright, J.R., 232

Wyeth, John, 17

Wyeth, Mrs. John, 42

Wykoff, J.P., 140, 141

Y shopping center, 122; established, 270

Yant, Ann (Linnel), 110

Yeomans, Edward, founding of OVS 75-76; chairman building committee, Presbyterian Church, 85; donated to library fund, 138

Ylla, Fr. E., established Villanova Cemetery, 41; building of Catholic Church 88, 89

YMCA, 166

Zimmerman, Ed P. (builder), 68, 144